Alec Soth / Magnum Photos

MARILYNNE ROBINSON is the author of the novels *Lila* (winner of the National Book Critics Circle Award), *Home*, *Gilead* (winner of the Pulitzer Prize), and *Housekeeping*, as well as four books of nonfiction: *When I Was a Child I Read Books*, *Mother Country*, *The Death of Adam*, and *Absence of Mind*. Winner of the Pak Kyung Ni Prize, she taught at the University of Iowa Writers' Workshop for twenty-five years and, in 2016, was named one of *Time*'s 100 Most Influential People in the World.

ALSO BY MARILYNNE ROBINSON

FICTION

Housekeeping

Gilead

Home

Lila

NONFICTION

Mother Country: Britain, the Welfare State and Nuclear Pollution

The Death of Adam: Essays on Modern Thought

Absence of Mind: The Dispelling of Inwardness from the Modern Myth of the Self

When I Was a Child I Read Books

Additional Praise for *The Givenness of Things*

"A sense of wonder pervades the powerful essays in *The Givenness of Things*. . . . Robinson's heroic lamentation is magnificent. . . . Robinson's insistence, throughout these essays, that we recognize the limitations of our knowledge is timely and important."
—Karen Armstrong, *The New York Times Book Review*

"These are beautiful essays . . . beautiful in thought and beautiful in expression." —*The Dallas Morning News*

"A new book of essays by Robinson is a major American literary event." —*The Buffalo News*

"These bravely and brilliantly argued, gorgeously composed, slyly witty, profoundly caring essays lead us into the richest dimensions of consciousness and conscience, theology and mystery, responsibility and reverence." —*Booklist*

"The prose is as finely wrought as in any of Robinson's novels. . . . Any reader not tone-deaf will be enchanted by her grave, urgent music." —*Bookforum*

"Eloquent, persuasive, and rigorously clear, this collection reveals one of America's finest minds working at peak form, capturing essential ideas with all 'the authority beautiful language and beautiful thought can give them.'" —*Publishers Weekly*

Praise for *The Death of Adam*

"A valuable contribution to American life and letters."
—Kathleen Norris

"A useful antidote to the increasingly crude and slogan-loving culture we inhabit." —Doris Lessing

"Robinson's thinking is all in the service of humanity's survival, spiritually and environmentally." —Charles Baxter

"One of Robinson's great merits as an essayist is her refusal to take her opinions secondhand. Her book is a goad to renewed curiosity." —*The New York Times Book Review*

Praise for *When I Was a Child I Read Books*

"Elegant essays . . . Reading [them] is like taking a draught of water from a cold spring. They offer us something rewarding, deeply essential, and long-sought." —Roxana Robinson, *The Washington Post*

"A broadside defense of literature and classic liberalism . . . Her defense of our national character and the systems it created can swell your heart." —*Los Angeles Times*

"One of the most remarkable of modern writers . . . This is a rare writer about America and one it seems to me we need."
—*The Buffalo News*

"The indomitable Marilynne Robinson radiates genius in her collection of essays." —*Vanity Fair*

THE GIVENNESS OF THINGS

```
    365
    6.5
  -----
  1825
 2190
 ------
 2372.5
```

THE GIVENNESS OF THINGS

ESSAYS

MARILYNNE ROBINSON

PICADOR FARRAR, STRAUS AND GIROUX NEW YORK

 Printed in the United States of America. For information, address Picador, 175 Fifth Avenue, New York, N.Y. 10010.

picadorusa.com • picadorbookroom.tumblr.com
twitter.com/picadorusa • facebook.com/picadorusa

Picador® is a U.S. registered trademark and is used by Macmillan Publishing Group, LLC, under license from Pan Books Limited.

For book club information, please visit facebook.com/picadorbookclub or e-mail marketing@picadorusa.com.

"President Obama and Marilynne Robinson: A Conversation in Iowa, Parts I and II" was previously published in slightly different form in the *New York Review of Books*.

Designed by Jonathan D. Lippincott

The Library of Congress has cataloged the Farrar, Straus and Giroux edition as follows:

Robinson, Marilynne.
[Essays. Selections]
The givenness of things : essays / Marilynne Robinson. —First edition.
p. cm.
Includes bibliographical references.
ISBN 978-0-374-29847-0 (hardcover)
ISBN 978-0-374-71431-4 (e-book)
1. Philosophical theology. 2. Christianity—Philosophy. 3. Christian philosophy. I. Title.
BT40.R57 2015
814'.54—dc23 2015022216

Picador Paperback ISBN 978-1-250-09731-6

Our books may be purchased in bulk for promotional, educational, or business use. Please contact your local bookseller or the Macmillan Corporate and Premium Sales Department at 1-800-221-7945, extension 5442, or by e-mail at MacmillanSpecialMarkets@macmillan.com.

First published by Farrar, Straus and Giroux

First Picador Edition: October 2016

10 9 8 7 6 5 4 3 2 1

For Bob and Peg Boyers,
with much love and many thanks

CONTENTS

THE GIVENNESS OF THINGS

HUMANISM

Humanism was the particular glory of the Renaissance. The recovery, translation, and dissemination of the literatures of antiquity created a new excitement, displaying so vividly the accomplishments and therefore the capacities of humankind, with consequences for civilization that are great beyond reckoning. The disciplines that came with this awakening, the mastery of classical languages, the reverent attention to pagan poets and philosophers, the study of ancient history, and the adaptation of ancient forms to modern purposes, all bore the mark of their origins yet served as the robust foundation of education and culture for centuries, until the fairly recent past. In muted, expanded, and adapted forms these Renaissance passions live on among us still in the study of the humanities, which, we are told, are now diminished and threatened. Their utility is in question, it seems, despite their having been at the center of learning throughout the period of the spectacular material and intellectual flourishing of Western civilization. Now we are less interested in equipping and refining thought, more interested in creating and mastering technologies that will yield measurable enhancements of material well-being—for those who create and master them, at least. Now we are less interested in the exploration of the glorious mind, more engrossed in the drama of staying ahead of whatever it is we think is pursuing us. Or perhaps we are just bent on evading the specter entropy. In any case, the spirit of the times is one of joyless urgency, many of us preparing ourselves and our children to be means to inscrutable ends that are utterly not our own. In such an environment the humanities do seem to have little place. They are poor preparation for economic servitude. This spirit is not the consequence but the cause of our present state of affairs. We have as good grounds for exulting in human brilliance as any generation that has ever lived.

The antidote to our gloom is to be found in contemporary science. This may seem an improbable stance from which to defend the humanities, and I do not wish to undervalue contemporary art or literature or music or philosophy. But it is difficult to recognize the genius of a period until it has passed. Milton, Bach, Mozart all suffered long periods of eclipse, beginning before their lives had ended. Our politics may appear in the light of history to have been filled with triumphs of statecraft, unlikely as this seems to us now. Science, on the other hand, can assert credible achievements and insights, however tentative, in present time. The last century and the beginning of this one have without question transformed the understanding of Being itself. "Understanding" is not quite the right word, since this mysterious old category, Being, fundamental to all experience past, present, and to come, is by no means understood. However, the terms in which understanding may, at the moment, be attempted have changed radically, and this in itself is potent information. The phenomenon called quantum entanglement, relatively old as theory and thoroughly demonstrated as fact, raises fundamental questions about time and space, and therefore about causality.

Particles that are "entangled," however distant from one another, undergo the same changes simultaneously. This fact challenges our most deeply embedded habits of thought. To try to imagine any event occurring outside the constraints of locality and sequence is difficult enough. Then there is the problem of conceiving of a universe in which the old rituals of cause and effect seem a gross inefficiency beside the elegance and sleight of hand that operate discreetly beyond the reach of all but the most rarefied scientific inference and observation. However pervasive and robust entanglement is or is not, it implies a cosmos that unfolds or emerges on principles that bear scant analogy to the universe of common sense. It is abetted in this by string theory, which adds seven unexpressed dimensions to our familiar four. And, of course, those four seem suddenly tenuous when the fundamental character of time and space is being called into question. Mathematics, ontology, and metaphysics have become one thing. Einstein's universe seems mechanistic in comparison, Newton's, the work of a tinkerer. If Galileo shocked the world by removing the sun from its place, so to speak, then this polyglot army of mathematicians and cosmologists who offer always new grounds for new conceptions of absolute reality should dazzle us all, freeing us at last from the circle of old Urizen's compass. But we are not free.

There is no art or discipline for which the nature of reality is a matter of indifference, so one ontology or another is always being assumed if not articulated. Great questions may be as open now as they have been since Babylonians began watching the stars, but certain disciplines are still deeply invested in a model of reality that is as simple and narrow as ideological reductionism can make it. I could mention a dominant school of economics with its anthropology. But I will instead consider science of a kind. The study of brain and consciousness, mind and self—associated with so-called neuroscience—asserts a model of mental function as straightforward, causally speaking, as a game of billiards, and plumes itself on just this fact. It is by no means entangled with the sciences that address ontology. The most striking and consequential changes in the second of these, ontology, brings about no change at all in the first, neuroscience, either simultaneous or delayed. The gist of neuroscience is that the adverbs "simply" and "merely" can exorcise the mystifications that have always surrounded the operations of the mind/brain, exposing the machinery that in fact produces emotion, behavior, and all the rest. So while inquiries into the substance of reality reveal further subtleties, idioms of relation that are utterly new to our understanding, neuroscience tells us that the most complex object we know of, the human brain, can be explained sufficiently in terms of the activation of "packets of neurons," which evolution has provided the organism in service to homeostasis. The amazing complexity of the individual cell is being pored over in other regions of science, while neuroscience persists in declaring the brain, this same complexity vastly compounded, an essentially simple thing. If this could be true, if this most intricate and vital object could be translated into an effective simplicity for which the living world seems to provide no analogy, this indeed would be one of nature's wonders.

Neuroscience has, as its primary resource, technology that captures images of processes within the living brain. Fear lights up a certain area, therefore fear is a function of that area, which developed for the purposes of maintaining homeostasis. It prepares the organism to fight or flee. Well and good. But fear is rarely without context. People can be terrified of spiders, dentists, the Last Judgment, germs, the need to speak in public, thirteen, extraterrestrials, mathematics, hoodies, the discovery of a fraud in their past. All of these fears are the creatures of circumstance, of the history and state of health of a specific brain. They identify threat, interpreting an environment in highly individual terms. They, not threat in the abstract, trigger alarm, and they are the products of parts of the brain that do not light up under technological scrutiny and would elude interpretation if they did. If they are not taken into account, the mere evidence of an excitation has little descriptive and no predictive value. A fearful person might take a pill, faint, or commit mayhem. The assumptions behind the notion that the nature of fear and the impulses it triggers could be made legible or generalizable for the purposes of imaging would have to exclude complexity—the factor that introduces individuality with all its attendant mysteries. In fairness, however, the neuroscientists seem well content with the technology they have, extrapolating boldly from the data it yields. Refinements that introduced complication might not be welcome.

This all appears to be a straightforward instance of scientists taking as the whole of reality that part of it their methods can report. These methods are as much a matter of vocabulary as of technology, though the two interact and reinforce each other. Here is an example. Neuroscientists seem predisposed to the conclusion that there is no "self." This would account for indifference to the modifying effects of individual history and experience, and to the quirks of the organism that arise from heredity, environment, interactions within the soma as a whole, and so on. What can the word "self" mean to those who wish to deny its reality? It can only signify an illusion we all participate in, as individuals, societies, and civilizations. So it must also be an important function of the brain, the brain aware of itself as it is modified by the infinite particulars of circumstance, that is, as it is not like others. But this would mean the self is not an illusion at all but a product of the mind at other work than the neuroscientists are inclined to acknowledge. Of course the physical brain is subject to every sort of impairment, the areas that light up during imaging as surely as any others. Impairments that seem to compromise the sense of self may be taken to demonstrate that it is rooted in the physical brain, that same fleshly monument to provident evolution the neuroscientists admire, selectively. If the physical disruption of the sense of self is taken to prove that the self is an experience created by the physical brain, then there are no better grounds to call its existence into question than there would be to question equilibrium or depth perception. Obviously there is a conceptual problem here—equilibrium does not "exist" except in the moment-to-moment orientation of an organism to its environment. Say as much of the self, mutatis mutandis, and it is granted the same kind of reality.

•

But to take a step back. It is absurd for scientists who insist on the category "physical," and who argue that outside this category nothing exists, to dismiss the reality of the self on the grounds that its vulnerabilities can be said to place it solidly *within* this category. How can so basic an error of logic survive and flourish? There is a certain Prometheanism in this branch of science that would rescue us mortals from entrenched error—for so they see the problem of making their view of things persuasive. For this reason—because questions might seem a betrayal of science as rescuer—its tenets enjoy a singular immunity from the criticism of peers. And their proponents feel confirmed by doubt and objection on the same grounds, that their origins and motives can be taken to lie in a hostility to science. On scrutiny the physical is as elusive as anything to which a name can be given. The physical as we have come to know it frays away into dark matter, antimatter, and by implication on beyond them and beyond our present powers of inference. But for these scientists it is a business of nuts and bolts, a mechanics of signals and receptors of which no more need be known. Their assertions are immune to objection and proof against information. One they dismiss and the other they ignore.

The real assertion being made in all this (neuroscience is remarkable among sciences for its tendency to bypass hypothesis and even theory and to go directly to assertion) is that there is no soul. Only the soul is ever claimed to be nonphysical, therefore immortal, therefore sacred and sanctifying as an aspect of human being. It is the self but stands apart from the self. It suffers injuries of a moral kind, when the self it is and is not lies or steals or murders, but it is untouched by the accidents that maim the self or kill it. Obviously this intuition—it is much richer and deeper than anything conveyed by the word "belief"—cannot be dispelled by proving the soul's physicality, from which it is aloof by definition. And on these same grounds its nonphysicality is no proof of its nonexistence. This might seem a clever evasion of skepticism if the character of the soul were not established in remote antiquity, in many places and cultures, long before such a thing as science was brought to bear on the question.

I find the soul a valuable concept, a statement of the dignity of a human life and of the unutterable gravity of human action and experience. I would add that I find my own soul interesting company, if this did not seem to cast doubt on my impeccable objectivity. This is not entirely a joke. I am not prepared to concede objectivity to the arbitrarily reductionist model of reality that has so long claimed, and been granted, this virtue. The new cosmologies open so many ways of reconceiving the universe(s) that all sorts of speculations are respectable now. We might have any number of other selves. If most or all these speculations are only flaunting new definitions of the possible, the exercise is valuable and necessary. Possibility has been captive to a narrow definition for a very long time, ourselves with it, and we must expect to blink in the light. These new cosmologies preclude almost nothing, except "the physical" as a special category. The physicality enshrined by the neuroscientists as the measure of all things is not objectivity but instead a pure artifact of the scale at which and the means by which we and our devices perceive. So to invoke it as the test and standard of reality is quintessentially anthropocentric.

I am content to place humankind at the center of Creation. We are complex enough, interesting enough. What we have learned, limited as we must assume it to be, is wonderful even in the fact of its limitations. This is no proof, of course. Be that as it may. It is not anthropocentricity that is a problem here, but the fact that it is unacknowledged and misapplied, and all the while imputed to the other side of the controversy, as if it were, *eo ipso*, a flagrant error. The objectivity claimed by neuroscience implies that it is free of this bias. Yet there could be no more naive anthropocentricity than is reflected in the certainty and insistence that what we can know about the nature of things at this moment makes us capable of definitive judgments about much of anything. That we have come to this place is not a failure of science but a glorious achievement, the continuous opening of insights science itself could never have anticipated. Nothing can account for the reductionist tendencies among neuroscientists except a lack of rigor and consistency, a loyalty to conclusions that are prior to evidence and argument, and an indifference to science as a whole.

This kind of criticism is conventionally made of religion. I am not attempting some sort of rhetorical tae kwon do, to turn the attack against the attacker. My point is simply that neuroscience, at least in its dominant forms, greatly overreaches the implications of its evidence and is tendentious. Its tendency is to insist on the necessity of a transformation of our conception of human nature—to make it consistent with a view of reality that it considers clear-eyed and tough-minded, therefore rational and true. Its ultimate argument seems to be that we all really know better than to subscribe to the mythic foolery that sustains us in a lofty estimation of ourselves and our kind. The evidence they offer is secondary to this conclusion and inadequate to it because it is based in a simplistic materialism that is by now a nostalgia. The profound complexity of the brain is an established fact. The depiction of a certain traffic of activation in it can only understate its complexity. One might reasonably suspect that the large and costly machines that do the imaging are

very crude tools whose main virtue is th[illegible]
kind of data their users desire and no mor[illegible]

Is it fair to say that this school of thou[illegible] humanism? This seems on its face to be true. [illegible] took the works of the human mind—literature, mus[illegible] losophy, art, and languages—as proof of what the mind is and might be. Out of this has come the great aura of brilliance and exceptionalism around our species that neuroscience would dispel. If Shakespeare had undergone an MRI there is no reason to believe there would be any more evidence of extraordinary brilliance in him than there would be of a self or a soul. He left a formidable body of evidence that he was both brilliant and singular, but it has fallen under the rubric of Renaissance drama and is somehow not germane, perhaps because this places the mind so squarely at the center of the humanities. From the neuroscientific point of view, this only obscures the question. After all, where did our high sense of ourselves come from? From what we have done and what we do. And where is this awareness preserved and enhanced? In the arts and the humane disciplines. I am sure there are any number of neuroscientists who know and love Mozart better than I do, and who find his music uplifting. The inconsistency is for them to explain.

A type of Darwinism has a hand in this. If evolution means that the species have a common ancestry and have all variously adapted and changed, that is one thing. Ovid would not object. If it means that whatever development is judged to be in excess of the ability to establish and maintain homeostasis in given environments, to live and propagate, is less definitive of the creature than traits that are assumed to reflect unambiguous operations of natural selection, then this is an obvious solecism. It is as if there are tiers to existence or degrees of it, as if some things, though manifest, are less real than others and must be excluded from the narrative of origins in favor of traits that suit the teller's preferences. So generosity is apparent and eed is real, the great poets and philosophers toiled in the hope of making themselves attractive to potential mates—as did pretty well every man who distinguished himself by any means or tried to, from Tamburlaine to Keats to anyone's uncle. (Women have little place in these narratives—they are the drab hens who appraise the male plumage.) This positing of an essential and startlingly simple mechanism behind the world's variety implies to some that these pretenses, these very indirect means to the few stark ends that underlie all human behaviors, ought to be put aside, if only for honesty's sake. So, humanities, farewell. You do not survive Darwinian cost-benefit analysis.

If there is a scientific mode of thought that is crowding out and demoralizing the humanities, it is not research in the biology of the cell or the quest for life on other planets. It is this neo-Darwinism, which claims to cut through the dense miasmas of delusion to what is mere, simple, and real. Since these "miasmas" have been the main work of human consciousness for as long as the mind has left a record of itself, its devaluing is a major work of dehumanization. This is true because it is the great measure of our distinctiveness as a species. It is what we know about ourselves. It has everything in the world to do with how we think and feel, with what we value or despise or fear, all these things refracted through cultures and again through families and individuals. If the object of neuroscience or neo-Darwinism were to describe an essential human nature, these disciplines would surely seek confirmation in history and culture. But these things are endlessly complex, and they are continually open to variation and disruption. So the insistence on an essential simplicity is understandable if it is not fruitful. If I am correct in seeing neuroscience as essentially neo-Darwinist, then it is affixed to a model of reality that has not gone through any meaningful change in a century, except in the kind of machinery it brings to bear in asserting its worldview.

A nematode is more complex than a human being was

thought to be fifty years ago. Now biology is in the course of absorbing the implications of the fact that our bodies are largely colonies of specialized microorganisms, all of them certainly complex in their various ways and in their interactions. It is the elegance of nature that creates even the appearance of simplicity. The double helix as a structure expedites fluent change, modifications within the factors it contains, or that compose it, that baffle determinist associations with the word "gene." Elegance of this kind could be called efficiency, if that word did not have teleological implications. I think the prohibition against teleology must be an arbitrary constraint, in light of the fact that we do not know what time is. It is not respectable to say that an organism is designed to be both stable as an entity and mutable in response to environment, though it must be said that this complex equilibrium is amazing and beautiful and everywhere repeated in a wealth of variations that can *seem* like virtuosity regaling itself with its own brilliance.

I am a theist, so my habits of mind have a particular character. Such predispositions, long typical in Western civilization, have been carefully winnowed out of scientific thought over the last two centuries in favor of materialism, by which I mean a discipline of exclusive attention to the reality that can be tested by scientists. This project was necessary and very fruitful. The greatest proof of its legitimacy is that it has found its way to its own limits. Now scientific inference has moved past the old assumptions about materiality and beyond the testable. Presumably it would prefer not to have gone beyond its classic definitions of hypothesis, evidence, demonstration. And no doubt it will bring great ingenuity to bear on the questions that exceed any present ability to test responses to them. It seems science may never find a way to confirm or reject the idea of multiple universes, or arrive at a satisfactory definition of time or gravity. We know things in the ways we encounter them. Our encounters, and our methods and assumptions, are determined by our senses, our techniques, our intuitions. The recent vast expansion and proliferation of our models of reality and of the possible bring with them the realization that our situation, on this planet, and within the cocoon of our senses, is radically exceptional, and that our capacity for awareness is therefore parochial in ways and degrees we cannot begin to estimate. Again, to have arrived at this point is not a failure of science but a spectacular achievement.

That said, it might be time to pause and reflect. Holding to the old faith that everything is in principle knowable or comprehensible by us is a little like assuming that every human structure or artifact must be based on yards, feet, and inches. The notion that the universe is constructed, or we are evolved, so that reality must finally answer in every case to the questions we bring to it, is entirely as anthropocentric as the notion that the universe was designed to make us possible. Indeed, the affinity between the two ideas should be acknowledged. While the assumption of the intelligibility of the universe is still useful, it is not appropriately regarded as a statement of doctrine, and should never have been. Science of the kind I criticize tends to assert that everything is explicable, that whatever has not been explained will be explained—and, furthermore, by their methods. They have seen to the heart of it all. So mystery is banished—mystery being no more than whatever their methods cannot capture yet. Mystery being also those aspects of reality whose implications are not always factors in their worldview, for example, the human mind, the human self, history, and religion—in other words, the terrain of the humanities. Or of the human.

Now we know that chromosomes are modified cell by cell, and that inheritance is a mosaic of differentiation within the body, distinctive in each individual. Therefore the notion that one genetic formula, one script, is elaborated in the being of any creature must be put aside, with all the determinist assumptions it has seemed to authorize. Moreover, the impulse toward generalization that would claim to make the brain solvable should on these grounds be rejected, certainly until we have some grasp of the deeper sources of this complexity and order, the causal factors that lie behind this infinitesimal nuancing. The brain is certainly more profoundly individuated than its form or condition can reveal.

So if selfhood implies individuality, or if our undeniable individuality justifies the sense of selfhood, then there is another mystery to be acknowledged: that this impulse to deny the reality, which is to say the value, of the human self should still persist and flourish among us. Where slavery and other forms of extreme exploitation of human labor have been general, moral convenience would account for much of it, no doubt. Where population groups are seen as enemies or even as burdens, certain nefarious traits are attributed to them as a whole that are taken to override the qualities of individual members. Again, moral convenience could account for this. Both cases illustrate the association of the denial of selfhood with the devaluation of the human person. This would seem too obvious to be said, if it were not true that the denial of selfhood, which is, we are told, authorized by the methods of neuroscience and by the intentionally generalized reports it offers of the profoundly intricate workings of the brain, persists and flourishes.

There are so many works of the mind, so much humanity, that to disburden ourselves of ourselves is an understandable temptation. Open a book and a voice speaks. A world, more or less alien or welcoming, emerges to enrich a reader's store of hypotheses about how life is to be understood. As with scientific hypotheses, even failure is meaningful, a test of the boundaries of credibility. So many voices, so many worlds, we can weary of them. If there were only one human query to be heard in the universe, and it was only the sort of thing we were always inclined to wonder about—Where did all this come from? or,

Why could we never refrain from war?—we would hear in it a beauty that would overwhelm us. So frail a sound, so brave, so deeply inflected by the burden of thought, that we would ask, Whose voice is this? We would feel a barely tolerable loneliness, hers and ours. And if there were another hearer, not one of us, how starkly that hearer would apprehend what we are and were.

REFORMATION

The Reformation, a movement that touched or transformed thought and culture across the breadth of Europe, must inevitably have different histories in various cities and countries and classes and language groups. It would be impossible to begin to do justice to the complexity of the phenomenon as a whole. Since the Reformation in Britain has had exceptional importance for us in North America, I will devote most of my time to this branch of it—not to the Tudor break with the Papacy but to the Puritans and Separatists who were early immigrants to these shores. Granting that the example of Luther and his writing as well had great influence in Britain, an even greater influence for our purposes was Jean Calvin, known by us as John Calvin, the sixteenth-century French Reformer whose career unfolded in Geneva.

Calvin was in the second generation of the European Reform movement, his *Institutes of the Christian Religion* first appearing in 1536, almost twenty years after Luther published his Theses. Important works of Calvin were printed in English soon after they appeared and were widely circulated during his lifetime. The Reformation itself came a little late to England, but when it came, it came with a vengeance, leading finally, in the seventeenth century, to civil war and then a mass migration of Puritans to New England. It had had important precursors in Britain, in the work of the Oxford professor John Wycliffe, for example, a central figure in the making of the earliest complete translation of the Bible into English, which first appeared in 1386.

The history of the Reformation is very largely a history of books and publication, a response to the huge stimulus given to intellectual life by the printing press. It was in considerable degree the work of professors, men of exceptional learning who were intent on making the central literature of the civilization accessible to the understanding of the unlearned, those who could not read or understand Latin. Luther made his profoundly influential translation of Scripture, which became the basis of the development of German as a literary language. Calvin did not make a translation of the Bible into French—that was done by a cousin, Pierre Robert. For the purposes of his commentaries, Calvin made translations from Hebrew and Greek into Latin. But he also wrote and preached in French. His work was read so widely that he is credited with creating French as a literary and discursive language, and an international language as well. His influence and Luther's are both very comparable to the impact on English of the Bible in English, generally attributed to the Authorized or King James Version. So one immediate and remarkable consequence of the Reform movement was the emergence of the great modern languages out of the shadow of Latin, with their power and beauty and dignity fully demonstrated in the ambitious uses being made of them.

The cultural dominance of Latin persisted even though there was a great period of vernacular English poetry in the fourteenth century, when Geoffrey Chaucer, John Gower, William Langland, and Julian of Norwich flourished. It is hard now to imagine a world in which virtually everything of importance—

law, humane learning, science, and religion—was carried on in a language known only by an educated minority. The dominance of Latin did have the advantage of making the learned classes mutually intelligible across the boundaries of nationality. But this advantage came at the cost of the exclusion of the great majority of people from participation in the most central concerns of their own civilization. And it was enforced by contempt for ordinary spoken languages and for the ordinary people whose languages they were. Thomas More was scathing on this subject. Despite the examples of John Gower and Julian of Norwich, More scoffed at William Tyndale's rendering *agape* by the word "love" in place of the conventional "charity." Love, he said, was a word that might be used by "any Jack." This is the same William Tyndale who made the translations of the New Testament and portions of the Old Testament that became the basis of all subsequent English versions of the Bible.

It would not occur to us now to find the word "love," commonplace as it is, unsuitable in the context of the sacred. This is one measure of the transformation that has resulted in the rise of the vernacular brought about by the Reformation, and an aspect of the embrace of the secular with which the Reformation is always identified. Thomas More was a man of great influence with the king, Henry VIII. His objections to Tyndale's work led him to call for Tyndale to be burned at the stake, as he was, though his martyrdom is less well-known than that of Thomas More himself, who was beheaded a few years later for refusing to acknowledge King Henry as the head of the English church.

All the conflict and denunciation, all the bitter polemic and violence, tends to distract attention from a remarkable and very beautiful fact: the learned men in Bohemia, Germany, France, and Britain who articulated the faith of the Reform and who created its central documents were devoted to the work of removing the barrier between learned and unlearned by making

Christianity fully intelligible in the common languages. They were devoted to the work of ending an advantage they themselves enjoyed, by making learning broadly available through translation and publication.

The modern languages surely benefited from their being brought into literature by these extraordinary scholars and humanists. But a more remarkable fact is that these writers heard the beauty in common speech, the very different speech of their various regions, and produced that beauty faithfully in their own use of these languages. To be sensitive to the aesthetic qualities of anything a culture has stigmatized as a mark of ignorance, or as vulgar in both senses of the word, would have required respect and affection that saw past such prejudices. The ability to hear the power and elegance of these languages would have been simultaneous with the impulse to honor the generality of people by giving them, first of all, the Bible.

The fourteenth-century Middle English translation of the Latin Vulgate associated with the Oxford professor John Wycliffe was widely circulated, and important in its own right. I have read that it did not have the literary value of later translations because it adhered closely to the Latin of the original. I cannot confirm this from my own reading of it. In any case, its greatest influence on literature was perhaps indirect, since it set off or encouraged a movement called Lollardy. The Lollards, also called "poor priests," wandered through the countryside, preaching and teaching from the Wycliffe Bible, which was clearly adequate to conveying the simple, radical force of the Gospels: "Blessid be ye, that now hungren, for ye schulen be fulfillid. Blessid be ye, that now wepen, for ye schulen leiye."

The fourteenth century was a time of great hardship and profound civil and religious unrest among the poor in England. In the years 1348 to 1350 the Black Plague ravaged and reduced the population. In 1381 Wat Tyler led the Peasants' Revolt, a major though ultimately failed insurrection whose demands included an end to serfdom. Lollardy took its character from this period. It was a radically popular movement, critical or dismissive of many teachings of the church of that time, and claiming an exclusive authority for Scripture over priesthood and Papacy as Wycliffe himself seems to have done. Parliament responded with an act titled De Haeretico Comburendo, which declared that those who continued to exercise "their wicked preachings and doctrines . . . from day to day . . . to the utter destruction of all order and rule of right and reason," if they did not repent of their error, were to be burned "before the people, in a high place . . . that such punishment may strike fear into the minds of others." Though it was harshly suppressed, Lollardy persisted until the time of the Reformation. Wycliffe himself, who had died a natural death in communion with the Catholic Church and had lain in his grave for years, was declared a heretic, dug up, and burned.

The poet and priest William Langland, contemporary with these events, wrote in Middle English the long visionary poem *Piers the Ploughman*, composed between 1362 and 1394. One voice of the poem, describing theologians at dinner, says, "Meanwhile some poor wretch may cry at their gate, tormented by hunger and thirst and shivering with cold; yet no one asks him in or eases his suffering, except to shoo him off like a dog. Little can they love the Lord who gives them so much comfort, if this is how they share it with the poor! Why, if the poor had no more mercy than the rich, all the beggars would go to bed with empty bellies. For the gorges of these great theologians are often crammed with God's Name, but His mercy and His works are found among humble folk."

Ne were mercy in mene men more þan in riche,
Mendinantȝ meteles miȝte go to bedde.
God is moche in þe gorge of þise grete maystres,
Ac amonges mene men his mercy and his werkis . . .

Complex as the history is, the Bible may be fairly said to have entered English as a subversive document. It continued to be a forbidden document in England for more than a hundred years, in law if not in fact. Meanwhile, off in Germany, the priest William Tyndale worked away at his translation, from the original Greek and Hebrew into the spoken language of his time. Tyndale could only have been aware of the probable consequences for himself of his labors. Yet, according to John Foxe's sixteenth-century *Acts and Monuments of the Martyrs*, disputing with a learned man at dinner Tyndale said something any Lollard would approve: "If God spare my life, ere many years I will cause a boy that driveth the plough shall know more of the Scripture than thou dost." The *Acts and Monuments* is a compendium of anecdotes about the heroes of the English pre-Reformation and Reformation. If the words attributed to Tyndale are hearsay, or even supplied by Foxe himself, this would only underscore the degree to which the Ploughman held place as a standard in the Protestant imagination.

The Ploughman was, of course, the archetypal poor man in the countryside, to whom the Lollards had preached. Toward the end of Langland's poem, Piers the Ploughman appears as the suffering Christ. More than a century later John Calvin will take this physical identity of Christ with the poor to a startling extreme, saying that "being born in a stable, all His life He was like a poor working man" and that he "was nourished in such poverty as to hardly appear human." This language reminds us how extraordinarily bitter poverty was in premodern Europe, how reduced and disfigured by hardship were those laboring people in whom Tyndale and the others acknowledged the image of Christ. The movement that preceded the Reformation and continued through it was one of respect for the poor and oppressed—respect much more than compassion, since the impulse behind it was the desire to share the best treasure of their faith and learning with the masses of unregarded poor whom they knew to be ready, and very worthy, to receive it.

The bookishness of the Reformation might be said to have generalized itself to become an expectation of legibility in the whole of Creation. If Tyndale felt he was effectively giving Scripture to the unlearned in the fact of translating it with art and skill, he was necessarily dismissing the interpretive strategies—allegorical, tropological, and anagogical—that were traditionally applied to the reading of it, and which gave it meanings only available to those who were especially trained in these methods. This sense that revelation, scriptural and natural, was essentially available to everyone, pervades Reformation thought.

Calvin described the heavens as intelligible in their deepest meaning to the unlearned as well as the learned. He said,

> In disquisitions concerning the motions of the stars, in fixing their situations, measuring their distances, and distinguishing their peculiar properties, there is need of skill, exactness, and industry, and the providence of God being more clearly revealed by these discoveries, the mind ought to rise to a sublimer elevation for the contemplation of his glory. But since the meanest and most illiterate of mankind, who are furnished with no other assistance than their own eyes, cannot be ignorant of the excellence of the Divine skill, exhibiting itself in that endless, yet regular variety of the innumerable celestial host—it is evident, that the Lord abundantly manifests his wisdom to every individual on earth.

The eighteenth-century English Puritan Isaac Watts, known to us for the hymns he wrote, was also the author of books on logic and pedagogy used in British and American colleges for generations. He said,

> Fetch down some knowledge from the clouds, the stars, the sun, the moon, and the revolutions of all the planets.

> Dig and draw up some valuable meditations from the depths of the earth, and search them through the vast oceans of water. Extract some intellectual improvements from the minerals and metals; from the wonders of nature among the vegetables and herbs, trees and flowers. Learn some lessons from the birds and the beasts, and the meanest insect. Read the wisdom of God, and his admirable contrivance in them all; read his almighty power, his rich and various goodness, in all the works of his hands.

Both Romanticism and early modern science are strongly associated with the Reformation. Passages like these show how they could have sprung from the same root. An intelligible Creation addressed itself in every moment to every perceiver, more profoundly as the capacities of perception were enlisted in the work of understanding. The most persistent and fruitful tradition of American literature from Emily Dickinson to Wallace Stevens is the meditation on the given, the inexhaustible ordinary. Ralph Waldo Emerson and William James wrote about the subtle and splendid processes of consciousness in this continuous encounter.

Clearly there was no condescension whatsoever in Tyndale's feelings about the people for whom his Bible was intended. The best proof of this is the fact that by far the greater part of the King James Version New Testament, universally considered to be among the glories of English literature and to be the source of much that is best in it, is in fact Tyndale's work. In writing for the common people, in writing for the Ploughman, who would not only have been ignorant of Latin but illiterate altogether, he created a masterpiece. This great generosity of spirit, this great respect, is perfectly consonant with his accepting the likelihood that he would suffer a terrible death for taking on this very great labor. Putting aside all other difficulties, the fact that he made himself proficient enough in Greek and Hebrew to carry out the work is remarkable in itself. These two ancient languages had been almost unknown in Europe for centuries and were just beginning to be studied again when Tyndale wrote.

Perhaps because I am sometimes a writer and sometimes a scholar I think I have a little sense of the labor and concentration represented in all these books. I know I can't imagine the care that went into the Bibles the Lollards carried, made small to be easily concealed, each one handwritten since there was still no printing press, and each one ornamented with delicate strokes in its margins. I have a collection of Calvin's writings, nowhere near complete but daunting all the same, dozens of volumes of disciplined and elegant explication from the hand of a man whose health was never good, who shouldered for decades the practical and diplomatic problems of Geneva, a city under siege, and whose writings inspired and also endangered the individuals and populations across Europe who read them, whether or not they were persuaded by them. To say these things are humbling would be to understate the matter wildly.

I do happen to know what goes into the writing of a book—granted, not a book that requires a mastery of ancient languages, or that addresses the endless difficulties of translation—nor one that sets out to make literary use of a disparaged language or that attempts to render or to interpret a sacred text. I have no idea what it would be like to write in prison or in hiding or in a city full of refugees. I have no idea what it would be like to live with the threat of death while trying to write something good enough to justify the mortal peril others accepted in simply reading it. I have just enough relevant experience to inform my awe. I find the achievements of these writers unimaginable. When I see Calvin in his commentaries pausing once again over the nuances and ambiguities of a Hebrew word as if his time and his patience and his strength were all inexhaustible, I am touched by how respectful he is, phrase by phrase and verse by verse, of the text of Scripture, and therefore how respectful he is of any pastor and of all those to whom that pastor will preach.

And this is why it seems important to me to remember the special popular origins of the movement that became the English Reformation, and the Reformation in general. Indeed, the intellectual genealogy of the movement is straightforward—Professor John Wycliffe of Oxford was read by Professor Jan Hus of Prague, who in turn was read by Professor Martin Luther of Wittenberg, whose work exerted enormous influence on William Tyndale. And it deeply influenced the brilliant young humanist scholar John Calvin, who would echo the psalmist and anticipate Hamlet in his praise of "the manifold agility of the soul, which enables it to take a survey of heaven and earth; to join the past and the present; to retain the memory of things heard long ago; to conceive of whatever it chooses by the help of imagination; its ingenuity also in the invention of such admirable arts." He is describing the universal and defining mysteries of human consciousness, which he says are "certain proofs of the divinity in man."

The argument could be made that we are now living among the relics or even the ruins of the Reformation. One relic is a continuing attachment to the Bible that is culturally particular to America, even in the absence of any great impulse to honor the Promethean work of the Reformers by reading it. A ruin may be the respect for one another as minds and consciences that is encoded in the First Amendment to the Constitution and institutionalized in the traditionally widespread teaching of the liberal arts, the disciplines that celebrate human thought and creativity as values in their own right and as ends in themselves. The fine colleges founded in the Middle West when it was still very much a frontier—Oberlin, Grinnell, Knox, and so many others—offered demanding curricula from the beginning, assuming that the young men and women who found themselves on the prairie would want to be educated to the highest standards. Rather than tuition, the colleges required all their students to do the chores necessary to the functioning of these little academic outposts, to make logic and classical history available to the figurative—or literal—Ploughman on equal terms with anyone.

It seems these days as if the right to bear arms is considered by some a suitable remedy for the tendency of others to act on their freedoms of speech, press, and assembly, and especially of religion, in ways and degrees these arms-bearing folk find irksome. Reverence for the sacred integrity of every pilgrim's progress through earthly life seems to be eroding. The generosity to the generality of people that gave us most of our best institutions would be considered by many pious people now to be socialistic, though the motives behind the creation of many of them, for example, these fine colleges, was utterly and explicitly Christian. If I seem to have strayed from my subject, it is only to make the point that forgetting the character of the Reformation, that is, the passion for disseminating as broadly as possible the best of civilization as the humanist tradition understood it, and at the same time honoring and embracing the beauty of the shared culture of everyday life, has allowed us to come near to forgetting why we developed excellent public libraries, schools, and museums.

We tend to break things down into categories that are too narrow. It is hard to call the motives behind the development of these institutions self-seeking, though there can be no doubt that they have contributed mightily to our prosperity and have in some cases redounded to the credit of philanthropists. We cannot call the motives altruistic, though many people have given selfless and devoted support to them. The motives were and are of another order. We are moved to respond to the fact of human brilliance, human depth, in all its variety, because it is the most wonderful thing in the world, very probably the most wonderful thing in the universe. The impulse to enjoy and enhance it is by no means originally or exclusively—or consistently—Protestant or Christian. It has its roots in Renaissance humanism, in classical tradition, and before either of them in the ancient Hebrews' assertion that a human being is an image of God.

In the forms we have known it, however, it is especially related to the Reformation because the rise of the vernacular languages with all they embodied in unacknowledged beauty and in the capacity for profound meaning made the broad dissemination of learning possible and urgent, and a labor of aesthetic pleasure and very great love. Isaac Watts wrote of one who teaches that "he should have so much of a natural candour and sweetness mixed with all the improvements of learning, as might convey knowledge into the minds of his disciples with a sort of gentle insinuation and sovereign delight, and may tempt them into the highest improvements of their reason by a resistless and insensible force." He recommended the reading of poetry so that one may "learn to know, and taste, and feel a fine stanza, as well as to hear it."

Now we are more inclined to speak of information than of learning, and to think of the means by which information is transmitted rather than of how learning might transform, and be transformed by, the atmospheres of a given mind. We may talk about the elegance of an equation, but we forget to find value in the beauty of a thought. At the same time we live, if we choose, in what amounts to a second universe. With the rise of mass literacy, printing, and publishing came an outpouring of books of many kinds, at first religious, classical, philosophical, polemical, and quasi- or protoscientific. Then there came as well any number of newly created works of the literary imagination. To this day the phenomenon accelerates. The universe of print we live in now, on page and screen, is an infinitely capacious memory and an inexhaustible reservoir of new thought. That its best potentialities are not often realized, that its best moments often pass unobserved or unvalued, only certifies its profound humanity.

Cultural pessimism is always fashionable, and, since we are human, there are always grounds for it. It has the negative consequence of depressing the level of aspiration, the sense of the possible. And from time to time it has the extremely negative consequence of encouraging a kind of somber panic, a collective dream-state in which recourse to terrible remedies is inspired by delusions of mortal threat. If there is anything in the life of any culture or period that gives good grounds for alarm, it is the rise of cultural pessimism, whose major passion is bitter hostility toward many or most of the people within the very culture the pessimists always feel they are intent on rescuing. When panic on one side is creating alarm on the other, it is easy to forget that there are always as good grounds for optimism as for pessimism—exactly the same grounds, in fact—that is, because we are human. We still have every potential for good we have ever had, and the same presumptive claim to respect, our own respect and one another's. We are still creatures of singular interest and value, agile of soul as we have always been and as we will continue to be even despite our errors and depredations, for as long as we abide on this earth. To value one another is our greatest safety, and to indulge in fear and contempt is our gravest error.

Sigmund Freud called Americans Lollards, intending no compliment. Still, I hope he was right. I hope that, whoever we are and by whatever spiritual or cultural path we arrive at Lollardy, we do and will share a generous and even a costly readiness to show our respect for all minds and spirits, especially for those whose place in life might cheat them of respect. It may be that the variety of cultures exists to show us that the histories that form them differently all yield value. The spiritual and intellectual wealth of nations has flowed into this country, enriching it in the degree that those who brought their histories and traditions have been good stewards of their special wealth and good interpreters of it to the larger society. The Reformation is another beautiful and very worthy heritage, another stream of cultural and spiritual wealth, also well deserving of advocates and interpreters.

GRACE

Among the most striking sentences in the English language is one spoken by Prospero to his treacherous brother, Antonio, in the fifth act of *The Tempest*. He says, "For you, most wicked sir, whom to call brother / Would even infect my mouth, I do forgive / Thy rankest fault—all of them." The shock is in the language itself, the stark sequence of contempt and forgiveness. Prospero has already told his attendant spirit, Ariel, of his intentions toward Antonio and the others:

> Though with their high wrongs I am struck to th' quick,
> Yet with my nobler reason 'gainst my fury
> Do I take part. The rarer action is
> In virtue than in vengeance. They being penitent,
> The sole drift of my purpose doth extend
> Not a frown further.

And again, while those subject to his magic stand "spell-stop'd," unable to move, he says:

> Flesh and blood,
> You, brother mine, that entertain'd ambition,

Expelled remorse and nature . . .
I do forgive thee,
Unnatural though thou art.

So there is no suspense at all about what Prospero will do, how, powerful as he is, he will treat the brother who has slandered him and usurped his dukedom, and who must have assumed that he had caused Prospero's death and his child's death as well. He is at Prospero's mercy, and the mercy he receives is perfect, insisted upon in these repetitions, qualified only by the fact that in no case does it forget, minimize, or extenuate his crimes.

I propose that Shakespeare is turning over a theological problem here. How do forgiveness and grace not deprive evil of its nature, its gravity? Granted, Prospero does subject the malefactors in his power to a minor purgatory of "inward pinches," which presumably have the effect of conscience. But no one except the king Alonso actually acknowledges fault or asks to be forgiven, nor does Prospero require it or even pause for them to ask it of him. He has already chosen virtue over vengeance before he has restored their ability to speak and to ask his pardon, if they choose to.

Debates had raged throughout Europe, at least since the time of Luther, about how sin and grace were to be reconciled. The Reformist side rejected purgatory as unscriptural, and therefore rejected indulgences and prayers for the dead as well. It rejected the canonization of saints and the treasury of merit. It rejected auricular confession and absolution by priests. It rejected "salvation by works," by which was meant pilgrimages and donations, vows, crusades, and anything else that was undertaken with the thought that it would mitigate sin in God's eyes. In place of all this it insisted on faith alone, Scripture alone, Christ alone, grace alone. This was a very profound stirring in the deeps of Western civilization, having to do with the structure of society and even of individual consciousness.

Rather than recruiting Shakespeare to one side or another, as critics and biographers often do, or supposing that these questions that absorbed so many of the best minds in England and Europe had no place in his thoughts, as critics and biographers do characteristically, let us say that he took an intelligent interest in them, as he did in so many things. How is guilt in others, real or imagined, to be dealt with? How is one's own sense of guilt to be borne or relieved? Histories and tragedies, and comedies, too, turn on these issues, and on one even larger. How is life to be lived in this fallen world, with all its dangers and temptations, if grace is taken to be the standard of a virtuous life? Who can rise to such a standard or be loyal to it? What response will it find where it is manifested? And what is the soul, the human essence for which all these questions are of infinite significance?

"Grace is grace, despite of all controversy." These words are spoken by the character Lucio in Shakespeare's *Measure for Measure.* Lucio is a fool and a scoundrel, a fantastic, according to the dramatis personae. But he is also the loyal friend who takes steps to save a man from suffering death as a penalty for an offense that is only made punishable by an extremely rigid interpretation of law. These words are part of a half-serious exchange with two anonymous gentlemen in a house of ill repute, and Lucio ends his remark with a jibe, "as for example, thou art a wicked villain, despite of all grace."

In this scene Lucio and the gentlemen are playing back and forth between two meanings of the word "grace," as "the thanksgiving before meat," and as a central concept of Christian theology, by which, in Lucio's taunting instance, a villain might be rescued from his wicked proclivities in this life. Still, Lucio's words are worth pausing over. "Grace is grace"—simply itself, not accessible to paraphrase. This would indeed put it beyond controversy, since there is no language in which it can be controverted, and it would give it a special character, most notably in the Shakespearean world, where associations among words, figures, similes, are constant and central. Lucio's exchanges with the gentlemen mention that table grace is to be heard in any religion, with the further implication that one would be better for hearing it. In this sense also it is put beyond controversy, and every religion is, so to speak, graced by it. I propose that, in his later plays, Shakespeare gives grace a scale and aesthetic power, and a structural importance, that reach toward a greater sufficiency of expression—not a definition or a demonstration of grace or even an objective correlative for it, but the intimation of a great reality of another order, which pervades human experience, even manifests itself in human actions and relations, yet is always purely itself. Hamlet speaks of ideal virtues, calling them "pure as grace." Prospero, after the scene of rather detached and unceremonious reconciliations, speaks his amazing epilogue to the audience, asking them to release him from his island, "As you from crimes would pardoned be." He says, "My ending is despair, / Unless I be relieved by prayer, / Which pierces so that it assaults / Mercy itself and frees all faults." Prayer opens on something purer and grander than mercy, something that puts aside the consciousness of fault, the residue of judgment that makes mercy a lesser thing than grace.

•

The word "Reformation" suggests that the primary source and effect of the controversy that fascinated Europe was a change in church polity. In fact, in this period people were pondering the deepest thoughts and traditions they shared as Christians. The powerful intervened and criminalized the expression of one or another theology, depending on the regime in power at the time, and this created a factionalism and repressiveness that perverted a rich conversation. Critics and historians have followed this precedent, often eager to identify the sympathies of any figure who did not, himself or herself, make them absolutely clear, as if a leaning were an identity, and might not change from year to year, depending on whom one had spoken with lately, or what one had read, or how an argument settled into individual thought or experience. In answer to the question, Which side are you on? "I'm still deciding," or "I see merit in a number of positions," would not have been more pleasing to the enforcers of any orthodoxy than outright heresy would have been. High-order thinking is not so readily forced into preexisting categories. If we step back from seeing the period as a political struggle first of all, the official view of it, we might see it as passionate and profoundly interesting, entirely consistent with the richness of its philosophic and literary achievements. What *is* grace, after all? What *is* the soul?

Again, I eschew any attempt to identify Shakespeare as the partisan of any side of the controversy, with a few provisos. First, to express any opinion or attitude that offended authority was extremely dangerous, to life and limb and also to the whole phenomenon of public theater. So tact must be assumed. I think it is appropriate to see Shakespeare as a theologian in his own right, though the perils that attended religious expression made his theology implicit rather than overt. Second, Shakespeare tests various and opposed ideas, giving each one extraordinarily just consideration. He appreciates a good idea.

My third point is a little more complex. Broadly speaking, English religious culture during this period was divided into three parts, Catholic, Anglican, and Protestant. Catholicism was traditional, and had major support from the Continent. Anglicanism was the British withdrawal from communion with Rome and from papal authority, with selected aspects of Catholicism and of Reformed teaching retained or absorbed. The Protestants, as I call them here, are elsewhere called Calvinists or Puritans. They were the faction that became strong enough by the beginning of the seventeenth century to carry out a successful revolution and to depose, try, and execute the king

Charles I. This happened after Shakespeare's death, but a movement of such strength would have to have been formidable for decades. This is only truer because it absorbed radical popular traditions, notably Lollardy. Calvinism was already well established in France and French Geneva, and in conflict with the French government. The name Puritan dissociates it from its Continental origins, and lends to the very fixed impression that it existed mainly to spread gloom and corrosive disapprobation, particularly with regard to the arts, poetry, and the theater, and, more generally, the Renaissance passion for pagan antiquity. In fact, Ovid's *Metamorphoses*, the most influential classical text in the English Renaissance, was translated by Arthur Golding, who also translated Calvin extensively, including his three-volume *Commentary on Psalms*. Calvin's *Institutes* was translated by Thomas Norton, one of the writers of *Gorboduc*, the first tragedy written in English. The first sonnet cycle in English was written by Anne Vaughn Lok and published with her translation of a set of Calvin's sermons. One of the popular plays of the period was *Abraham's Sacrifice*, translated from the French by Arthur Golding, the first tragedy written in a modern European language. Its author was Théodore de Bèze of Geneva, the closest associate of John Calvin. This is to say that these so-called Puritans were literary people in the classic Renaissance mold. I have seen Golding's authorship of the translation of Ovid disputed on the grounds that he was a Puritan (that is, a Calvinist) and Ovid is rather salacious. But this is in fact typical when seen in relation to France. Marguerite de Navarre, the French patroness of the Renaissance and Reformation, whose court produced Anne Boleyn, wrote rapturous religious poetry and also the *Heptameron*, which can startle even the jaded modern reader. Clément Marot, who made the translations of the Psalms that, set to music, were the joy and ornament of Protestant France, wrote many secular poems, also startling. Geneva itself scandalized Europe by printing ancient literature elsewhere banned, including other and more salacious works of Ovid. The historical characterization of so-called Puritanism precludes our looking to neighboring France for context, though Calvin was French and was widely read in England. English Protestants went to France and French Protestants came to England during periods of persecution. Shakespeare would have been following a familiar pattern in writing *Venus and Adonis*, which was published in a famously beautiful edition by a French Huguenot émigré printer in London. So the Puritans were not puritanical. Nor were they anti-intellectual or obscurantist. And they drew directly on the Continental Renaissance.

All this is to make the point that there were three highly distinctive, theologically articulate religious cultures in Elizabethan England, not the usual triad of Catholics, Protestants, and misanthropes. When the Acts of Uniformity were passed under Elizabeth, they criminalized both Catholic and Protestant forms of worship in that they departed from Anglican practice. Both Catholics and Protestants lost most of their civil rights, which were restored to both in the nineteenth century. Both suffered persecution and martyrdom. So, if Shakespeare seems cautious and elusive, it could mean that he was Catholic, or that he was Protestant, or that he did not want to align himself with or against any faction. His younger contemporary, René Descartes, was similarly elusive, probably on these same grounds. He described himself as masked, like an actor. It was the nature of the times.

But if Shakespeare did take seriously the great questions bruited in his civilization during the whole of his lifetime, then he might have reflected on the meaning behind, or beyond, it all—not the geopolitics of it, but the essential, shared truth that underlay these aggravated differences. Grace is grace. How would this be staged?

•

I wrote my doctoral thesis on Shakespeare, and I am very glad I did, even though, in retrospect, I think I was wrong about a great many things. I suppose there is enough money in the world to induce me to read it again sometime, foreign currencies being taken into account. Still, the research that went into the writing of it did acquaint me with the times a little, and also with critical and historical approaches to them. I have been a truant these many years, so I am not abreast of new work in the field. I have glanced now and then at a historicism that does not seem to me to be particularly attentive to history. I have diverted myself with arguments in support of the Earl of Oxford's authorship of the works conventionally attributed to Shakespeare. And I can only say that if Oxford was secretly their author, the perfection of his disguise is the fact that poetry the earl is known to have written is strikingly inferior to the work he published pseudonymously, under the name Shakespeare. It would have required phenomenal effort in a great poet to have written work so undistinguished.

As a student I was mystified though not interested by the elaborate concluding acts of so many of the later plays, thoroughgoing reconciliations, sometimes among a great many characters. Critics and professors excused these endings, and dismissed them, as the sort of thing the audience would have wanted. Old Will was a canny businessman. Our groundlings seem to prefer concluding mayhem of some kind, a shootout or an act of war, merciless and mindless retaliation for unforgivable crimes. So it might be interesting to consider what sort of crowd it was that could be pandered to with these long scenes of gratuitous pardon. The use of the word "gratuitous" is considered. Grace is gratuitous. Etymologies are lovely things.

I think it is probably an error to suppose that any serious artist allows considerations like these—i.e., what will bring in the crowds, and what will appeal to their presumedly unrefined tastes—to govern important choices, certainly not with the frequency they would have done in Shakespeare's case. *Cymbeline, Antony and Cleopatra, Measure for Measure, The Winter's Tale, The Tempest*, all end with elaborate scenes of reconciliation that all of them are designed from the first act to bring about. This is to say, reconciliation is their subject. If this is conventional in comedy, it is odd in plays as grave as these are. And what happens in these scenes is no sorting out of grievances, no putting of things right. Justice as that word is normally understood has no part in them. They are about forgiveness that is unmerited, unexpected, unasked, unconditional. In other words, they are about grace.

There are perils in attempting a distinction between characteristics of a particular writer's work and the conventions that prevailed among writers active when he was. Christopher Marlowe is as close to being Shakespeare's peer as any of his contemporaries, and he died young, leaving just a few plays, so the value of comparisons between the two is limited. Still, Dr. Faustus goes to hell, Tamburlaine brutalizes the eastern world without compunction, Aeneas abandons Dido without a backward glance, and Edward II dies onstage, a wretched victim, leaving the child king Edward III to avenge him by sending his own mother to the Tower. Nowhere is there a glimpse of anything that might be called grace, divine or human.

Shakespeare could imagine a world without grace as well, as he did in *Macbeth*, *Timon of Athens*, *Coriolanus*, and the appalling *Titus Andronicus.* These plays are all set in pagan antiquity, but so, for example, is *Pericles, Prince of Tyre*, in which Diana of Ephesus emerges as the giver of grace, felt among its characters as profoundest human love. If reconciliation scenes pleased the crowd, then Marlowe might have tried his hand at one. But he had a formula of his own for pleasing them, one that seems to have appealed to unembarrassed resentment and a taste for violence. He anticipates the relentless dramas of the Jacobean theater, as Shakespeare does also in the plays I have just named.

It is the movement toward reconciliation, toward act 5, that makes many of Shakespeare's plays exemplify the kind of drama we call Elizabethan, and might as well call Shakespearean, since I at least am not aware of any other playwright who shaped his plays in this way.

Let us consider a hard case: *Hamlet*. *Hamlet* raises a great many questions. Why has Horatio been at the Danish court since old Hamlet's funeral, for months, that is, without encountering Hamlet until he feels he must speak to him, having seen the king's ghost? He is on familiar terms with the castle guards, who defer to him as a "scholar." And he seems impressively informed about state affairs. Yet he seems to have stayed below stairs, as it were. By comparison with Rosencrantz and Guildenstern, he is never greeted by Claudius or Gertrude or addressed by them otherwise than as a servant, though Hamlet calls him "fellow student" and mentions his "philosophy." Clearly he has been at Wittenberg with Hamlet. Poor students often paid their way by acting as servants to wealthy students, and this might explain Horatio's ambiguous status.

The title of the play, *Hamlet, Prince of Denmark*, is also ambiguous. The word "prince" could mean the son of a king, or it could mean a ruler, as in Machiavelli's use of it. Putting aside the fact that Hamlet is male and adult, the obvious successor to his dead father, there is the fact that old Hamlet has been murdered. These are the makings of a tragedy of revenge, Prince Hamlet being the "avenger of blood," the one singled out by ancient tradition to "set things right." This is only truer because Claudius's crime is beyond the reach of any other authority. And the legitimacy of a king had everything to do with the health of a kingdom, so Hamlet would have had an obligation to act even weightier than revenge.

Hamlet is a Renaissance man captive to a medieval world, and, as Laertes says, he is subject to his birth. He is a learned prince of the Renaissance type. He longs to go back to school at Wittenberg and is forbidden to. Kings kept those who might challenge them at court close at hand, where they could be watched, and Claudius has very good grounds for suspecting Hamlet, having at the least "popp'd in between the election and [his] hopes." He is intensely aware of his nephew's demeanor, reading in his mourning and melancholy not merely grief and disillusionment but also sinister intent.

But Hamlet does not want his traditional roles, as king or as avenger. He really does want to return to his life as a student. This is apparent in the eagerness with which he greets Horatio, who at first deflects Hamlet's shows of friendship by insisting on his own subordinate place. Hamlet is a classic Shakespearean character, a king who is and is not a king. His rank makes his intentions toward Ophelia presumptively dishonorable, deprives him of freedom to go where he wishes and live as he wishes, and deprives him of friendship as well, which in Horatio is at first reduced to self-protective deference, and in Rosencrantz and Guildenstern to feigning and informing. Granting the endless complexities of the play, the drift of it brings Hamlet back to himself, so to speak. From the first he is in some ways remarkably innocent. His father has died under doubtful circumstances, the crown has been usurped. Yet he seems to entertain no suspicions until a ghost comes from the grave to lay things out for him. He is appalled by his mother's disloyalty to his father, but does not reflect at all on her marriage to Claudius as having been meant to help legitimize him as king. He chooses to doubt the ghost, setting a snare for Claudius with a play that enacts the murder as described by the ghost, and Claudius is terrified, losing composure altogether, so suspicion is confirmed and Hamlet tells himself he is resolved to act. Then he comes upon Claudius praying and bethinks him that if his uncle dies at his prayers he will go to heaven—an interesting assumption, considering the theological weightiness of usurpation, incest, and the murder of a king. Claudius himself remarks on the ineffectuality of repentance when the penitent intends to go on enjoying the benefits of his sins.

It is not that Hamlet cannot make up his mind, but that he refuses proof that would persuade anyone else, then, finally convinced, talks himself out of an opportunity to be avenged. In a sense the prince descends for a while into the roles that are expected of him, treating Ophelia with vicious contempt, using royal authority, both feigned and real, to have Rosencrantz and Guildenstern killed. But a strange innocence in Hamlet, recovered or never really lost, allows the ending to unfold as it does. When he receives the challenge to duel with Laertes, he takes it in good faith, seeming to anticipate nothing worse than "taking the odd hit" from his opponent's foil. At the same time he tells Horatio, "Thou wouldst not think how ill all's here, about my heart." He has just recounted to Horatio Claudius's plot to have him killed in England, which he thwarted in obedience to "a kind of fighting" in his heart. He has recounted his uncle's crimes and asks, "Is't not perfect conscience, / To quit him with this arm? and is't not to be damn'd, / To let this canker of our nature come / In further evil?" And now he has accepted Claudius's request that he engage in a sword fight with a man who holds him responsible for the deaths of his father and sister. He feels again an intuitive dread, which Horatio encourages. Yet, even after Gertrude is poisoned and Hamlet is wounded by Laertes's unbated sword, he reacts as if the plot could have come from anywhere. He shouts, "O villainy! Ho! Let the door be lock'd: Treachery! Seek it out." *Laertes* is obliged to *tell* him that treachery "is here," and murderous old Claudius is to blame.

In the first scene of the play we hear about Fortinbras, the Norwegian prince who means to make Denmark answer for his father's death. Claudius, his judgment perhaps wassail-impaired, sees good news in the fact that the king of Norway is pleased with Fortinbras for saying he has given over his plan to invade, and has rewarded him with a great deal of money and an invading army—bound for Poland, the ambassadors are told. And could they please pass through Denmark on their way. So Fortinbras is spared the trouble of invading, and all the great labor of defense described in the first scene is for nothing. The play does not allow any certain judgment about Fortinbras's intentions, whether his low estimate of Claudius and of the state of things in Denmark is being acted on in this very transparent ruse, if ruse it is. Hamlet's one act as king is to give his endorsement to things as they are, to Fortinbras, who has brought armed men into the Danish court. The endorsement hardly seems necessary, in the circumstances. But it does mean that Hamlet sees the presence of Fortinbras as fortuitous, and him as someone to be trusted with the welfare of a country toward which his intentions not long before had been vengeful. When Claudius lays out his plot for the murder of Hamlet to Laertes, he says Hamlet will suspect nothing, "being remiss, / Most generous and free from all contriving." Not himself deceptive, Hamlet does not look for deception in others—even after he has fallen victim to another flagrant deception. Through it all, his mind is not tainted. This seems to be what we are seeing in the matter of Fortinbras.

Hamlet's madness is both feigned and real, and it consists in his descent into the reality of his circumstances. He cannot naturalize himself to this reality, and, consciously, at least, he cannot see his way beyond it—except, perhaps, in the thought of death. As prince, and as madman, he is flattered, manipulated, spied on. His world would compel him to an act of homicide that, thoroughly as he can rationalize it in the world's terms, and despite continuing provocations of the darkest sort, he finally seems to have put out of mind. And when he does this, he is restored to himself. He will die because he is a generous, uncontriving man in a world where these virtues are fatal vulnerabilities. Since he seems to have forgotten to despise

Claudius and to condemn Gertrude, his mother, toward whom he acts with great courtesy and tenderness, he should also be called a gracious man. He would seem to have freed all faults.

If death seems a poor reward for his having stepped almost free of this corrupting and entangling reality, among the things that were true in Shakespeare's time was the fact that to die for one's faith or one's conscience was not altogether unusual. Many heroes of the age went calmly to the stake when capitulation would have spared them. And their ends crowned their lives. In Shakespeare's plays there tends to be a strong awareness of life after death. Both life and death are appraised differently than we moderns appraise them, for this reason. The dying Laertes says, "Exchange forgiveness with me, noble Hamlet: / Mine and my father's death come not upon thee, / Nor thine on me." Hamlet replies, "Heaven make thee free of it! I follow thee." The efficacy implied here for simple human forgiveness is to be noted. These two right noble youths pass into eternity together, as if the madness of earth had never contrived to make them enemies.

Still, death is grave and terrible here and in all the plays, graver because the state of the soul at death is crucial to its immortal fate. What does Hamlet fear will be remembered of him if Horatio does not live after him to tell the tale aright? That the final scene will be interpreted by its appearance, and he will be thought to have carried out a brutal revenge intentionally, as his world would have expected, rather than as the agent of a destiny he could not evade. He might have said, "At least I have avenged the crimes against my father." Instead he reacts to the catastrophe as a potential slander on his memory. Misinterpretation would be the final snare the world could deploy to make Hamlet less than Hamlet.

It is a part of my argument for Shakespeare's theological seriousness to point out that this consciousness of the heavens is quite particular to him among the playwrights, at least so far as I know. I may rely too heavily on Marlowe in making this comparison. But there is a tendency among critics, in my experience, to relegate striking elements in Shakespeare's work to cultural backdrop—Elizabethans simply assumed certain things, so (the reasoning here is not really clear to me) these things should not be taken to be especially important to Shakespeare. The further I look into the period, the more inclined I am to doubt that we have equipped ourselves to make such generalizations about worldview. More to the point, no great statement about reality, for example, that the heavens are attentive to our thoughts and actions and will determine the fate of our souls, can be static, like simple information. It implies a profound relationship that unfolds continuously and compels, among other things, extraordinary self-awareness. Then in this way Shakespeare's theological seriousness is simultaneous with his greatness as a dramatist.

•

Antony and Cleopatra are two fabulous, aging reprobates who toy with the fate of the world as few people in history have had the power to do. Power is prominent among Shakespeare's fascinations, and in this ancient moment it is so hypertrophic that the influence of individual men can be reckoned at half the known world, or the whole of it. Preposterous and true. Shakespeare studies power in its waning, its dissolution. What does it consist of? So long as it retains its integrity it seems simply to define itself, to be self-evident. When it disintegrates it is revealed to be compounded of will, custom, kinship, loyalty, and opportunism, together with a magnetism of its own, which in some part always inheres even in fallen greatness. Its ebbing exposes the fact that it has always depended on the acquiescence of people in general, as well as of its servants and lieutenants and its potential competitors.

Granting all this, why does power center itself in certain individual figures, all of whom eat bread, need friends? How does this web of dependencies manifest itself in society and history as a force not to be resisted? Monarchy in Shakespeare's time and place claimed to take legitimacy from royal descent. But his history plays are studies in the difficulties that beset hereditary kingship, including, in its worst moments, the violent removal of some cousin claimants to the advantage of others. Still, volatile as it was, violent as it often was, it provided a theoretical basis, at least, for deference and acknowledged right. Antony, Octavius, Lepidus, and Pompey are all aristocrats, but none of them can make a claim to a dynastic right of succession, since the disaster that has elevated them to the power they hold, share, and contend for is the collapse of a republic. From the first we are shown a cold Octavius, a doting Antony, a foolish Lepidus, all of them drunkards except Octavius. The soldiers who attend them regard them with discreet contempt. Yet they are all powerful still, commanders of immense fleets and armies, and of the obedience of the familiars who see them at their worst and nevertheless are prepared to give their lives for them. When warfare among them leaves only Antony and Octavius as competitors, in battle between them great Antony disgraces himself, his fleet following Cleopatra's in uncompelled retreat. He tries to recover in a second battle, is betrayed by Cleopatra's forces, and fails. Cleopatra is then so fearful of him that she sends a messenger to tell him she is dead, and in his grief at this message he wounds himself fatally, botching his suicide. Hearing of this, she stages her own death.

On its face, this is not an especially attractive story. It is remarkably uncomplicated by Shakespeare's standards, though its movement is familiar—the waning of power and status in characters for whom status and power are so habitual and defining that the loss of them confounds identity itself. There is, however, a remarkable countermovement. Even as Antony and Cleopatra decline, as the world measures such things, the play affirms them by casting a golden, one might say celestial, light over their very human failings. This is an effect of the great irony that embraces the events the play embodies. This Octavius Caesar, in defeating Antony, or rather in enjoying the consequences of his self-defeat, will become Caesar Augustus the unrivaled emperor, mighty enough to decree that all the world should be enrolled. Antony's defeat, which is his utter though not honorable, virtuous, or politic love for the disreputable queen of Egypt, fulfills a great cosmic intent. Augustus brings the peace that was the prophesied condition for the coming of the Messiah. If anyone, in all Shakespeare's plays, is the chosen of the Lord, it is this unlikable Octavius, who is entirely overshadowed by those he has conquered.

What might Shakespeare the theologian be pondering here? The acceptance by the Renaissance and Reformation of material we might find morally doubtful has been noted. Clearly the much mooted question of destiny, of divine determination, arises with singular clarity at the moment of this break in historic time, when the engrossing turmoil of earth is preparing the occasion for a consummate act of divine grace. Antony is destined to lose, brought down by what pagans and Christians would agree were license, vice, and folly, but destined to lose in any case so that order-imposing Caesar Augustus can establish his great peace. Then, since divine intent unfolded as it did, must it be true that God willed the transgressions of this grandly decadent pair? Or does the vast graciousness of divine intent not only forgive but even transform—therefore free—all faults? If this were to happen, what would it look like? How could it be staged?

Almost from its beginnings Christianity has attempted to reconcile the indubitable virtue of many great pagans with the fact that they seemed to fall outside the scheme of salvation. But these particular pagans were not virtuous, so Shakespeare has set himself an interesting variant of the problem. Let us say that he was exploring another thought, controversial in his time, that the Greek *agape*, traditionally translated into Latin as *caritas*, or charity, actually meant love. This change is reflected in the Geneva Bible, which Shakespeare knew well. However close *caritas* may have been to *agape* when Jerome flourished, "charity" had drifted a very long way from "love" in early modern English, a distance still marked in our own usage. And what we learn at the end of this play is that Antony and Cleopatra really do love each other. This might seem trivial. But Thomas More pointed out that the word "love" could refer to a commonplace, even base, human emotion and relationship. Granting his point, then Scripture would seem intentional in its permitting this association to be made. The note on 1 Corinthians, chapter 13, in the Geneva Bible says that in "the life to come . . . there at length shall we truly and perfectly love both God, and one another." And perhaps Antony and Cleopatra participate in this greatest of the theological virtues, the one that makes conditional all the others, even faith. Certainly this understanding would resolve the anomaly of the implied exclusion of every kind of pagan and infidel from the divine love and grace Christians call salvation.

I feel justified in this speculation by the importance of love in Shakespeare. The great acts of grace at the end of many of his plays are the restoration of lost loved ones. Human love in the purest forms we can know it, wife and husband, parent and child, has the aura and the immutability of the sacred. And it is surely to be noted that the settings of these plays are typically non-Christian.

In act 1, in his first appearance and his second sentence, Antony tells Cleopatra that, to find a limit to his love, "Then must thou needs find out new heaven, new earth," alluding to a text he would not have known, the book of the prophet Isaiah. Isaiah is, for the New Testament, the great prophet of the world transformed. Aside from allusions to Herod of Jewry, another important contemporary, there are ironies in the speeches of both of them. Chiding him for faithlessness, Cleopatra reminds

Antony that once "Eternity was in our lips and eyes, / Bliss in our brows' bent; none our parts so poor, / But was a race of heaven." When he hears of her (supposed) death, Antony says, "I will o'ertake thee, Cleopatra, and / Weep for my pardon." And he says, "Where souls do couch on flowers, we'll hand in hand, / And with our sprightly port make the ghosts gaze"—his imagination of a life to come continuous with all the particular luxurious and whimsical charm of the life they have lived together. And his perfect forgiveness of Cleopatra, who has not only destroyed his greatness but has now caused his death, is striking against the false promise of Caesar's grace, ending with the aside "You see how easily she may be surprised," that is, captured. And Cleopatra has her "dream" of an Antony "past the size of dreaming." She says, "Methinks I hear Antony call . . . husband, I come: / Now to that name my courage prove my title."

These immortal longings have the authority beautiful language and beautiful thought can give them. The Renaissance and the Reformation loved these great souls who, in their way, haunted pagan antiquity uniquely, offering instances of the unquestionable power of human love, with all this might imply about their having a place in divine love. Nothing is asserted in this play. They die, and the rest is silence. Shakespeare, my theologian, never asserts but often proposes that we participate in grace, in the largest sense of the word, as we experience love, in the largest sense of that word. Beauty masses around the moments in which these thoughts are spoken and enacted. In the words of the Geneva Bible, love "is not provoked to anger; it thinketh no evil." Finally both Antony and Hamlet are gracious after unthinkable, then fatal, provocations. In this they are at last fully themselves, purely the souls God gave them.

SERVANTHOOD

So late in my life I have learned that theological writings of John Wycliffe survive in significant numbers, a substantial part of them never to this day translated from his Latin. My interests being what they are, I have done more than most people to put myself in the way of knowing this, but the discovery came as a complete surprise to me. I was aware of Wycliffe's influence on Hus and Luther, assuming that the example of the fourteenth-century vernacular Bible associated with him was the reason for his importance to them and to the Reformation in general. Now I have a collection of Wycliffe's and his followers' writings published in the valuable Masters of Western Spirituality series, and I find that there is much more to be surprised about. Despite its obvious importance, the treatment of religion by historians and critics as an element in the English Renaissance is odd and unsatisfactory.

The influence of earlier Reformation and Renaissance on the Continent, especially in France, tends to go unmentioned before the massacres of St. Bartholomew's Day in 1572. This is true despite the fact that the French Reform was indisputably the greatest contemporary influence on religious thought and literary culture in Renaissance England. Given the importance of French literature for Chaucer, Gower, and the writer of *Sir Gawain and the Green Knight*, and for the later *Morte d'Arthur* of Thomas Malory, this influence might be assumed to be established and continuous, and absorbed into the English vernacular tradition.

Even if they arose among Oxford scholars and were influential in the universities, dissident movements in England tend to be dismissed by historians and critics, including our contemporaries, on the basis of polemical associations with the lower orders, peasants in the case of the Lollards, shopkeepers in the case of that important group history has taught us to call Puritans. Of course it is very much to the credit of both Lollards and Puritans that there were a great many peasants and shopkeepers among them, as well as scholars and aristocrats. But these associations with the lower orders tend to obscure the fact that in both cases the impetus they gave to the culture was literary and intellectual. Worse, these conventional views of Lollards and Puritans are effectively dismissive on grounds that should themselves have been discredited long since, because they enlist the historical enterprise in a hermeneutics of snobbery, neither more nor less. In 1394 twelve "Lollard Conclusions" were anonymously posted on the door of Westminster. They were objections to the special spiritual status claimed for the Catholic priesthood, to priestly celibacy, to the doctrine of transubstantiation and the veneration of the host, to exorcisms, to the holding of clerical and secular offices simultaneously, to prayers for the dead that give preference to those who have left money for this purpose, to icons as encouraging practices amounting to idolatry, to auricular confession, to manslaughter in war or through judicial process, to celibacy of women religious, to the costly material elaboration of the churches. The leading humanists of the Reformation, men of great learning, raised objections very similar to these more than a century later. In other words, we know enough about this sect, despite all efforts to suppress and destroy it, to see that it was intellectual as well as popular, neither of these excluding the other.

From the thirteenth century until the eighteenth century, Western civilization expended enormous wealth and energy in suppressing ideas that were considered by religious and political authorities to be disruptive or heretical. Lollardy, the movement associated with Wycliffe, which continued and grew after his death, moved Henry IV and his parliament to pass De Haeretico Comburendo, a law whose object was to destroy this sect utterly. The law required that their books be surrendered, that their preaching and teaching cease, and that those who persisted in this heresy should be burned. Words meant to stigmatize do have this very potent effect over centuries, "Lollard" and "heretic" being two excellent examples. The extraordinary severity of the punishments suffered for heresy, defined by its prosecutors as the entertaining of questions, and of opinions different from those taught by the church, has caused heretics to be thought of as egregious misanthropes and fanatics. But the beliefs of the Lollards or Wycliffites are so unobjectionable, at least to those who consider it no crime to read a Bible in English or to doubt certain doctrines and practices of medieval Catholicism, that allusions to them stand little chance of being noticed by modern readers. Lollards believed that the image of God in any human being, themselves included, is properly the basis for all Christian life and worship, as well as charity and personal integrity. Charity should go directly to the needy poor, confession should be made directly to whomever one has wronged. This made them regard themselves as sufficient to the requirements of Christianity, and capable of its joys, with minimal dependency on the rites of the church, including even for the sacraments of marriage and baptism. Their piety centered on the Ten Commandments, enlarging on them to make them the core of a strongly articulated ethics and ecclesiology.

•

Suppression tends to obscure evidence of its own failures, since fear is as likely to inspire ingenuity and stealth as it is compliance. Lollardy persisted in England until it merged with the Reformation. The Protestant writer John Bale, in his preface to *The Examinations of Anne Askew,* written in 1546, the year of the young woman's death at the stake, says, "Great slaughter and burning hath been here in England for John Wycliffe's books, ever since the year of our Lord 1382. Yet have not one of them thoroughly perished. I have at this hour the titles of one hundred and forty-three of them, which are many more in number."

In England, literature in the vernacular at least from the time of John Wycliffe is associated with religious dissent. For this reason, I propose, the concerns and the loyalties of the movement crossed the lines of class and economic status. To challenge the dominance of Latin was to diminish the potency of a great distinction among social strata. "Benefit of clergy," that is, some acquaintance with Latin, could save one from hanging. To challenge it was also to broaden access to knowledge and understanding of the texts that were said to provide the theological basis of the existing order. Again, though the word "Lollard" was derisive, suggesting the speech of the uneducated, Wycliffe, an Oxford professor, was supported by Oxford faculty and members of the gentry and nobility, including John of Gaunt, the father of King Henry IV. Geoffrey Chaucer was associated with figures called the "Lollard knights," or "hooded knights," adherents and protectors of the sect's preachers. Some of these knights were also close to Richard II, a fact that sheds interesting light on Henry IV's attempts at suppression. Certainly it demonstrates that the sect's having adherents in the highest ranks of society did nothing to secure its safety or its acceptance. Though the emphasis of the critique offered by the movement fell largely on evil in the form of the impoverishment of the lower classes by an abusive established order, civil and religious, nevertheless some who enjoyed the privileges of that order seem to have seen beyond their own worldly interests. Despite whatever wisdom is contained in our darkest hermeneutics, this does happen. Many of the surviving Wycliffe Bibles are beautiful and would have been costly, the property of wealthy people. Yet the movement was much broader than its learned and aristocratic expressions. The Piers Ploughman tradition arose at this time and flourished for generations, until the boy who followed the plow could serve as William Tyndale's ideal reader.

The English vernacular movement had its great resurgence in the Renaissance, which was simultaneous with the Reformation and hardly to be distinguished from it. This time the forbidden Bible in English translation was Tyndale's New Testament, and when it arrived, the Geneva Bible as well. Under Mary Tudor the De Haeretico Comburendo, in relative abeyance under Henry VIII and Edward VI, was again enforced. People in those days were of course inured to horrors. There were always plenty of decapitated heads on London Bridge. English monarchs were never at a loss for means to terrorize and execute, and suppression and extermination of sects as government policy was hardly novel in England or Europe. So this return to the burning of heretics might not have had the impact it did if it had not called up an earlier era, extraordinary for the literature it left and inspired, a rich religious and secular literature written in the popular tongue. The second-largest-selling book of the sixteenth century in England was Foxe's *Book of Martyrs*. This continuously larger, beautifully printed and illustrated compendium of accounts of the suffering and death of the heroes of dissent made an unbroken narrative of executions of fourteenth-century Lollards and sixteenth-century Protestants. The exhumation and burning of the remains of John Wycliffe are as vividly realized as the famous sixteenth-century torture and burning of the young gentlewoman Anne Askew.

•

My intention is to open the question of the mind-set of Shakespeare's audience, a self-selecting crowd of Londoners with no more in common than a free afternoon and the price of admission. The argument that Shakespeare was actually someone else, the Earl of Oxford, say, is based on his apparently extensive knowledge of court life. But what we know of court life is largely what Shakespeare tells us about it. And, for the most practical reasons, the knowledge that was actually crucial to him was the kind that would make his plays intelligible and engrossing to his public. This would place him closer to the man or woman in the street than to more rarefied circles, a perspective that would have come naturally to him, if Shakespeare was Shakespeare. Obviously his career depended on his making a sound estimate of their interests and capacities. And here we are, centuries on, granting him more weight and subtlety than we grant any theologian or philosopher, on the basis of his estimate of his audience. There seems to be an assumption among critics that the deep parts of his plays were written for that small class trained in the universities or sophisticated by some other means, while the groundlings were there for the clowns and the sword fights. But what if there was an intellectual tradition shared by Shakespeare and his larger audience, so strong and well established that it was capable of serving as a medium for ideas of great complexity, yet so long stigmatized as subversive or heretical, and still, rightly, so much a source of anxiety to those in power, that allusions to it are oblique and implicit? What if this tradition, unacknowledged by modern scholars and critics, was a robust conceptual frame, brought to the plays by the audience and shared and explored by the playwright? If there is a continuity of thought and perspective between William Langland's *Piers the Ploughman*, written in the fourteenth century, and John Bunyan's seventeenth-century *Pilgrim's Progress*, both masterpieces of the vernacular tradition, an ongoing vernacular culture accounts for this continuity.

Under Edward VI there was indeed a surge of interest in the works of Chaucer, Langland, Lydgate, and Gower. Then the fashion changed, and they, together with contemporary writers in the popular style, were ridiculed by Elizabethan critics such as Philip Sidney. But Spenser was among those who emulated the old style. Shakespeare foregrounded "ancient Gower" in the late play *Pericles, Prince of Tyre*. With archaisms of verse and language, he drew explicit, even emphatic, attention to his source. This might account for the great popularity of the play as well as the fact that it was omitted from the First Folio. Again, if Shakespeare's view of Shylock and Othello seems anomalously generous and complex in a culture from which Jews had been expelled in 1290 on the pretext of blood libels, and which they would not be permitted to enter again until 1657, *Piers the Ploughman* may shed light on popular feeling toward them. Perhaps cynicism about the motives of a king who made himself wealthy by this expropriation preserved an unofficial memory of the Jews among the people, as having been wronged in a way that was familiar to them. Or perhaps there were Jews who remained in England and were not betrayed to the authorities. Repression discredits law, after all, and dignifies resistance. A century after the expulsion, William Langland wrote this:

> "But all the clergy of the church," I said, "say in their sermons that neither Saracens nor Jews nor any other creature in the likeness of Christ can be saved without baptism."
>
> "I deny it," said Imagination, frowning, for the Scripture says, "The just man shall *scarcely* be saved on the Day of Judgment. Therefore he shall be saved . . . For there is a baptism by water, a baptism by the shedding of blood, and a baptism by fire, which means by

> steadfast faith—The divine fire comes not to consume, but to bring light.
>
> "So an honest man that lives by the law that he knows, believing there is none better (for if he knew of a better he would accept it)—a man who has never treated anyone unjustly, and who dies in the same spirit—surely the God of truth would not reject such honesty as this. And whether it shall be so or not, the faith of such a man is very great, and from that faith there springs a hope of reward. We are told that God will give eternal life to His own, and His own are the faithful and true."

And this: "Faith alone is sufficient to save the ignorant. And that being so, many Jews and Saracens may be saved, perhaps before we are."

•

Here Langland compares the spiritual state of Muslims, whom he takes to have strayed from an original Christianity, to that of good Christians who are misled by incompetent priests. Clearly there is no reason to think of the dominant classes in fourteenth-century society as more generous and sophisticated in their thinking than the popular audience of Langland's book, nor to suppose that the past is more naive or intolerant than the present. This is certainly relevant to the question of Shakespeare's audience.

It is usual for scholars to say that these old writers were inappropriately made to serve the purposes of Puritanism—there may be no meaning at all in the fact that the Puritan Oliver Cromwell negotiated the return of the Jews to England, many of whom had by then found refuge in the tolerant and Calvinist Low Countries. In any case, it is difficult to know what such an assertion means, since scholars never offer a definition of Puritanism. If the movement was so diffuse as to make definition impossible, then statements that treat it as unitary, as this one does, are misleading. We can say that Puritanism was a popular political movement, whatever else. History is unambiguous on this point. Phenomena of its kind, broad-based and durable, never simply fall from the sky. If the old masterpieces of the vernacular style seemed to English readers of the Reformation period to be in harmony with then contemporary grievances and aspirations, this should surely be taken as good evidence that they were indeed in harmony with them. Modern critics cannot claim equal standing. And of course those who identified with these books would also have been formed by them. The strongly biblical language in *Piers the Ploughman*, Langland's emphasis on the concern for the poor that is so strongly insisted upon in both Testaments, and on the poverty of Christ, would make the English Bible, Wycliffe's, then Tyndale's, the text that created continuity between the earlier writers and the Puritans. Beyond question, if one were to venture a definition of Puritanism, it would include their deep interest in the Bible and deep knowledge of it. The meaning of the existence of the Bible in English, the assertion of the dignity and beauty of the language of the common people implicit in these works of translation, as in original works, is consistent through the centuries, and religious and political in its implications.

Roger L'Estrange, censor to Charles II after the Restoration, called for the proscription of older as well as current books and pamphlets, on the grounds that "being Written in times of Freedom, and Menag'd by great Masters of the Popular Stile, they speak playner and strike homer to the Capacity and Humour of the Multitude." Suppressions were to be accomplished by means of the suite of penalties usual at the time—"Death, Mutilation, Imprisonment, Banishment," etc. Penalties were to fall upon anyone involved in the dissemination of proscribed material, including sailors, ballad singers, and carters, unless they informed on others. It is reasonable to wonder what was lost, and interesting to note that writers for the multitude could be acknowledged masters of their style. L'Estrange says, "For the Authors, nothing can be too Severe, that stands with Humanity, and Conscience. First, 'tis the Way to cut off the Fountain of our Troubles. Secondly, There are not many of them in an Age, and so the less work to do." The demand for the kind of literature to be suppressed is reflected in the difficulties L'Estrange anticipates in banning it. Printers would be expected to fail if they could not sell it, and therefore would be inclined to sell banned books for the greatly enhanced value they would have as a consequence of their being banned. As the merest aside, I will mention here that the writer most widely read in England while Shakespeare wrote was the French theologian John Calvin. This is a fact of such obvious significance that its eclipse amounts effectively to another proscription. It is no accident, after all, that the revolutionary side in the civil war were and are called Calvinists.

Considering the variety of Protestantisms already active on the Continent, it is striking that Calvin should have had so singular an impact among the English. Arthur Golding, uncle by marriage to the Earl of Oxford, best known now for his translation of Ovid's *Metamorphoses,* was also an important translator of Calvin's sermons and commentaries from French and Latin, including a three-volume *Commentary on Psalms.* Golding's *Metamorphoses* is, of course, the book most frequently alluded to by Shakespeare after the Bible, typically the Geneva Bible. And there were a number of important printers and booksellers in London at this time who were French Protestant refugees, including Shakespeare's first publisher.

More important, I would suggest, is the similarity between Lollard or Wycliffite theology and Calvin's theology, for example, in their interpretation of Communion or Eucharist. Many critics, taking transubstantiation to be the one understanding of the sacrament that realizes the presence of Christ in the

Supper, repeat the canard that for Protestants the rite is symbolic only. In fact the rejection of transubstantiation had to do with the role it asserted for priests, the teaching that they uniquely are capable of making the presence of Christ real, in effect interposing themselves between the faithful and the Lord's gift of Himself. The twentieth-century Reformed theologian Karl Barth describes Calvin's conception of the Eucharist as of a high and holy mystery. "We must listen to the words. We are told to take, and that means that it is ours; we are told to eat, and that means the other thing that we cannot see or take or eat becomes one substance with us. The whole force of the sacrament, says Calvin, lies in the Word: 'given for you,' 'shed for you.' Those who take in the language of the sign truly take the thing signified." A poem attributed to the young Queen Elizabeth expresses the same understanding:

Hoc est corpus meum
'Twas Christ the Word that spake it.
The same took bread and brake it,
And as the Word did make it,
So I believe and take it.

I pause over this because Puritanism especially is treated as having been a stripping away of the poetics of the traditional faith, out of some supposed shopkeeperish impatience with the beautiful. This notion in turn occludes the indisputable fact that much of the literature and poetry of the English Renaissance was the work of people who were Puritans and Calvinists. Here I will mention only Spenser and the Sidneys, Milton and Marvell, though it is relevant that Arthur Golding translated *Abraham's Sacrifice*, the first play written on the model of classical drama in a modern European language. Its author was Théodore de Bèze, Calvin's closest associate in Geneva. The play went through twenty-three editions in the sixteenth and seventeenth centuries. Calvin himself was a famous stylist in French and

Latin, though the way historians and critics speak of him makes his reputation for eloquence seem an anomaly. His dozens of volumes might as well have "predestination" and "depravity" inscribed in blackletter on every page for all the information these scholars offer, or have, that might be more sufficient to the subject. In any case, it is true that the arts of English Renaissance culture were markedly weighted toward the literary rather than the visual. A dispassionate appraisal might not find the world poorer for this fact.

To say that Calvin was widely read is by no means to say that everyone who read him agreed with him. Nor is it to say that there was a considerable overlap of his readership and Shakespeare's audience. Still, it seems arbitrary to dismiss the significance of this readership. The society was moving toward civil war, and the insurgent and militarily successful side was called Puritans or Calvinists or Roundheads, the last a derisive term for the lower classes. This would imply that Calvinism was popular in the way Lollardy was popular also, despite and because of the learning and prestige of their great theologian and the power of his thought. The affinity between Wycliffe and Calvin, Lollardy and Calvinism, is strong enough to permit the thought that Calvinism, from an English popular point of view, was less an innovation than a restoration, a boldly public assertion of beliefs it had been perilous to utter for generations. The source of this affinity is not obvious. I know of no mention of Wycliffe by Calvin, though if Hus and Luther were aware of him, no doubt he was aware of him, too. In some sense Wycliffe and Calvin may have had a common source. The Reformers were not the first European critics of priestly celibacy or of transubstantiation. Long before the Reform there were the Waldensians in Italy and southern France, a persecuted egalitarian sect whose piety, like the Lollards', was formed around vernacular Bibles and who also merged with the Reformation. Before Calvin joined the Reform, his cousin Pierre Robert had made a new translation of Scripture for the Waldensians.

Since celibacy and transubstantiation became doctrine and dogma only in the thirteenth century of the life of Christianity, isolated communities or groups committed to another experience of the church might have continued to adhere to the customs and teachings of those earlier centuries. The claim these movements made to having origins in the primitive church, often dismissed as crude biblicism, may have had a real basis. When beliefs are driven underground, it is difficult to gauge their actual importance. When their adherents are persecuted they tend to scatter, taking their faith with them into new territories and populations, as for example the Huguenots in Renaissance London had done.

•

It is broadly assumed that the Elizabethan population subscribed to an ideology that enshrined the existing order of things. I have seen a recent history that invokes in all seriousness E.M.W. Tillyard's old variant on Arthur O. Lovejoy's *Great Chain of Being.* Tillyard asserts that the resourceful Elizabethan mind simply could not think beyond the manifest goodness and necessity of the divinely established hierarchy that ordered not only physical nature but also human social and political relations. Again, this was a society drifting toward civil war, toward the startlingly modern trial and execution of a reigning king. In their own recent history, the English had seen repeatedly that notionally hereditary monarchy with all its uncertainties and complications could and did untune the string of social order to disastrous effect. Shakespeare opens his first history play with the hero king Henry V dead on the stage, leaving as successor an infant who would live into adulthood yet never really come of age. The conquests in France, which were unsustainable, in the plays and in fact, left England overextended and impoverished, without authoritative leadership. In more recent history the boy king Edward VI died too young to have left an heir. His half sister Mary, whose father had declared her and his daughter Elizabeth illegitimate in order to bar them from succession, did succeed Edward, and in turn left no heir. Elizabeth, famously, did not marry. Monarchies and dynasties in dissolution, the disintegration of powerful persons, are subjects to which Shakespeare returns persistently. If there was a divinely ordained and inviolable order of things, it was in fact violated so continuously and so profoundly as to disappear in the endless turmoil of the actual world. It is hard to imagine how God's will could be inferred from a system that at best constantly threatened collapse even while it sustained a violent order. When at his trial Charles I invoked the sacredness of hereditary succession, his judges could reply that half the kings of England after the Norman conquest were not in fact lawful heirs to the throne. I will concede that William Shakespeare might have looked in at a bear baiting. With a little difficulty I grant the possibility that he sometime danced around a May pole. But I draw the line at the thought that he, the most brilliant mind in a brilliant age, could have given a moment's actual credence to a Tillyardian Great Chain of Being, a God-ordained social order intrinsic to reality like the relative status of oysters and angels. Certainly this view of things is not to be found in Wycliffe, or Aristotle, in Raleigh or even in Hooker. The list of writers in whom it is not affirmed or reflected would be very long, but one or two are sufficient to dispel the notion that Elizabethans could only imagine the world in these terms. And one on any list should be Elizabeth herself. She said, "I know the inconstancy of the people of England, how they ever mislike the present government and has their eyes fixed upon that person that is next to succeed; and naturally men be so disposed: 'More to adore the rising than the setting sun.'" She said this in reply to the urging of those who believed that by bearing a child, producing a clear successor, she would ensure political stability and order.

On the subject of royal authority, the historian Christopher Hill quotes Calvin's commentaries on the Book of Daniel. "Earthly princes deprive themselves of all authority when they rise up against God, yea, they are unworthy to be counted among the company of men. We ought rather to spit in their faces than to obey them when they . . . spoil God of his right." While assumptions now prevailing might lead to the thought that Calvin's influence would have been conservative, monarchical, in fact Calvin says a great deal more that makes clear his opinion of kings, with unmistakable contemporary relevance, this for example:

> In the palaces of kings we often see men of brutal dispositions holding high rank, and we need not go back to history for this. In these days kings are often gross and infatuated, and more like horses and asses than men! Hence audacity and recklessness obtain the highest honors of the palace . . . we ought to weep over the heartlessness of kings in these days, who proudly despise God's gifts in all good men who surpass the multitude in usefulness; and at the same time enjoy the society of the ignorant like themselves, while they are slaves to avarice and rapine, and manifest the greatest cruelty and licentiousness. Since, then, we see how very unworthy kings usually are of their empire and their power, we must weep over the state of the world, for it reflects like a glass the wrath of heaven, and kings are thus destitute of counsel.

The last sentence expresses Calvin's belief that even the worst monarchs or figures of power are in place by the will of God, a clear consequence of his understanding of God as both omnipotent and deeply involved in human affairs. And as a consequence of the same understanding, he believes they are overthrown by the will of God. "Whence, then, does it happen that Christ strikes kings with an iron scepter and breaks, and ruins, and reduces them to nothing? Just because their pride is untamable, and they raise their heads to heaven, and wish, if possible, to draw down God from his throne." Clearly, to other eyes this "iron scepter" would seem to be wielded by ordinary men. On the other hand, times being ripe, ordinary men might feel that they were enacting the will of Christ in taking part in rebellion. Revolution could therefore have the blessing of heaven as surely as any existing order. Calvin does urge obedience under most circumstances to magistrates, a word that refers not only or primarily to kings, but also to elected authority, the kind that governed Geneva. In expressing this degree of ambivalence he is perhaps more conservative than Christopher Marlowe and his roaring audience, for whom the humiliation of kings seems to have been subject enough.

•

Some might suspect me of wanting to make a Calvinist of Shakespeare. I would, if I felt that there was good evidence to justify it—though never without reservations. I think it is more faithful to what we can know to think of him as broadly and impartially engaged in a period of then unprecedented intellectual richness, testing one idea, then another. His subscribing to a single theological system and adhering to it would seem to me to be out of character. I would argue that there are important Calvinist elements in *Hamlet*, and I note that the figures in *Cymbelline* who want to end England's ancient tributary relationship to Rome, as, mutatis mutandis, Wycliffe urged they should and Henry VIII saw to it that they did, are grasping scoundrels. The plays could be Reformist in that they never treat virginity as a thing to be valued in itself, only as a kind of fidelity in anticipation of marriage. There is the matter of Sir John Oldcastle, a friend of Henry V in his youth who led a Lollard rebellion against the king and was hanged and burned for it. Oldcastle is the name Shakespeare first gave to Falstaff, strangely enough, given the Lollard knight's famous courage in war and his piety. He is among Foxe's martyrs, emaciated in the woodcut of him.

Clichés of English life in Shakespeare's time feature a great deal of rollicking and ale quaffing and lute strumming. These images stand in the place of the cultural and intellectual life of the Elizabethans, those theology-reading generations, possessed as many of them were, discreetly or secretly, of beliefs they might die for. But there must have been street preaching and disputation and sailors' tales of alien gods and unimagined coasts, and pamphlets and ballads and books of every kind passed hand to hand among those for whom literacy was a new privilege. Troupes of actors passed through the country, performing plays meant to advocate religious reform. There was the return of the Marian Exiles, the hundreds of Protestants who had gone to the Continent, to Reformed communities in Geneva, Antwerp, Frankfurt, and elsewhere, to escape the persecutions of Catholic Mary, and who brought back the thought and experience of the Reformation in Europe, as well as the epochal Geneva Bible, which they assembled and printed while in Geneva. If Shakespeare's eye now and then wandered from the text to the margins of this possibly smuggled volume, he found a compendium of interpretation drawn from the leaders of the Reform, British and European. Perhaps he could not have done anything more radical at the time than to stand aloof from the claims of all these contending loyalties.

At the same time, what could have been of greater interest to a dramatist than to see them embodied and articulated, with the resources of thought and language brought into play, and the blindnesses and unacknowledged motives revealed, that enabled or undercut their exponents. The misconstrued Latin and the random scraps of learnedness in his comic scenes must reflect this period, in which the printed book rather abruptly assumed such importance in the consciousness of ordinary people. Shakespeare's dramatizations of stories from North's Plutarch, the chronicle histories, Gower, and the rest would be an exploitation of these excitements. I am assuming that truly effective repression of political as well as religious ideas would have been impossible in the culture of the time, and that the horrors of the public executions of Protestants under Mary and Catholics under Elizabeth were meant to accomplish what public authority could not. Friends, the like-minded, the inebriated, the aristocratic, could no doubt say what they thought among themselves without great fear of consequences. And Shakespeare could watch and listen, thinking his own thoughts, his sympathies offered as a moment invited them.

As for these thoughts of his. It occurred to me to consider the figure of the servant in his plays, as a sort of sight line for the audience I propose. The word "servant" has always carried a very strong charge in Christian theology, as in the following passage in *Piers the Ploughman*:

> If the poor man is pursued by Sloth and fails to serve God well, then Adversity is his teacher, reminding him that his greatest helper is not man, but God, and that Jesus is truly his servant (for He said so Himself) and wears the poor man's livery. And even if God does not help him on earth, yet he knows that Jesus bears the sign of poverty, and saved all mankind in that apparel.

Wycliffe writes of a "servant God." If the phrase is a little startling, I think most Christian traditions would be willing to endorse it. The differences among them, however embattled, generally come down to differences of emphasis. So if, as I suggest, there are theological or political elements that recur with important consistency in Shakespeare's plays, bearing in mind his speaking within the conceptual terms, and also within the experiential world, of his audience, servants onstage would have had more interest and meaning than might be apparent to a modern audience. In those days anyone who could have servants kept as many as he could afford to maintain. A great many people were or had been servants. They would have had relatives and friends who were servants. Masterless men of the lower orders were treated as vagrants, a criminal class subject to branding and hanging, and this would have given many of the poor reason to seek out and remain in the role of servant, however notional, as Shakespeare and his company were obliged to do. Then, too, the conventional manners that reinforced deference and were the common coin of flattery imposed at least the pretense of humility and obedience throughout society. Shakespeare establishes at some length that Hamlet's bonnet-doffing water fly Osric is a wealthy man, "spacious in the possession of dirt." Peers were, ideally, servants of the king or queen, the monarch servant of the commonwealth, priests of the church and faithful, lovers of their idealized beloved, and everyone of Christ, who took the form of a servant and made himself subject to death. So the language and conventions of servanthood were pervasive and value laden. At the same time, while for some these conventions were largely a form of politesse, for most they were tedium and drudgery. Worse, the most brutal and shameful acts seem to have been relegated to servants, leaving the possibility of denial of guilt to Henry IV in the death of King Richard, to King John in the supposed death of Prince Arthur, to Ferdinand in the death of the Duchess of Malfi. Soldiers also confronted the ethical problems of subservience. In the words of a Wycliffite writer, "Manslaughter is committed not only by the hands but also by consent, advice, and authority. And since priests consent to false wars and many thousands of deaths, they are cursed murderers and unfit to perform their duties, by God's law and man's, and by reason as well." Such thinking could well lie behind *Henry V*, from the fraudulent business of seeking and being given a theological justification for invading France to the haunting questions posed to the disguised king in the night before battle.

The speaker in Shakespeare's Sonnet 58, in the voice of "slave" or "vassal," clearly in that of a servingman, says, "I am to wait, though waiting so be hell; not blame your pleasure, be it ill or well." This metaphor relies on the fact of the morally ambivalent circumstance of the servant, frequently an issue in the plays. The servant is required to be loyal and obedient to, and is deeply dependent on, a master who might put him to uses that are contrary to his own moral feelings and to the good of his own soul, and in doing so might expose him to revenge or to the rigor of the law.

Wycliffe and his followers had an answer for this, asserted in their vernacular moral teaching. The subordinate was indeed guilty who carried out an order to do a sinful thing or who consented to sin, that is, who did not object to or strongly oppose sinful behavior in a superior. "Among all the sins by which the fiend beguiles men, none is more subtle than this consent . . . But cowardice and lack of love for God makes us start back from doing so [that is, refusing consent] as traitors do." This kind of teaching is the consequence of the dignity and value of the human person in Wycliffite thought, without reference to status or condition. Wycliffe wrote that though, according to the philosophers, friendship occurs only between equals or near equals, "the simple response is that humanity is in its nature equal," this in a context which asserts the apostles were the friends of Christ, no less. In a gloss on the commandment "Thou shalt not take the name of the Lord in vain," a Wycliffite writer said, "We should know, first, that both prayer and speech have more to do with action than with words spoken by the mouth. Every man on earth bears the name of God printed in his soul, for otherwise he might not have being. So when any man abandons what he should do, or does what he should not do, on pain of the hate of God, he takes his holy name in vain. For no man is ordained for any purpose but to serve God, and he must take his name if he has being, and so he takes his name in vain when he fails in achieving his proper purpose." Society has its hierarchies, but, in reality, everyone has the same master. Wycliffe wrote, "One can be saved without obedience to someone superior, since obedience does nothing unless it leads one in obedience to the Lord Jesus Christ. But without obedience to Christ, no one can be saved." The authority of earthly masters seems to have been reinforced by oaths. Lollards forbade oaths. Loyalty to Christ might bring down affliction. This was a thing Lollards were always ready to accept.

Let us say no more than that Lollard thinking had had an influence over time on the thinking of England at large, and more particularly on those who felt the condition of subordinate or servant without the compensations that would have come with being served in turn—groundlings, in a word. Or let us say that these teachings reinforced a sense of things congenial to the English people more generally. Then the issue of individual moral dignity in circumstances that would penalize its expression would have been live, even pressing, since this very dignity meant their souls were at stake when obedience to an earthly master would have put them at odds with the will of God. John Webster's dark play *The Duchess of Malfi* turns on the pathological obedience of Bosola to Duke Ferdinand, who, in his own defense, can plausibly claim to be mad. *Othello* is another version of the destructive power of a trusted subordinate. In light of the dependency of anyone having servants on their loyalty and discretion, that is, in light of the master's vulnerability to the effects of a servant's disloyalty and indiscretion, or his uncritical obedience, these relationships must have been at least as complex as marriages. Servanthood is strongly foregrounded in *King Lear*, *Cymbeline*, and *The Winter's Tale*. In each of these plays, disobedience motivated by a higher loyalty is central to the drama. The Duke of Kent takes the form of a servant, disguising himself as what he is in fact, dutiful and loving as would become an ideal liege man, in order to continue to attend on and protect Lear even after he has been banished by him. In the horrific scene of the blinding of Gloucester, only a servant has the courage or the moral sense to attempt to intervene. Other servants, at peril to themselves, care for the old man's injuries and arrange his escape. The dying thought of the superserviceable Oswald, servant to Goneril, is to attempt to ensure that the letter she has entrusted to him will be delivered, his obedience a consent to evil in Wycliffite terms, in contrast to the refusals of the other servants, whose disobedience is true to their consciences and would mitigate the evil being done. *Cymbeline* depends altogether on the refusal of a servant to obey an order to kill his master's wife. In *The Winter's Tale*, Camillo refuses to murder a king who is a guest in the court of his master, King Leontes. Another servant carries out the king's order to leave an infant to die of exposure. He loathes the act, which is to say that he is violating his own conscience in doing it, and he is, famously and remarkably, killed by a bear, and eaten by it, too. As bad befalls the ship he came in. The servant Leonidas in *Pericles* is ordered to kill the young woman Marina, refuses at first, then resolves to do it. Though she has been carried away before he can act, he is poisoned and dies. Even Nym and Pistol, half the ragtag entourage of Falstaff, recoil from his scheme to seduce two wives of Windsor for access to their husbands' wealth. They plot to defeat him in it, his little page assisting. Pistol will not become Sir Pandarus of Troy, Nym will keep the 'havior of reputation. Literal servanthood being a widely shared condition, and the expectation of loyal subservience being a powerful social norm, to obey is nevertheless a complex moral choice, equally so when peers or people are forced to decide to whom their obedience is owed. This is an issue that brought England to disaster in the fifteenth century, the period of Shakespeare's history plays, and more recently threatened or haunted the country in the persons of Lady Jane Grey, Mary Queen of Scots, the Earl of Essex, and other less significant claimants and pretenders.

On the other hand, the servants who are faithful and comforting to Webster's Duchess, and to Cleopatra, to the boy Arthur, to the imprisoned Richard II, and to Lear as well, bring the audience into the drama, enacting the kindness the audience feels toward these desperate and bewildered souls, the selflessness of ideal servanthood. At the same time they make the sufferers more sympathetic by revealing them as they are in their private and intimate lives. These servants are deeply normative figures, figures of grace. The character Hamlet would be impossible if there were not Horatio, his "poor servant ever," self-possessed and unpresuming, to whom the prince can speak without feigning or irony or contempt, who in turn can speak the simple and perfect blessing and farewell, and would die with Hamlet, if the prince had not asked him to live on and serve him further. In their servanthood these figures are not so much Christian as they are Christlike. The dignity of their courage and generosity, so costly to themselves, epitomizes the deep core of value the civilization had claimed for a millennium and more, a fierce, barbarous civilization, but with an ember of beauty at the center of it for which our egalitarianism and our pride have perhaps denied us a name. Then again, our egalitarianism was once inspired by this early recognition of the high dignity of servants and the lowly, the saving paradox at the heart of wild old Christendom. To quote again from *Piers the Ploughman*, "Our joy and our healing, Christ Jesus of Heaven, always pursues us in a poor man's apparel, and looks upon us in a poor man's likeness, searching us as we pass with looks of love, and forever seeking to know us by our kindness of heart; and he sees which way we cast our eyes, and whether we love the lords of this earth before the Lord of Heaven."

GIVENNESS

I have been reading Jonathan Edwards lately, notably the *Treatise Concerning Religious Affections*, "affections" being the eighteenth-century term for emotions, more or less. He lists these "affections"—joy, love, hope, desire, delight, sorrow, gratitude, compassion, and zeal, as well as fear and dread—and demonstrates from Scripture their intrinsic part in the experiences of faith. I have been impressed for some time by American philosophical pragmatism, at least as I understand it, or as I find it useful in my own thinking. The great pragmatist William James, in his *Varieties of Religious Experience*, seems to be making much the same argument Edwards had made more than a century earlier, in his case centering the question on the meaning of the profoundly emotional and sometimes transformative character of many religious conversions. His posture of objectivity, scrupulous because it is tentative, different as it is from Edwards's intensely scriptural and theological approach, makes the same assertion Edwards makes, which is that a kind of experience felt as religious and mediated through the emotions does sometimes have formidable and highly characteristic effects on personality and behavior that are available to observation. Many of my nineteenth-century American heroes passed through the alembic of what they, like Edwards, called conversion, this qualitative leap in religious intensity and commitment that typically changed solidly pious Presbyterians or Methodists or Congregationalists into Congregationalists or Methodists or Presbyterians capable of prodigies of selflessness and discipline and generosity. I am and am not of their tradition, a mainline Protestant who has a vested interest in believing they overstated the importance of these singular, threshold experiences, and who takes it to be true that the grace of God works as it will, even gradually, patiently, quietly. This is not by any means to question the authenticity of the visions and passions they passed through, or to suggest that these were anything but enviable. These enthusiasms struck whole classes of Andover and Yale divinity graduates, sending them out to the frontier to establish churches and colleges that would help to create a culture of enlightened self-sufficiency, that is, a culture resistant to the spread of slavery or committed to its abolition. Their works speak for them still. Their devotion to their purpose is an impressive, if forgotten, proof that, in a great many ways, faith forms life and drives behavior. In their case, it engaged them in truly urgent work, and gave them an extraordinary steadiness of purpose. It made them realists, pragmatists.

Thus are we plunged into the mysteries of consciousness. There is nothing unusual about this—we are so deeply immersed in these mysteries that we have no way of establishing an objective view of them. The behavioral sciences have toiled for generations to explain how we think, why we act as we do. The models they proceed from are generally either reactions to environment that are measurable by them, or presumptively delusional states like the intuitions and experiences that sustain religious belief, or that sustain the sense of the self. My Yale divines believed heroically in a kind of personal agency that allowed them to see and engage reality and to change it, and they did this in the thrall of a kind of visionary experience it would be very difficult to describe in the reductionist terms our science of the mind allows us. They are forgotten historically, perhaps because they and their labors resist description in reductionist terms.

Granted, throughout history brutal and disastrous crusades have been carried out by leaders acting at the urging of visions and ecstasies. And brutal and disastrous customs have thriven in the humdrum of ordinary life, in the absence of anything to be called vision, slavery, for example. We are a strange species.

In all circumstances complex, higher-order thinking is called for, among contemporaries and certainly among historians. Scientific reductionism, good in its place, is very often used to evade the great fact of complexity. It has no vocabulary for higher-order thinking, which it often dismisses on the grounds that it chooses not to address it. This science begins with the assumption and ends with the conclusion that subjective experiences are not as they present themselves to individual or to common experience, though, as in the case of moral judgment, they are only and always subjective.

(I find myself using the terms "objective" and "subjective" though they imply a clean and simple distinction where no such thing is possible. A neuroscientist might see herself as the arbiter in such matters, an apostle of the objectively true with machinery to prove it. And to me she might seem like someone intoxicated by her role and loyal to its orthodoxies. In this she is like a great many of us who are specialists in one way or another, though readier to exempt herself from suspicion of bias and fallibility than most of us are. Alexis de Tocqueville described the emergence in the Europe of his day of "men who, in the name of progress, seek to reduce man to a material being." He says, "They look for what is useful without concern for what is just; they seek science removed from faith and prosperity apart from virtue." They style themselves "champions of modern civilization," and so on. My point is simply that the posture often assumed by the behavioral scientists, the ones who claim to be the agents of social transformation as they dispel illusion and reveal the hard fact of our materiality, has been around for a long time. It is an established role in Western society, refreshed from generation to generation by claims to newness and rigor, always bringing this same bold, irrefutable truth. It has proved impervious to the demonstrations by physical science that materiality, however defined, is profoundly amazing, uncanny, in no way suited to the antique rhetorical uses made of it in Tocquevilles's time and ours. All this tells strongly against positivist claims to objectivity, which are after all an essential part of this role.)

Recently I heard a neuroscientist in Europe explain that what we call fear is in fact a pattern of heightened activity, synapses firing in a certain region of the brain. This seems to some to dispel the mystery, to refute the illusion of selfhood—aha! there it is! a bright spot on a screen. No doubt if I and a higher ape encountered a lion, there would be an interesting similarity in the pattern of excitation in our nervous systems. And much would be made of this. But if I and the ape were confronted with a subpoena or a pink slip, all similarity would vanish. This is to say that human emotion is conditioned profoundly by culture and society and one's individual history of interaction with them both, in other words, by being human. Reaction to a subpoena would vary radically from one human being to another, depending again on personal history. In other words, neuroscience might tell us something about the processes by which fear becomes a physical sensation. But the sensation in most cases means only that a predisposition compounded of memory, association, information or the lack of it, temperament, and circumstance has been triggered and physiologically expressed. Fear as sensation is too late in the causal sequence to define fear itself. And its true origins would be dispersed throughout the brain, raising questions about the meaningfulness of the apparent relative quiet of the parts of consciousness where it has its origins, therefore about the meaningfulness of the local excitation of particular neurons. Its quiet could imply that the workings of the mind, or brain, are not of a kind existing instruments are designed to capture.

Jonathan Edwards knew that the emotions have a physical component, and he knew it could be argued that this is all they amount to. He said, "The motion of the blood and animal spirits is not the *essence* of these affections . . . but the *effect* of them . . . There is a sensation in the *mind* which loves and rejoices, *antecedent* to any effects on the fluids in the body." He is arguing here for the capacity for emotion in spirits, disembodied souls. He is speaking within a set of religious and cultural assumptions, just as our neuroscientists do when they tell us that fear is the firing of certain synapses in the brain. Their culture and moment allow them to say, in effect, it is not you who are afraid—a little patch of gray matter is responding to stimuli in the environment. Then is there a self, at all? The point is now actively disputed.

Medical science does not know what life is, but it is very careful to distinguish it from death just the same, and very little inclined to question the reality of the phenomenon on the grounds that it lacks a satisfactory account of it. Neuroscience does not know what the mind or the self is, and has made a project of talking them out of existence for the sake of its theories which exclude them. They have banished the dichotomy called Cartesian by excluding one major term, the mind, that is.

•

Jonathan Edwards is a pragmatist by my definition because he has a very active sense of the givenness of things. We know what love is—he uses the word without definition or modifier. Like every Christian moralist since Jesus, he knows love can attach itself to the wrong things, things of the world, things like power and wealth that are usually implicated in exploitation and impoverishment, if the prophets are to be believed. Still it is love he is speaking of, and we understand what he means by it. Modern English speakers may be a little less discriminating in their use of the word than the ancients were, but perhaps not. When poor old Isaac expresses his love for a stew of game, he uses the same verb Moses uses in the commandment that we love God with all our heart, soul, and strength. Of course Isaac associates the stew with rugged Esau and his life in the fields and the sunlight, so, like most things we love, it exists in a web of meaning and memory. Early translations into Latin and English made distinctions the Hebrew Bible did not make, sometimes introducing *caritas*, or charity, where the context implied holy love. Sometimes, as in the Vulgate's version of the words of Isaac, it employs paraphrase.

Scriptural and modern usage does reflect experience. Love, however elusive, however protean, however fragmentary, seems to have something like an objective existence. It can be observed as well as tested. Perhaps it is better to say, language reflects a consensus of subjectivities. We seldom agree in our loves, we vary wildly in our ability to acknowledge and express them, we may find that they focus more readily on cats and dogs than on justice and mercy, neighbors and strangers. And yet, for all that, we do know what love is, and joy, gratitude, compassion, sorrow, and fear as well.

Fear is an easier subject than love because it relates more directly to environment, complex as that is. The human impulse to fear is antecedent to any construction, even though, as I have said, it is *shaped* and triggered by culture and personal history. We all know that there are people in this country right now who acquire arsenals and gold coins and shipments of freeze-dried hamburgers and then sit in their basements waiting for the first clap of Apocalypse. However peculiar to culture and temperament this may be, the fear behind it all is just plain fear. In principle, in order to empathize, anyone who has ever had a bad dream or sat in a dentist's chair need only scale the experience up. It would help if the empathy could factor in a near-certainty that subversives are beaming dreams into her brain or that world history is an international conspiracy of dentists. Failing this, we still know what fear is, how it feels, and how it both sharpens and distorts our perceptions.

On the other side of the question there are those who feel the objectivity of their view is established in the fact that they have produced accounts of subjective experience that are impossible to affirm on the basis of subjective experience. People may accept the meaningfulness, the truth value, of the claim that an emotion is identical with a patch of cerebral activity registered by a machine. This might well influence their own experience and worldview, that is, their subjectivity. Still, it is hard to see the point of defining emotion, or subjectivity, by depriving it of the character that defines it. If you happened to have a thousand-dollar bill, and I told you it was in fact a slip of paper with the image of Grover Cleveland printed on it, you would not accept this as true in any important sense, no matter how true it might be in the impossible absence of history, culture, society, and the rest, no matter that a higher primate would drop it in favor of a candy wrapper. It is indeed arbitrary, purely an effect of cultural consensus, that a slip of paper has value in the total absence of intrinsic value, simply because a certain number of zeros follow a one. My basement dweller has given much thought to this conundrum. The slip of paper will likely prove for human purposes to be highly negotiable all the same, on the strength of subjective consensus.

For Edwards the existence of the emotions and their character are arbitrary phenomena, in the sense that they reflect the intent of God in creating humankind. If his intent had been different we, like every created thing, would be utterly different as well. But God made us in his image, that is, with attributes that we share with him. Since religious thought assumes that he has made us one by one, so to speak, our participating in these attributes is arbitrary, too. Their existence need not be arrived at as the consequence of evolution or as an effect of self-interest or by making any other account of them that would rationalize and compromise them. This is the anthropology of the soul, and, besides its cultural and political importance—we are created equal, we are endowed by our Creator—it is entirely compatible with the pragmatism that accepts things in their complex and veiled givenness, extrapolated neither to nor from. God so loved the world. God is love. Love one another as I have loved you. These sentences are intelligible to us because we do, in however misdirected or dilute a form, participate in this attribute.

For Edwards our nature is a reflex of the expectations God has of us. We are told to hope. To fear. To feel compassion and gratitude. All these things we can do, can scarcely refrain from doing. The Bible is a compendium of passions, emotions, and meditations. The whole traffic of interaction among human beings, and between the human and the divine, is essentially a matter of inward experience—often it is dread, loneliness, homesickness, and regret, interpreted as alienation from God, or as the fear of alienation. Skeptics have always taken this kind of thinking for anthropomorphism, a primitive or wistful projection onto the unreadable universe that makes human traits into divine attributes. Skeptics can't prove that this is true, and believers can't prove that it is not true. Faith takes its authority from subjective experience, from an inward sense of the substance and meaning of experience. The same is true of disbelief, no doubt. Objective proof cannot be claimed on either side.

•

From the point of view of Jonathan Edwards, these "affections" he names exist apart from any particular human being who might be their locus, no matter how much they are colored by temperament and by occasion. They are full of meaning intrinsically, as they are felt and expressed and as they are suppressed and denied. The aesthetic and moral order of the universe to which they are essential, and in which we are assumed by him to participate, are freestanding as well. They are intrinsic to the meaning of the whole of Creation, as our minds and perceptions are also.

William James very wisely cautioned against extrapolation from what we know, or think we know, to what it seems to us this knowledge must imply. If we approach the question of the affections or emotions or the inward life as Jamesian pragmatists, allowing always for the fact that they often mystify us, we will take our feelings as we know them, not only as physical states rooted in all the processes of our brains that reflect and condition our motives, but more especially as the continuously variable inward weather in which we live from birth to death. That our feelings, things so familiar to us, so near to us as to be in a sense identical with us, should be defined primarily or exclusively as the mechanistic triggering of neurons is the consequence of a particularly remarkable extrapolation, from the observation of localized activity in the brain to the assertion that human experience is of a kind to be describable in its essence on the basis of the information, if this is the proper name for it, accessed by these means.

Here is another assumption Edwards makes, one that seems confirmable from experience. Like Descartes and any number of earlier thinkers, he assumes that we are not passive in relation to our emotions. There is, experientially, a second self, a self who can wish we would not be afraid of what frightens us, that we would not be angered by what angers us, a self-awareness that regrets an incapacity for the kind of joy the best moments of life should afford us or the kind of compassion circumstance seems to demand of us. As intimate as our emotions are, we continuously stand apart from them, appraising. Why should one possibly snide remark by someone we hardly know ruin a whole day, even a week? Why do we talk too much when we are nervous? Drugs and therapies are marketed to the voice in our heads that is so alert to our failings, and so frustrated by them. It is this second self, always tacking against the impulses in us that are least acceptable to us, which makes us feel, quite rightly, that others never know us as we really are. Edwards could preach to the difference his congregation would have felt between appropriate experience—an overwhelming love of God, an overwhelming gratitude for existence, a ravishing sense of the divine beauty manifest in Creation on one hand, and the comparatively dull and meagre experience of unconverted life on the other. He could try to induce in them the state of mind or soul that would lift them out of their insensibility. Again, this is all articulated in highly particular cultural terms, and yet it does acknowledge a complexity in experience that religions generally acknowledge, for which the concepts of neuroscience offer no equivalent. To put the matter in secular terms, who can read about this speck of glittering planet in gravitational thrall to a star at the fringe of a whorl of galaxy in a roaring, surging universe that, as Edwards says, might be no more than a water drop beside the grander systems that are possible and not feel how minor and grudging our wonder is at what we are and what we can know and imagine? Add to this the belief that we are created to marvel at Creation, as Edwards and his tradition believed we were, and our bizarre fixation on lesser things becomes a part of the difference between our circumstance and our awareness of it that his tradition called our fallenness.

As in the matter of the water drop, theologians often had appropriately hyperbolic notions about the nature and reach of Creation, expressing them long before physicists could begin to confirm them or were disposed to. This aside, for them the theological universe had a grand moral architecture as well. Reality was structured around good and evil, humankind being uniquely capable of both. There was no greater scale than this architecture by which reality could be measured, even granting as they often did heavens beyond heavens. Let us say that human beings would have proceeded from a sound intuition of this moral structure if they had fed the hungry, clothed the naked, given drink to the thirsty, and, needless to say, beaten their swords into ploughshares. Clearly this would have gone far toward assuring the long-term viability of the planet, an argument for a high order of objective facticity behind teachings whose truth value is routinely slighted when it is not dismissed outright. If we had not heard these verses as poetry or as piety, to the extent we have heard them at all, we'd have a much sounder basis for dealing with reality, from the point of view of peace and human thriving, and might not now be so starkly confronted with the alternative realities of war and disease. Here history has made a more irrefutable proof than science could ever dream of.

We cannot know that conscious life has appeared only on earth, but we have good grounds for assuming that it is rare and extraordinary enough that its vanishing would be an incalculable impoverishment of the sum of things. An insect is more complex than a star. So how is the scale of change to be reckoned if life itself is the thing lost, recent and local as the phenomenon seems to be? Stars burn out and the nature of the universe is more or less unaltered. But if we say that, for all we know to the contrary, there is just one minor planet in a limitless field of stars where apple trees blossom and where songs are sung, then most of us would probably grant an important centrality to that planet. The parable of the Pearl of Great Price is not apt here, since it assumes something imaginable, a near equivalence of exchange value between the whole of a man's wealth and a single pearl. But if this strange planet is the pearl, what could even seem to be of equivalent value? Say the universe has no boundary and the stars are numberless. Still there is an infinite qualitative difference between life and the most opulent and glorious reaches of lifelessness. I may seem to be offering a very available defense of the ecosystem. But my point is of another kind. If life is as extraordinary as it appears to be, if it is unique to this planet, as it may well be, then it is within human power to make an infinite qualitative difference in the cosmos by erasing this singularity. Objectively speaking, this change would be imponderable, because the difference between life and lifelessness is imponderable. The very notion of scale, with its implication of commensurability, collapses. From this perspective, the argument for the alternative architecture proposed by religion, that moral structures are essential elements of cosmic reality, taking precedence over space and time and gravity, matter and force, is formidable.

And this returns me to pragmatism, givenness, what Edwards called the arbitrary constitution of the Creator. We know only what we know, only in the ways that we know it or can know it. It is only reasonable to assume that the physical world is accessible to other modes of perception than we are capable of. Our instruments project and refine human perceptions and query reality in order to address whatever questions we think to pose. However triumphant our achievements may seem to us, to an all-competent observer we might appear entangled in a small, dense web of our own weaving. As civilizations, polities, ethnicities, professions, and families, we certainly are entangled, in webs of status and honor and custom and piety that can seem inevitable to us and utterly arbitrary to outsiders, as in fact they are, though no more so than are the standards an outsider's view would bring to bear on them. So we have models, after our human fashion, of realities composed of givens of our own creation that yield the profoundest effects on our minds and our lives. I mention here gender and race, concepts of indeterminable meaning and great practical power, variously active in every social order, every culture.

It is in his defense of the doctrine of original sin that Edwards makes his most explicit and extended argument for creation's arbitrary character, that is, for its being composed so as to reflect the intentions of a creator, not as the elaboration of an order intrinsic to itself. Edwards can speak of natural system and order+revelatory beauty+the moral contest of good and evil, and be wholly unembarrassed by the heterogeneity of components of the reality he describes. Pre-Reformation theology, influenced by the thought of Aristotle and Ptolemy, tended to resolve all being into one system. Edwards is indebted to Calvin in that he makes the phenomenon of consciousness, rather than an objective cosmic order, the central reality. Calvin could be agnostic in the matter of the Copernican hypothesis because his theology was not dependent on any model of structured ontology. Edwards was thoroughly knowledgeable in the Newtonian science of his time, but for him no more than for John Locke did it imply a closed system, one that could in principle be described or explained exhaustively in terms of established physical properties or laws.

Positivist science, dominant among us, resembles pre-Reformation theology in its drive to unite all knowledge in one vocabulary of description. But, since for it God is emphatically not a given, the elements of reality that were consistent with reality's divine origins in the Thomist scheme are not to be accommodated in the new system. Those "affections" Edwards makes much of are, in the modern understanding, anomalies or delusions. True, now and then something is sighted that looks like love or compassion among members of another species. Under current assumptions this would be better evidence of their reality than any number of seeming altruisms among human beings, certainly better than the surges and twinges we take for love or pity when we are subject to them ourselves.

But skepticism is mighty. Such human evidence is anecdotal and open to interpretation.

There is a very strict principle of selection at work here, which looks rational to us, being strict. Obviously, to invoke the will of God to explain anything, to the exclusion of other ways of accounting for it, would be to disable the knowledge-acquiring, problem-exploring brilliance that for Calvin and his tradition were proof of the existence of the human soul. But for the positivist model of reality humanity itself is not really a given. Indeed, the positivist exclusions of articulate experience, the report we make of ourselves, is as rigorous as its exclusion of theism. This is generally accepted as something objectivity requires, but as strong a case could be made that it is a thing objectivity forbids.

William James proposed that ideas should be tested in their playing out in the real world, a theater of occasion clearly more splendid and momentous in his understanding than anything the phrase implies in ordinary use. Let us say, as a thought experiment, that someone in authority in a country equipped with doomsday weapons fears attack by another country and strikes preemptively. There would be thousands of years of cultural history and some few decades of personal history behind the decision. Madman though he might be, he would have brought the species to a culmination that humankind had been preparing for eons. To say that a spasm of activity in a region of his brain was crucial to the event would be utterly trivial, laughable, it being so thoroughly overdetermined. Yet we are encouraged to accept as hard truth a conception of reality that deprives us of the means to talk about ourselves in clearly necessary terms, as precious, for example, or tragic, or epochal, since we do have a terrifyingly profound impact on this strange little garden leafing and blooming in the frozen, fiery tempest of cosmic reality, a garden entrusted to our care in irresistible fact, even if there were no creator God present to charge us with it.

The impact of our presence in the world, which is far too consistent over time to be excluded from any objective account of our nature, as any reader of history will know, is emerging as an urgent reality, an objective, unequivocal reality, at a point when principled ignorance of ourselves is called science. Say only that the Genesis narrative reflects no more than sad wisdom and long, if primordial, experience. It makes a kind of statement about our divided selves of which we moderns, on principle, are wholly incapable. And it tells us that we are no ordinary participants in nature, that what we do is a matter of the highest order of importance, however minor our transgressions may seem to us. Edwards would say that God in his freedom can impute the sin of Adam to every human being and generation, re-creating as true what he wills, who alone creates and perpetuates all Being—that is, all that is in fact true. To me this seems a long way of saying that we are Adam, singly and together, and that the etiology of our behavior, so remarkably splendid and terrible, is to be traced directly and exclusively to our humanity. There simply is a bias toward error we share only with one another, with the beasts not at all. Recognition of this bias would surely yield humility and mutual forgiveness, if we were not so intractably human.

•

I admire Calvin more than I do any of the Calvinists, Edwards included. Edwards's defense of the doctrine of original sin seems to me more brilliant as ontology than persuasive as theology. And as ontology it is not original with him. Yet for me this ontology in the context he gave it was a godsend. It was in reading this text many years ago that I was rescued from the determinist, even mechanistic implications of positivism, a determinism more constraining than either original sin or predestination, the first of these implying to me a realism that profoundly and appropriately complicates the impulse to lay blame, the second entering so far into the mysteries of time and causality that only incomprehension could see it as determinist. There is probably no cruder moral statement possible than to say that people get what they deserve, and this is only truer when rewards or punishments are to be felt everlastingly. So it is reasonable to suppose that other considerations must be in play.

The prodigal son, of whom we know nothing good, is predestined to receive welcome and embrace because his judge is his father. Perhaps the parable would lose its authority if the youth had had a door slammed in his face, though perhaps not, since people are much impressed with the notion of just deserts. In any case, polemic and ignorance have made cartoons of both these famous doctrines, original sin and predestination, which were not aberrations of Puritanism but were in fact virtually universal in Christian theologies, Catholic and Protestant, for as long as meaningful theology was written.

•

There is at present an alienation from religion, even among the religious, that is a consequence of this privileging of information, for want of a better word, over experience, or of logic over history. The faithful are baffled by the problems that have come with the loss of the conceptual vocabulary of religion, and, more generally, of the language that can speak of and for the radical, solitary, time-bound self. The authority of a model of reality that excludes the former on principle and the latter out of a simplistic confidence in the adequacy of its own terms, its own small sphere of reference, has distracted and demoralized the faithful, as it would not have done if they were a little inclined to reflect. They are not alone in being talked out of the meaningfulness of their own experience, but they are perhaps more at fault for it than others, having had their souls as a conscious and in theory a cherished and cultivated part of their inwardness. If they have displaced the Holy Ghost with the zeitgeist, the choice is entirely their own. And if they feel this as an impoverishment, it is for them to consider why this is true and what it might mean. I hasten to add that fundamentalism that makes the same naive truth claims positivism makes is still more impoverished than religious thought that attempts to be reconciled with positivism. Certainly every problem of extrapolation is present in the insistence on basing cosmogenesis on texts that are brief and ancient and culturally remote, and, for those who take them to be sacred, should induce humility in their interpreters. There is more reverence, intended or not, and in any case more awe, in the hypotheses that ponder unperceived dimensions and abrupt cosmic inflation than in the construction of these temporally tiny models of reality which reject the freedom of God to act as mysteriously as his nature assures us he would do, as observation assures us he has done. Where were they when he laid the foundations of the earth? Extrapolation always entails presumption. To quote Jonathan Edwards, "We have got so far beyond those things for which language was initially contrived, that, unless we use extreme caution, we cannot speak, unless we speak exceeding unintelligibly, without literally contradicting ourselves—Coroll. No wonder, therefore, that the high and abstract mysteries of the Deity, the prime and most abstract of all beings, imply so many seeming contradictions."

The great given, the medium of all gain and all loss, the medium within which change is possible and inevitable and constancy persists through endless transformations, the medium of act, accident, and thought, disruption and coherency, is time. No one knows what time is, or whether it began when the universe began or is a constant in a system of Being that preexists the one we know. For our purposes it accommodates everything that has existed or will exist, utterly indiscriminate but by no means neutral, transparent, or passive. The ideas we all live by change over time, inverted, eroded, distorted, amplified, recombining in time, which might seem to be a space that permits movement and change, or a kind of liquidity that irresistibly effects movement and change, though the inadequacy of both metaphors makes the point that it is something else entirely. It might seem to occur as quanta, ticks of a cosmic clock. The absolute and momentary present in which we all live might seem to be set apart by the slightest, most porous membrane from the moment that precedes or follows it. But this way of thinking excludes the fact that moments can differ in every property, and as they differ they change our experience of time. Only when we are presented with an astonishment of some sort, a threat or an insight, are we inclined to realize that a moment is potentially capacious and transformative, and that we are subject to time far otherwise than in the most predictable of events, our mortality.

This is to say that the primary condition of our existence is a mystery as virginal as it has always been. Science may at some point be able to say meaningful things about time. I can't imagine what even a tentative account of it would look like, but I am no scientist, certainly no mathematician. And in fact the descriptions I read of epigenetics or of quantum phenomena might as well be of genies and dervishes for all the ground they seem to provide for extrapolation of the familiar kind, so long considered scientific. Our genes are not fixed like beads on a string, the physical world is not simple and solid, to be meaningful a statement need not be falsifiable, nor is it falsified in its not satisfying a particular, sometimes tendentious, standard of meaning or truth. The reality we experience is *given* in the sense that it is, for our purposes, lawful, allowing hypothesis and prediction, or available at least to being construed retrospectively in terms of cause and effect. It is *given* in a deeper sense in the fact that it is emergent. The genome accomplishes its microteleologies, a thought elaborates itself, finding its way to conclusion, recruiting memory, bias, and mood among other things all more or less persistent, most of them unconscious and unarticulable. Our singularity lies above all in the negotiations the mind makes with itself, of which we ourselves know very little. W. B. Yeats called it "the long-legged fly upon the stream, moving upon silence."

The word "emergent" implies a source, an "arising from." This is a mystery with analogs. If the universe expanded from a single particle, what did it expand into? Was everything that has been, is, and will be, through the whole of its eons of transformations, potential in that particle? My language here is no doubt far too crude to serve my argument well. My point is simply that there are other frontiers than this one we stand on continuously, where *what is* fronts on *what is to come*. It is an error of much scientific thinking to extrapolate—that word again—from our radically partial model of reality, a model curtailed, unaccountably and arbitrarily, by the exclusion of much that we *do* know about the vast fabric and the fine grain of the cosmos in which we live and move and have our being. Cosmic and microcosmic being are so glorious and strange that nothing marvelous can be excluded on the grounds of improbability, particularly nothing attested to by innumerable brilliant and distinctive voices in every corner of the world, for example human selfhood, the human mind. I invoke the stuff of Being because we are made of it. An etiology that implies a lower order of complexity than our given experience reports to us and through us only seems rational if we leave out of account the most basic knowledge we now have of the cosmos, knowledge that has as its signature a radical resistance to simplification, to understanding in terms of any known language of causality.

AWAKENING

It is an essential principle of American government and society that there should be a separation of church and state. As with all our essential principles, we argue endlessly about what this means. In eighteenth-century Britain and Europe there were laws that limited the civil rights of subjects who did not conform to the established church. So in America there was to be no established church, and there was to be no religious qualification for public office. State churches in Britain and Europe were subsidized by government. This was not to be true in America, though all the denominations have enjoyed the passive subsidy of tax exemption. In these respects the matter is straightforward enough. Still it is perhaps even truer of our society than of most that religion and public life are inextricably involved. Where most people are religious, where their values or at least their sense of identity are formed by Christian cultural influences, and where government is at least formally popular, it could hardly be otherwise.

For various reasons the bonds between politics and religion have begun to chafe in the last few decades, and not for the first time. Movements that present themselves as religiously motivated have now begun to regard the state as aggressively secular, and as enforcing secularism, precisely in maintaining institutional distance that was meant in the first instance to protect religious freedom. They have begun to regard the state with a hectic moral aversion, and at the same time to meddle in or to stymie public life by asserting a presence in governments national and local. The defense against these movements has often taken the form of a secularism that is contemptuous of religion—religion being for these purposes identical with the unbeautiful phenomenon that now so loudly claims the title for itself. This is a bad turn of events for church and for state, a separation of culture and ethos that truly amounts in certain quarters to deep mutual antagonism. It is a turn things have taken before, as a student of our history would be aware. Whether this fact is reassuring or alarming is hard to know. In any case, we have been reminded again lately how true it is that a small flame can cause a great fire. And that, to complete the allusion, the tongue is a flame.

•

My country has a relatively brief history, yet it has existed long enough to be patterned with certain recurrences. Owen Lovejoy, who became the close friend and confidant of Abraham Lincoln, was a Congregational minister and a passionate antislavery man. In 1842 he gave a sermon deploring the distinction he felt was customarily made between religion and politics. His text was from 2 Samuel: "He that ruleth over men must be just, ruling in the fear of God." Lovejoy said, "My general remark is, that every individual in this country that has arrived at years of discretion, and especially every voter, is responsible for the laws which are enacted and the manner of their execution." In a republic, he said, every person capable of asserting influence, male or female, as effective ruler, stands under the judgment of God. This view is still widely held in America, if not in precisely these terms, by people on every side of every question. It seems so right in the context Lovejoy gives it, preaching the day before an election in Illinois that would influence policy on the treatment of fugitive slaves. And there is no disputing in any case that the responsibility of the individual citizen is real and grave. But to put it this way is to introduce very stark language into what are after all contending opinions about what is just, or best, even when the issues involved are very grave. Some, in the fear of God, could never knowingly vote against the interests of the poor or of those who suffer discrimination, while others, in the fear of God, are content that the poor should be with us always, and would never vote for marriage equality. The very high standard of responsibility Lovejoy articulates has the effect of making political differences intractable. I will say at the outset that I do not know how this problem can be resolved. I cannot find any slightest inclination in myself to make concessions, precisely because I attach religious value to generous, need I say liberal, social policy. If it would be illiberal and unchristian of me to suppose that divine judgment might be brought down on the United States for grinding the faces of the poor (despite all the great prophet Isaiah has to say on the subject), I take no comfort from the certain knowledge that my opposite is struggling with just the same temptation, though mulling other texts. So, is this order of seriousness, the consequence of the compounded effects of relative democracy and a basically religious habit of mind, on balance stabilizing or destabilizing, good or bad? There is little point to the question, since these things are so engrained in the culture that they are no doubt our perpetual storm, raging in place like the red spot on Jupiter. If there is a dynamic equilibrium at work here, then it takes its stabilizing force from the belief in and expression of views that are opposed. Therefore I can in good conscience put aside my attempts at evenhandedness.

•

The First and Second Great Awakenings, religious revivals that swept through the midcolonies in the late eighteenth century and the northeastern states in the first third of the nineteenth century, were followed, I have come to realize, by a third awakening in the latter half of the twentieth century, just as I was coming of age. Historians usually treat the earlier awakenings as surges of religious enthusiasm primarily or exclusively, though they are attended by a characteristic cluster of reform movements—enhancements of the status of women, broadening of access to education, mitigations of social and racial inequality. These were consistent even while the demographics of the country changed. The religious and denominational character of the earlier awakenings seems to have been as much a consequence of the old centrality of the churches as centers of civic life as it was a result of their role in stirring religious passion. I hasten to say that in these instances religious passion—and there were occasions of hysteria, fainting fits, visions—led to, and was consistent with, stable and thoughtful social change. The period in the twentieth century I would call the third great awakening was led by the black church, and sooner or later had the support of all the major denominations. But it was not, and is not, understood as an essentially religious movement, though as I have said the distinction between civic and religious is never clear, and was certainly not clear in this case.

The Reverend Martin Luther King spoke in the language of what has been called the American civil religion—"We hold these truths to be self-evident, that all men are created equal, that they are endowed by their Creator with certain unalienable Rights." This is explicitly religious language, of course, based on a reading of the creation narratives in Genesis. But it functions as a powerful ethical statement for vast numbers of Americans who have no investment whatever in the authority of Scripture. Thomas Jefferson, that most complicated man who stands at the origins of our most complicated civilization, happened upon one bold sentence that, in course of time, overturned the society he lived in and the society Dr. King lived in, as well. It contains an energy that pushes its meaning far beyond his probable intentions, with the result, for example, that my life is vastly different from my mother's, as hers was from her mother's.

The sobering truth is, however, that these reform movements fall back. They exhaust themselves and trivialize themselves. The Second Great Awakening spent its last energies on cults and health fads and spirit photography. The awakening of my youth spun off into cults and drugs and health fads. The positive content of these movements tends to disappear except in the obverse image they impress on the reactions against them. There is comfort to be found in the fact that they are more expansive in each iteration. There is discomfort to be found in the fact that the baseline from which they begin is always inexplicably low. America had fine colleges integrated by race and gender decades before the Civil War. I saw the same integration occur in my own youth, as if it were an experiment never tried before. On every side the relevant history had slid into oblivion in the strictest sense of that word. In America the demographics and even the geographics of reform and reaction are relatively straightforward in the moments of change. But it is the collapse of the reformist side that punctuates our history decisively. The pattern is most strikingly apparent in our racial history. I know causes of the Civil War are widely disputed, but I have been reading the speeches and papers of leaders of the Confederacy, and for them the point at issue was slavery. Slavery plain and simple. They drew up a constitution very like the national Constitution, except in its explicit protections of slavery. Their defense of their sacred institutions means the defense of slavery. Their definition of states' rights means their insistence on their right to bring this "species of property" into states that did not acknowledge it, and to make these states enforce their claims on such "property" without reference to their traditions, to their own laws, or to their right to protect their own citizens. The North did not start the war, but the issue that erupted in war had been smoldering for generations, and the issue was slavery. That the point is still disputed seems to me now a lingering effect of reformist collapse, since it is among academics, who notoriously self-identify as liberals, that the question has currency. The immediate and vastly more important consequence of this collapse was the emergence after the war of the near-slavery called Jim Crow. This system emerged most strongly in the South, but it influenced law and practice throughout the country, buttressed by eugenics theories and "racial science," which were taken as real science in those same religious and intellectual circles that had been passionately antislavery decades before.

I was in high school and college when the civil rights movement emerged. That was a very troubled time, and it was for me a deeply important education. I came from a strongly conservative background. I can truly say that I was schooled in generosity and optimism by the great movements of that period. I understood them as an essential America bursting the bonds that had distorted and constrained it. We hold these truths to be self-evident. Nothing has ever persuaded me to think less of these movements or otherwise about them. Therefore the fact that they seem sometimes to be at risk of following precursor movements into collapse and oblivion alarms and appalls me. The word "liberal" has been effectively stigmatized, as the word "abolitionist" was and is. As if generosity were culpable. As if there were some more reasonable response to slavery than to abolish it. As I write, the Voting Rights Act is being challenged before the Supreme Court. If American civil religion can be said to have a congregation, I was a member in good standing—until certain shifts became apparent in the meaning and effect of religion in America. These changes made me realize that I had indeed allowed my culture to instruct me in my religion—to my benefit, during a period that was singularly worthy of the confidence I placed in it. This is to say, it was worthy as other periods, quite reliably, are not. I am not suggesting that this change is irremediable, irrevocable. Americans are always looking for trends and projecting them forward to their extremest possible consequences, as if there were no correctives or countervailing forces. "The crack in the teacup opens / A lane to the land of the dead." But trends can be counted on to reverse themselves. I take much comfort from this fact.

•

Still, in the last few decades a profound, if relative, change has taken place in American society. No doubt as a consequence of a recent vogue for feeling culturally embattled, the word "Christian" now is seen less as identifying an ethic, and more as identifying a demographic. On one hand I do not wish to overstate the degree to which these two uses of the word "Christian" are mutually exclusive, and on the other hand I think it would be a very difficult thing to overstate how deeply incompatible they can be. This drift is the American version of a phenomenon that is clearly widespread throughout old Christendom. A ferocious secularism can carry on its internecine wars under the names Catholic and Protestant. Notional Christians can align themselves against actual Muslims in defense of European culture and civilization, which are based on a system of belief that is no longer believed, and are therefore under a severer threat than any they could face from a competing religion. History has shown us a thousand variations on the temptations that come with tribalism, the excitements that stir when certain lines are seen as important because they can be rather clearly drawn. This is old humankind going about its mad business as if it simply cannot remember the harm it did itself yesterday.

What is at stake in these great struggles? Very few of us

know enough about a religion that is not our own to venture any judgment about its place in the cosmic scheme. We cannot know how another faith is felt by its real adherents, the peace or the sense of rightness or truth it brings to them in its own terms, by its own means. Even to broach the subject is to acknowledge the depth of the mystery that surrounds culture and consciousness. I used the word "truth," referring only to inward assent. A Muslim might say, God is merciful, and feel she has uttered an indubitable truth. A Muslim, a Christian, or a Jew might say, and deeply feel, that the judgments of the Lord are true and righteous altogether. With these words Abraham Lincoln anchored the argument that the suffering of the North in the American Civil War—they had lost two soldiers for every one the South lost—was deserved because of Northern complicity in the system of slavery. His meaning was that this suffering was not to be avenged as a grievance against an adversary. It was instead to be accepted as affirming the impartial justice of God. Insofar as Lincoln's words were taken to express an indubitable truth, the terrible war came to a less terrible and more final conclusion than civil wars generally do, granting as I must that it has not really ended yet. Granting that I do not now foresee circumstances that will end it. Granting, indeed, that in recent years its embers have been flaring up rather brightly. For the moment the words "secession" and "nullification" have currency.

The world is cruel and God is merciful. The sword draws blood on every side and God is righteous altogether. The great religions are counterstatements made against a reality that does not affirm them with much consistency at all. This can only have been truer in any earlier century, when life was more brutal than we in the West can readily imagine. The temptation has always been to hold affirmations of this kind up to given reality and then declare the two of them irreconcilable, the faith statements therefore unsustainable, weighed and wanting.

This is to deny the ethical meaning of such affirmations. Sigmund Freud said we cannot love our neighbor as ourselves. No doubt this is true. But if the reality that lies behind the commandment, that our neighbor is as worthy of love as ourselves, and that in acting on this fact we would be stepping momentarily out of the bog of our subjectivity, then a truth is acknowledged in the commandment that gives it greater authority than mere experience can refute. There is a truth that lies beyond our capacities. Our capacities are no standard or measure of truth, no ground of ethical understanding.

I have written more than a thousand words and not mentioned Calvin once, except implicitly. Lincoln spoke in Calvinist language to a population it might have been meaningful at the time to call Calvinist, as the historians generally do. He says, Accept suffering with humility. Both suffering and humility will serve you. This apparent fatalism is actually confidence that life is shaped by divine intention, which will express itself in ways that can be baffling or alarming but that always bring an insight, pose a question, or make a demand, to the benefit of those who are alert to the will of God. The activism, even radicalism, of this tradition is inscribed very deeply on modern and American history. At the same time it was characterized by a striking inwardness, based on an immediate, an unmediated, conversation between the Lord and the individual soul. God's language in his discourse with humankind was taken to be experience, personal and historical, intellectual and sensory, emotional. All this yielded some good novels and some fine poetry. It created a number of excellent universities. I put it in the past tense because I no longer see much trace of it in American culture. Perhaps I am too close to the situation to be a reliable judge.

I am not speaking here of our changed demographics. When I say Calvinism has faded, I am speaking of the uncoerced abandonment by the so-called mainline churches of their own origins, theology, culture, and tradition. I have spent most of my life in Presbyterian and Congregational churches, and I was well into middle age before I made the connection of these traditions with Calvin, though I had heard any number of times in other contexts about the all-pervading influence of this theology. What has taken the place of Calvinism in the mainline churches? With all due respect, not much.

I apologize. There are countless good souls in the mainline churches. No other tradition interests or attracts me. But through the whole of my experience I have had the sense that these churches were backpedaling, were evading, at last very effectively, the influence cultural history would have given them. I am sure they were wrong about some things, like all other churches. But I envy a time when an American president could speak as candidly as Lincoln did, and remind us that whom God loveth he also chastiseth, our adversaries and ourselves equally. That we must love our enemies because God loves them. Say what you will about "the Calvinist God," he is not an imaginary friend. Nor is he entangled in any sort of one-to-one relationship to human expectations. I don't know whether it is time or history or Calvin that has left me so profoundly convinced of the importance of human fallibility, and so struck by its peculiar character. But I wouldn't mind hearing the word "sin" once in a while. If the word is spoken now it is likely to be in one of those lately bold and robust big churches who are obsessed with sins Jesus never mentioned at all. On the testimony of the prophets, social injustice is the great sin—according to Ezekiel the reason for the destruction of Sodom. Oh, well. The Old Testament is so, you know, Calvinist.

Then again, all the theologies are fading away. America was populated in its early years by people seeking religious freedom. This is our way of saying that the early settlers were refugees from the wars of religion, and then from the suppression of dissent that followed outright war. In light of the fact that our ancestors were the belligerents on every side, oppressed and oppressors depending on circumstance, our religious traditions have gotten along remarkably well. We have spent four hundred years getting used to each other, making accommodations, and we have done so fairly successfully. In the course of achieving this general amity we have virtually erased all sense of the history that gave rise to our many denominations. It is a bitter history, in some ways well forgotten, even though it entails losses we would regret if we were aware of them. As one consequence denominations themselves are fading away. The theological coherency developed over the centuries within the denominations, each one in its own way, created a vocabulary of thought, a literature of hymns and prayers and testimony, that gave its adherents the means to conceive of the divine and of humankind. I assume they were all wrong and right in important ways, richer for the light they shone on one another in the very fact of their differences.

The religious monoculture we seem to be tending toward now is not a neutral averaging of the particularities of all the major traditions. It is very much marked by its cultural moment, when the whole focus is on "personal salvation," on "accepting Jesus as your Lord and Savior." Theologically speaking, the cosmos has contracted severely. The simple, central, urgent pressure to step over the line that separates the saved from the unsaved, and after this the right, even the obligation, to turn and judge that great sinful world the redeemed have left behind—this is what I see as the essential nature of the emerging Christianity. Those who have crossed this line can be outrageously forgiving of one another and themselves, and very cruel in their denunciations of anyone else. Somehow in their eyes this does not make them hypocrites, a word that for Jesus clearly had a particular sting. And no, this is not Calvinism. Calvin would have called it salvation by works, which for him was anathema. As corollary, his famous predestinarianism forbade the passing of judgment, since such matters must be left to God's inscrutable will. Max Weber saw anxiety in Protestants'—he meant Calvinists'—uncertainty about their own salvation. There are worse things than uncertainty, presumption being one.

So, we have an element newly prominent in American religious and political life, a new form of entitlement, a self-declared elect. What some have seen as a resurgence of Christianity, or at least a bold defense of American cultural tradition—even as another great awakening!—has brought a harshness, a bitterness, a crudeness, and a high-handedness into the public sphere that are only to be compared to the politics, or the collapse of politics, in the period before the Civil War. Its self-righteousness fuels the damnedest things—I use the word advisedly—notably the acquisition of homicidal weapons. I wonder what these supposed biblicists find in the Gospels or the Epistles that could begin to excuse any of it.

Well, life is full of surprises. I thought I knew more about American Christian culture than I did. When Martin Luther King was preaching to us all, there was a strong enough sensitivity among the public to the language he spoke in to stir deep assent, the recognition of truth in what he said that made the reality he spoke from and to appear as it was, mean and false. But he was a reverend doctor after all, learned in the difficult disciplines of historic Christianity, brought up in the richness of the black church. His educational attainments would no doubt disqualify him from respectful attention in certain quarters now, as President Obama's do him.

I still see the best impulses of the country expressed in its politics, and its worst impulses as well, the worst abetted by self-declared Christians, the best holding their own despite what seems to be silence and passivity on the part of those who might make the Christian case for them. Many have noted that the media do not find reasonable people interesting. Over time this has surely had a distorting effect. Nevertheless, the mainline churches, which are the liberal churches, in putting down the burden of educating their congregations in their own thought and history, have left them inarticulate. Christianity is stigmatized among the young as a redoubt of ignorance, an obstacle to the humane aspirations of the civilization. The very generosity and idealism of young people is turning them away. I know this is not unique to America. But there appears to me to be a dynamic at work that is new for us, a polarization of the good on one side and the religious on the other, which will be a catastrophe for American Christianity. And it will be an appalling deprivation on every side of the great body of art and thought and ethical profundity that has been so incalculable an enrichment of all our lives. Can a culture be said to survive when it has rejected its heritage? Every defense of Christianity is nonsense while in one way or another its loyalists are busy cutting it off at the root. I'm speaking here of the partisans who use it to put a lacquer of righteousness over fearfulness and resentment, and I'm speaking here of the seminaries that make a sort of Esperanto of world religions and transient pieties, a non-language articulate in no vision that anyone can take seriously.

I have mentioned the qualitative difference between Christianity as an ethic and Christianity as an identity. Christian ethics go steadfastly against the grain of what we consider human nature. The first will be last; to him who asks give; turn the other cheek; judge not. Identity, on the other hand, appeals to a constellation of the worst human impulses. It is worse than ordinary tribalism because it assumes a more than virtuous *us* on one side, and on the other a *them* who are very doubtful indeed, who are, in fact, a threat to all we hold dear. Western civilization is notoriously inclined to idealize itself, so it is inclined as well to forget how recently it did and suffered enormities because it insisted on distinctions of just this kind. If the claims to Christian identity we hear now are rooted in an instinctive tribalism, they are entirely inappropriate, certainly uninformed, because in its nature the religion they claim has no boundaries, no shibboleths, no genealogies or hereditary claimants.

However sound our credentials seem, we have it on good authority that the prostitutes and sinners might well enter heaven before us. It is difficult to respond to this assurance with a heartfelt amen if one has found comfort in despising people in whom our eponymous Christ clearly finds great value. In the seventh chapter of Matthew there is a text I have never heard anyone preach on. There Jesus says that in the last day "many will say to me, 'Lord, Lord, did we not prophesy in your name, and cast out demons in your name, and do many mighty works in your name?' And then will I declare to them, 'I never knew you; depart from me.'" It is for Christ to decide who the Christians are, who has in fact done the will of his Father.

I have recourse here to chapter and verse to make the point that all the praying on street corners, or, in contemporary terms, all the making of elaborate claims for one's special piety on cable channels, and, heaven help us, at political events, might be evidence of an upsurge of enthusiasms that assume the coloration of religion for purposes that are not, strictly speaking, terribly religious. People of good faith get caught up in these things in all times and all places. In the excitement of the moment who really knows he might not also shout, "Give us Barabbas!"

But, understandable or not, a mistake is still a mistake. And its consequences can be very grave indeed. For some time there have been interests intent on legitimizing bad ideas by creating an atmosphere around them that simulates mass passion—distrust or resentment or rage as the manufactured outcry of a virtual populace. These are not conditions in which religion is likely to retain its character as religion. Once, in a discussion of the passage in Ephesians where Paul speaks of "the sword of the Spirit, which is the word of God," a woman in the audience, making a two-handed figure eight in the air, said, "But if you have a sword, you're supposed to smite somebody." Where to begin. But it is just this kind of slippage, of the figurative into the literal, of affection for the traditions of Christianity into hostility toward those who are known or assumed not to share them, that makes the religion the opposite of itself. Does the word "stranger," the word "alien," ever have a negative connotation in Scripture? No. Are the poor ever the object of anything less than God's loving solicitude? No. Do the politics of those who claim a special fealty to the Bible align themselves with its teachings in these matters? No, they do not, not in contemporary America, certainly. We have been hearing a lot about "takers" lately. True, this interpretation of the social order sent a thrill of revulsion through enough of us to doom a candidacy. But those Americans who use the word as if it actually describes something are disproportionately self-identified as Christians.

Inevitably, this is how Christianity has come to be understood by a great many good people who have no better instruction in it than they receive from ranters and politicians. Under such circumstances it is only to their credit that they reject it. Though I am not competent to judge in such matters, it would not surprise me at all to learn in any ultimate reckoning that these "nones" as they are called, for the box they check when asked their religion, are better Christians than the Christians. But they have not been given the chance even to reject the beautiful, generous heritage that might otherwise have come to them. The learned and uncantankerous traditions seem, as I have said, to have fallen silent, to have retreated within their walls to dabble in feckless innovation and to watch their numbers dwindle. A recent article in *The New York Times* reported that the mainline traditions were actually gaining ground, relative to the so-called fundamentalists. The article concluded by quoting a professor in a mainline seminary to the effect that they spent a great deal of their time trying to adapt the methods of the fundamentalists to their own purposes. This I do truly believe. I would expect this to be the case for the next few decades, so that they and fundamentalism can lose the interest of the populace together. We poor dwellers in history. To what can our situation be compared? Only to earlier history.

Recurrences, atavisms, are by no means uniquely, or even especially, an American phenomenon. What are we to do? Prayer would be appropriate, and reflection. We should take very seriously what the dreadful past can tell us about our blindnesses and predilections. The haunting fact is that we are morally free. If everyone around us is calling for Barabbas, it is only probable, never necessary, that some of us join in. Since we have not yet burned the taper of earthly existence down to its end, we still have time to muster the dignity and graciousness and courage that are uniquely our gift. If we are making the last testament to the nature of human life, or if we are only one more beleaguered generation in a series whose end we cannot foresee, each of us and all of us know what human beauty would look like. We could let it have its moment. Fine, but would this solve the world's problems? It might solve a good many of them, I think.

DECLINE

A number of years ago a reporter from a prominent New York magazine was sent to interview the faculty and students at the Iowa Writers' Workshop. She came with a premise—that literacy was ebbing away, and that we Iowans were soon to be stranded on the shoals of time. She posed the question this way: Don't you feel that you are training auto mechanics, when soon there will be no autos? (She was British.) It is interesting that she couldn't produce a more telling vision of cultural atrophy than this, but never mind. We, faculty and students, were so unanimous in assuring her we felt no anxiety on this point that she was convinced we had colluded. This was during those years when the death of literacy was a dominant thought fad. Clearly we seemed to her to be in profound denial at best. She could not take into account the fact that she was speaking with people for whom writing is an art, not simply a commercial product in the early stages of manufacture, or that these were people who would still be writing, in their minds, at least, if they were crouched and hiding in a dystopian cellar while platoons of zombies plodded past. So it is with humankind. The siege of Paris did not suppress this impulse, this need to write, and neither did the siege of Stalingrad. Literacy came late into the world, but it spread as fast as resources and official tolerance would allow, and by now it is a sort of second nature for most of us. We translate arbitrary signs into language so instantly that we are not even aware of doing it. True, e-books are encroaching on the printed kind, but this has nothing to do with literacy. People are simply finding more ways and occasions to read. But putting the darkest construction on whatever people in general are doing or failing to do is not so much an impulse as a reflex.

The literacy-is-ebbing-away fad had an ugly cousin, the dumbing-down fad. The assumption was that the prototroglodytes of this reverse evolution would be offended and alienated by anything not already familiar to them, not expressed in the most elementary language. Nothing that mattered could be conveyed in prose forced into these constraints, but when one is sacrificing everything else to the contortions involved in lowering oneself to the level of dumbness then thought necessary, one has already abandoned all that nonsense about maintaining an informed citizenry. So the language-generating industries set about producing a more and more defective product. And their market shrank, confirming their darkest assumptions. Since the only solution seemed to be to make the product more defective still, this downward spiral might have continued, taking us finally to the printed versions of grunts and moans, I suppose. But this fad has also passed. I credit the Internet for our rescue. It turns out that there are audiences for science and economics and political history—wonkish, unembarrassed discussions of complex issues in complex language. This is not typical, of course. I grant the legitimacy of much criticism of the Internet. It is certainly open to abuse. Nevertheless, the information revolution did come along to save us from the assumption that the masses are uniformly hostile to information, and that fad passed.

I mention all this because on my next birthday I will be

seventy. Having experienced what is, by historical and global standards, a long life, I want to garner some of the benefits of it. I am seventy and the United States of America is two hundred thirty-seven. This means that I have lived through, witnessed, something between a quarter and a third of our national life. There are problems with my calculations—I should have allowed for my own infancy and early childhood, and also allowed for the fact that America had incubated for centuries before the Revolution. Still it is a striking thing to consider that my life spans so large a portion of the life of the country. What do I have to report from my decades of observation? All sorts of things. But today I will address our extraordinary proneness to thought fads and to what are called trends.

This should be diverting, a mere sidebar, since a great civilization ought to be navigating by the stars, shall we say. It should have its gaze fixed on higher things. If wisdom fails, then simple dignity should prevent it from losing itself in crazes that, in retrospect, when there is a moment of retrospect, seem baffling, even ridiculous. This is only truer because these trends and fads often have an edge, and more than an edge, of panic. Like an elephant balked by a mouse, we can persuade ourselves that our best option might be to stampede. I remember the Red Scare, *Sputnik*. But these moments of geopolitical alarm, full of consequence as they were, are like eruptions on the surface of the sun, startling displays of the substance of which they are made.

To consider the phenomenon in a relatively innocuous form: I have been involved in one way or another in higher education for most of my adult life. I have seen any number of scholarly fads come and go. A new approach can refresh a field of study, and when this happens it is an excellent thing. A new approach can have the relationship to its field of study that a very small lifeboat has to a large and sinking ship. Ill-advised crowding, unwholesome proximity, uncivil exclusion. And who knows for sure that the ship was really sinking after all. As a professor of literature, more or less, I have seen scholarly criticism given over to quasi-sociology, or -psychology, or -economic theory, or -anthropology, taking some sort of authority from the imposition of jargon that is either dubious in itself, wholly inappropriate to its subject, or both. This looks to me like the abandonment of literature as such, its reduction to data to be fed into theories. It is only logical in the circumstances that the individual student's encounter with a book should be marginalized in favor of a more knowing construction of its meaning. Nothing is lost except everything that makes literature the preeminent art. The music of it would clog the conceptual machinery. I have had students at the Workshop tell me that until they came there they had never heard the word "beautiful" applied to a literary text. Beside the great interest this phenomenon has always had in itself, beauty is a strategy of emphasis. If it is not recognized, the text is not understood.

I won't pause here to grumble over the critical assumption that the writer cannot intend anything more or other than his or her culture, class, gender, and so on would permit—as these are understood by critics with extraordinarily narrow definitions of all such terms. (I must say there are advantages in being a self-declared Calvinist from northern Idaho, from the point of view of evading easy categories.) It doesn't really matter what the writer, I in this case, thinks she means. The critic knows better than I do. That's just insulting. I freely grant, I preach, that the origins of a fiction in the writer's mind are mysterious. So are the origins of all complex thought, of dreams. Mysteries seem in their nature to invite remarkably convenient solutions, especially as they pertain to human nature or behavior. But some of us are closer to the phenomenon than others. We're in a position to say, no, that isn't it at all.

I may be blind to the virtues of theory. Some of my most interesting students would go to graduate school if they did not have to study theory. A loss to the profession. Nevertheless, if it were treated as an approach that for the moment is influential in certain circles, a recent phase in a project that began with Aristotle and has taken any number of forms since then, I would withdraw some of my objections. But it is above all an American thought fad, which means that its exponents feel that scales have fallen from their eyes. Why talk of the divagations of other decades? Context cannot catch revelation in its snares.

We know that somewhere a great conceptual wrecking ball is following its arc, and the immortals of theory and their pedestals and their shrines will go the way of Monsieur Mesmer and Madame Blavatsky and theirs, to be replaced by who knows what. And the exponents of who-knows-what will, in turn, be sure that scales have fallen from their eyes. I am not speaking here of anything as coherent as a dialectic. I am talking about a cultural habit of picking up the latest thing and discarding the second-latest thing without a thought or a backward glance. There is a great deal in our culture that encourages us to do this. The academy should not reinforce the habit. In this case, the conversation that should be carried on within the culture is in some degree impeded.

I mentioned the trend as a phenomenon. Obviously trends and fads are closely related, almost synonymous. The difference is that fads actually materialize. They have their effect and run their course. Trends are projections or speculations that are meant to anticipate events or conditions which may or may not materialize. If a trend is a projection of any desirable quality or tendency in American life, its direction is always alarmingly downward. If it is a projection of any negative quality, the arrow tips sharply upward. I became aware of this when I spent a year teaching in France. The French professors in whose house I lived were Americanists, and they had towering stacks of American news magazines. So I read backward through what was then our recent history, if history can be said to be composed primarily of things that never happen. Perhaps in our case it is appropriate to define it this way. The magazines were largely chronicles of dread and alarm. Some country somewhere had enjoyed an economic surge, which could only mean that our status was threatened and our schools were failing and we were losing the qualities that had made us great.

This narrative was recycled endlessly. What to do about those tiger economies? Well, we've forgotten now that there ever were tiger economies. Including that Celtic tiger. The projecting of trends never takes account of the endless variables involved. Remember when Japan seemed bent on buying every stick and stone of this perishing republic? At least so far as our journalism was concerned. Remember when they were instinctive mathematicians because of some association of numbers with their alphabet?

None of these things were the fault of the Japanese. They were simply the screen on which, for the moment, we projected our anxieties. It wasn't so long ago, in the era of the Japanese juggernaut, that we actually once more fell to ranking races by intelligence—Asians first, Europeans, i.e., white people, second. I will not go on with the list. It was such a heartbreaking lapse into the kind of thinking we might have hoped we had outgrown. Now Japan seems to have drifted away from its obsession with economic productivity, and it has had the terrible misfortune of Fukushima to deal with. So we have more or less forgotten it, too, together with the nonsense about racial intelligence. Now China looms. If it should prove unstable, if it should falter, India is waiting in the wings, and after India, Brazil. Russia might well make an appearance.

I distinctly remember when the flourishing of another country was considered a good thing. We did not need to be in competition with every patch of earth that happened to have a name and a flag. Competition is a questionable value, especially when it pits the very great power we are against countries that are small and fragile. I have my doubts about "creative destruction" under the best circumstances. But where whole populations and cultures are affected to their harm, it should in fact be called destructive destruction. As a matter of fact, this would also describe the competition between the United States and the Soviet Union, which left waste and warheads on earth and plutonium in the upper atmosphere. Since we are so fond of projecting, it might be interesting to estimate the number of casualties the Cold War, which might better be called the 25,000 Years War, will ultimately claim.

Be that as it may. Since it is so entrenched a habit with us to live in a state of alarmed anticipation, gearing up for things that do not happen, non-events have important real-world consequences. In recent years we have heard endlessly about our need to be competitive in the world economy. On these grounds we have been ransacking our public school system, and we have been turning a coldly utilitarian eye on our great universities. Meanwhile the world economy has more or less fallen into shambles. We had our crisis, too, and by the standards of the world at large we weathered it. This might be taken to imply that our society and economy are relatively stable and strong. But no, we are on the verge of becoming Greece. If that threat seems to have lost a little of its potency, we were staring into that potential abyss for months, some people absolutely mesmerized by it. It was an important pseudodatum that has influenced important social and government policy in this country. I am not optimist enough to suppose someone noticed that Greece has about the population of New York City and its environs, with far fewer economic resources. If only in the name of dignity and reasonableness, we really ought not to be comparing ourselves to countries one thirtieth our size.

While "Greece" was still the monosyllable that triggered in our minds the threat of precipitous downward slide, a woman remarked in my hearing that of course their economic situation was deplorable. She said, "Their malls aren't even open on Sunday." It is apparently to be assumed that economics, as the word is presently understood, not only can but should regiment national culture. Why might the Greeks choose to remember the Sabbath? Possibly because their country and language sustain an ancient religious tradition. A vast and absolute loss would be entailed in their abandonment of it. Then, too, the day of rest has other benefits. If there is any truth in relevant statistics—I doubt them all—perhaps health and longevity are not the effects of diet, of fish, vegetables, and olive oil, but of having a little time to oneself, with family and friends.

Research along these lines may well be underfunded. The Sabbath has a way of doing just what it was meant to do, sheltering one day in seven from the demands of economics. Its benefits cannot be commercialized. Leisure, by way of contrast, is highly commercialized. But leisure is seldom more than a bit of time ransomed from habitual stress. Sabbath is a way of life, one long since gone from this country, of course, due to secularizing trends, which are really economic pressures that have excluded rest as an option, first of all from those most in need of it.

•

I come at last to my main question. Has Greece somehow lost the right to be Greece? Granted, some individuals or interests there entangled the country in financial thickets and labyrinths that were meant to be impenetrable, harbored and sponsored by Britain, Germany, and the United States, whose regulators themselves claim not to understand them. Granted, Greece involved itself with the euro and has been whipsawed by the larger economies in that supposed union. Have we come to a place where essential elements of national life should be stripped away to conform every population to the disciplines of productivity, when earth itself is being worked to death? The rationale for this is competition, a notion that is symbiotic with our thinking in terms of trends. We are moving ahead in the race, or we are falling behind. There is no finish line, and there are most certainly no prizes for having led most of the way, or for leading now, when some potential competitor appears to be gaining on us. What is the nature of the race, the object of it? This changes from moment to moment. Just now it seems to involve making our children into maximally efficient workers. Whose idea was it to have them studying art and music, anyway? For a little while we were pretty serious about teaching them Japanese—why should they bother with French or Latin?—but it is clearly Chinese they should be learning, as a matter of urgency. Tomorrow it might be Hindi or Portuguese. Never mind. Trend thinking yields tunnel vision, which desperation reinforces. And the belief that is constantly urged on us is that if we are not desperate we are not paying attention.

•

As I have said on many occasions, I am a Calvinist. A bookish woman like myself, with a long, quiet life behind her, has few opportunities to shock, even scandalize, and that is part of the appeal of making this claim, I admit. But a disappearingly small part. I really am a Calvinist. And one aspect of Calvin's thought that appeals to me mightily is the famous work ethic. I work more or less constantly. Leisure bores me to death. But—this is the crucial thing—I have found my calling. Difficult as it is, my work is my pleasure and recreation. Calvin taught that all work was of equal dignity, and that one is called to a secular vocation just as one might be called to a religious vocation. Excellent. But this ideal is dependent on certain conditions. There must be an awareness of options to choose among and reasonable access to whatever tools or learning are required to make the choice. Historically, American education has provided an array of experience to allow students to discover their talents, their gifts. This practice is ending.

Our imagined future economy will supposedly require workers trained in math and science. So traditional options are falling away, denied to our children. Certainly students with a gift for math and science should be stimulated and encouraged. But the fact is that those workers who are our competitors are "efficient" because their labor is cheap. Their poverty and their defenseless environment are sold into the world market. They, and the poor who really do compete with them, will lose their terrible advantage the minute they begin to prosper a little. In any case, a factory that required its workers to be doing higher math would obviously not be efficient. The genius of mass production systems is what used to be called de-skilling, making every step in the process as simple and routine, as automatic, as possible. Those robots who will replace human labor are not mathematicians, and the technicians who design them are not working on the factory floor. But this association of math and science with efficiency is stuck so solidly in the American brain that it is never questioned, and we are stripping down our educational system in deference to it.

Historically, our ways of doing things have worked rather well. Maybe we need to reflect on this. I know, there aren't any prizes for not having lost yet. But what if there is not, need not be, should not be, a race to begin with? What if, ideally, Greece is a place for Greeks to be Greek, and—what a concept!—America is a place for Americans to be American? What would this mean for us, diverse as we are? Well, there is one thing it had better mean—that as a society we prepare ourselves and one another to be competent citizens of a democracy. One consequence of the obsession with competition, with all its attendant fears and anxieties, is that we are encouraged to forget that we are, in fact, a very great power. Account for this however we might, at this moment and into any foreseeable future it will be a fact, an important reality in the life of the whole world. Suppose we do by some calculus slide into second place, or third place. We will still be a very great power, with all the responsibilities that come with power. The world is volatile and fragile, as we all know. Too often we feel we are a blundering giant, invading countries of which we know nothing—which, as we are oddly fond of saying, most of us could not find on a map. Neither science nor math will help us to have an appropriately humane, a civilized, interest in the world, a respectful awareness of lives lived otherwise that might stay our hand, militarily and economically.

I hope I will not seem eccentric when I say that God's love for the world is something it is also useful to ponder. Imagine humankind acting freely within the very broad limits of its gifts, its capacity for discerning the good and just and shaping the beautiful. If God has taken pleasure in his creation, there is every reason to assume that some part of his pleasure is in your best idea, your most generous impulse, your most disciplined thinking on whatever is true, honorable, just, pure, pleasing, excellent, and worthy of praise. I am paraphrasing Paul, of course, but if you have read Cicero or *The Egyptian Book of the Dead*, for example, you know that pre-Christians and pagans made art and literature and philosophy, excellent and worthy of praise, out of love for the thought of all these things. When Solomon set about creating the temple where God would put his name, he went to the Tyreans, pagans with an established history of temple building. The houses they built were for Baal and El and Ishtar, true, but clearly in Solomon's eyes the Tyreans had developed an architecture entirely suitable for expressing the idea of the holy. My point is simply that, from the time the first hominid looked up at the stars and was amazed by them, a sweet savor has been rising from this earth, every part of it—a silent music worthy of God's pleasure. What we have expressed, compared with what we have found no way to express, is overwhelmingly the lesser part. Loyalties and tendernesses that we are scarcely aware of might seem, from a divine perspective, the most beautiful things in creation, even in their evanescence. Such things are universally human. They forbid the distinctions "us" and "them." We do not know what we obliterate when we drop a bomb. And neither math nor science can begin to make us realize.

So. If we are to be competent citizens of a powerful democracy, we must encourage the study of the aptly named humanities. The cultures of the world's people are complex and diverse, but they are manifestations of one phenomenon, the uniqueness of the human presence on earth. A student of the French Enlightenment knows at least something about the profound particularities of history and circumstance that invest any place and period. A student of Greek or German begins to understand that languages both constrain and enable the thought of those who speak them. Touch a limit of your understanding and it falls away, to reveal mystery upon mystery. The one great lesson we can take from the study of any civilization is the appropriateness of reverence, of awe, and of pity, too. This would be a good thing for the citizens of a powerful democracy to remember.

Are we, indeed, a democracy? Yes, relatively speaking, we are. Despite slovenliness and mendacity, which are usual in governments of every kind, and despite the predisposition to fads and trends that seems to characterize us more than others, we do have a very broad franchise and a demonstrated openness to suasion. That we are a democracy in this degree means that we have the option of making ourselves a much better democracy. This brings me back to the matter of fads and trends, especially as they affect higher education.

For many years the dominant thought fad was something called Marxism. This fad was basically coterminous with the Cold War. With the end of the Soviet Union and the rise of Friedman-ism it folded like a cheap tent. But when the fad was at its height, when people swept along in it felt bold and even dangerous, I began to learn that in the overwhelming percentage of cases, these Marxists had not read Marx. I assume some must have, but I never found a single one. The confession did not embarrass them. Of course anyone can call himself a Marxist, on the same grounds that I can call myself a Plantagenet if I want to. Absent the intent to defraud, which is possibly an issue in the case of those who pose as experts in and converts to a highly readable and available body of thought with which they have in fact no familiarity whatever. They were a voluble lot and seemed to be mutually intelligible in a through-the-looking-glass language that yielded, for example, preposterous misstatements about such things as Marx's view of the American Civil War—about which Marx wrote extensively. No doubt some part of their once great influence lingers. I was recently at a meeting of international scholars who were as one in resenting, rather in the manner of a *classe dangereuse*, their economic enslavement. So Marx is still unread. Perhaps the Marxist influence lingers in the principled neglect of primary texts and the principled reliance on esoteric language, which certainly contribute to the growing sense that higher education in general and the humanities in particular have nothing to do with anything.

Serious as all this is, it is trivial beside the fact that this self-declared Marxism did flourish in American universities during the Cold War. It is appropriate to wonder what Marx's thought ever had to do with the Soviet economic and social order. But they claimed him, and we in America used Marxism as a synonym for their ideology and their political system. Therefore, as a courtesy to the larger world, which has inevitably been deeply affected by the nuclear testing and the proxy wars and the defensive imperialism both sides engaged in, wouldn't it have been the proper thing, true, honorable, and just, to acquire some meaningful grasp of the nature of the argument? Was it not a disservice to humankind to provide instead tomes and decades of arcane nonsense?

This episode in the life of American higher education epitomizes for me the failure to live up to the standard of competency democracy requires. We depend on one another to deal truly, to provide one another with a basis for understanding and judgment. Anyone with higher education is likely to have an area or a role for which he or she is responsible in some degree. This is true very obviously for writers, scholars, teachers, journalists, lawyers. And it is true of scientists and mathematicians, whose work may contribute to the horrors of war, or to catastrophic failures in the global economy.

Lately I have been reading things written around the time of the Civil War by both Unionists and secessionists, most recently the memoirs of Thomas Wentworth Higginson. It is lodged immovably in the academic mind that Higginson undervalued and discouraged Emily Dickinson, though in fact he was in awe of her and wrote about her brilliantly. He was also a strong early feminist and a great abolitionist. The literary figures of the age who were committed to the abolition of slavery are often treated as so many fastidious and distant onlookers, but in fact many of them were in the thick of the fray. Higginson, for example, has good claim to having been the commander of the first black regiment to see combat in the Civil War. In the essay "Army Life in a Black Regiment," Higginson quotes from a report made by the army surgeon after an early skirmish. The surgeon wrote,

> Braver men never lived. One man with two bullet-holes through the large muscles of the shoulders and neck brought off from the scene of action, two miles distant, two muskets; and not a murmur has escaped his lips. Another, Robert Sutton, with three wounds—one of which, being on the skull, may cost him his life—would not report himself till compelled to do so by his officers. While dressing his wounds, he quietly talked of what

> they had done, and of what they yet could do . . . He is perfectly quiet and cool, but takes this whole affair with the religious bearing of a man who realizes that freedom is sweeter than life. Yet another soldier did not report himself at all, but remained all night on guard, and possibly I should not have known of his having had a buck-shot in his shoulder, if some duty requiring a sound shoulder had not been required of him.

Higginson says, "This last, it may be added, had persuaded a comrade to dig out the buck-shot, for fear of being ordered on the sick-list . . . An officer may be pardoned some enthusiasm for such men as these." Higginson is very insistent on the courage and discipline of his soldiers, his recording them being important, as he believed, to "the fortunes of a race." The book was published in 1869, four years after the war. William Dean Howells, reviewing it for *The Atlantic*, remarked rather dismissively that the country was tired of the Negro.

I have often wondered what abyss it was that opened and swallowed so much that was good and enlightened in the social thought and the many important experiments and reforms that emerged from the abolitionist movement before the Civil War. Perhaps this gives me an answer. We simply tired of justice and equality. They were out of fashion in the new era of eugenics and social Darwinism and their ugly brother, racial science. These new enthusiasms were considered highly intellectual for just a little less than a century, not least because they were so European. They were centered in our great universities. Only relatively recent scholarship has recovered the history of these black regiments. The Civil War and the decades that preceded it called up so much courage and intelligence and sacrifice, such an outpouring of lives, and it bought us a decade or two of sanity between chattel slavery and Jim Crow. What in God's name might we not tire of?

It is no small matter, how we conduct our intellectual lives, we who populate universities. We are used to the idea that sellers of tulip bulbs or lanolin or bad mortgages try to catch the nearest way to profit, which is after all the difference between the actual worth of a thing and what someone can be induced to pay for it. None of us is surprised if this reality is one in which demand is artificially stimulated in order to enhance the exchange value of some item of commerce that might be a drug on the market in sixty days. The wisdom-of-the-market fad, which survives though global markets have been dragging the world economy into the abyss for a number of years now, was and is embraced by the universities. The universities now seem obsessed with marketing themselves and ensuring the marketability of their product, which will make the institution itself more marketable—a loop of mutual reinforcement of the kind that sets in when thinking becomes pathologically narrow. Somehow, in a society that is extraordinarily rich by world standards, largely on the basis of wealth created by earlier generations, and one that is capable, if it or any other society ever has been, of giving its people the means to consider and appreciate their moment on this earth, we are panicked into reducing ourselves and others into potential units of economic production—assuming, as we never should, that we know what future circumstances will demand of us. The humanities teach us respect for what we are—we, in the largest sense. Or they should. Because there is another reality, greater than the markets, and that is the reality in which the planet is fragile, and peace among nations, where it exists, is also fragile. The greatest tests ever made of human wisdom and decency may very well come to this generation or the next one. We must teach and learn broadly and seriously, dealing with one another with deep respect and in the best good faith.

FEAR

America is a Christian country. This is true in a number of senses. Most people, if asked, will identify themselves as Christian, which may mean only that they aren't something else. Non-Christians will say America is Christian, meaning that they feel somewhat apart from the majority culture. There are any number of demographic Christians in North America because of our history of immigration from countries that are or were also Christian. We are identified in the world at large with this religion because some of us espouse it not only publicly but also vociferously. As a consequence, we carry a considerable responsibility for its good name in the world, though we seem not much inclined to consider the implications of this fact. If we did, some of us might think a little longer about associating the precious Lord with ignorance, intolerance, and belligerent nationalism. These few simple precautions would also make it more attractive to the growing numbers among our people who have begun to reject it as ignorant, intolerant, and belligerently nationalistic, as they might reasonably conclude that it is, if they hear only the loudest voices.

There is something I have felt the need to say, that I have spoken about in various settings, extemporaneously, because my thoughts on the subject have not been entirely formed, and because it is painful to me to have to express them. However, my thesis is always the same, and it is very simply stated, though it has two parts. First, contemporary America is full of fear. And second, fear is not a Christian habit of mind. As children we learn to say, "Yea, though I walk through the valley of the shadow of death I will fear no evil, for Thou art with me." We learn that, after his resurrection, Jesus told his disciples, "Lo, I am with you always, to the close of the age." Christ is a gracious, abiding presence in all reality, and in him history will finally be resolved. These are larger, more embracing terms than contemporary Christianity is in the habit of using. But we are taught that Christ "was in the beginning with God; all things were made through him, and without him was not anything made that was made . . . The light shines in the darkness, and the darkness has not overcome it." The present tense here is to be noted. John's First Letter proclaims "the eternal life which was with the Father and was made manifest to us." We as Christians cannot think of Christ as isolated in space or time if we really do accept the authority of our own texts. Nor can we imagine that this life on earth is our only life, our primary life. As Christians we are to believe that we are to fear not the death of our bodies but the loss of our souls.

We hear a great deal now about the drift of America away from a Christian identity. Whenever there is talk of decline—as in fact there always is—the one thing that seems to be lacking is a meaningful standard of change. How can we know where we are if we don't know where we were, in those days when things were as they ought to be? How can we know there has been decline, an invidious qualitative change, if we cannot establish a terminus a quo? I propose attention to the marked and oddly general fearfulness of our culture at present as one way of dealing with the problem. In the twenty-sixth chapter of Leviticus we find a description of the state the people of Israel will find themselves in if they depart from their loyalty to God. "The sound of a driven leaf shall put them to flight, and they shall flee as one flees from the sword, and they shall fall when none pursues. They shall stumble over one another, as if to escape a sword, though none pursues." Now, of course, there are numbers among us who have weapons that would blast that leaf to atoms, and feel brave as they did it, confirmed in their alarm by the fact that there are so very many leaves. But the point is the same. Those who forget God, the single assurance of our safety however that word may be defined, can be recognized in the fact that they make irrational responses to irrational fears. The text specifies the very real threat that fear itself poses—"you shall have no power to stand before your enemies." There are always real dangers in the world, sufficient to their day. Fearfulness obscures the distinction between real threat on one hand and on the other the terrors that beset those who see threat everywhere. It is clear enough, to an objective viewer at least, with whom one would choose to share a crisis, whose judgment should be trusted when sound judgment is most needed. Granting the perils of the world, it is potentially a very costly indulgence to fear indiscriminately, and to try to stimulate fear in others, just for the excitement of it, or because to do so channels anxiety or loneliness or prejudice or resentment into an emotion that can seem to those who indulge it like shrewdness or courage or patriotism. But no one seems to have an unkind word to say about fear these days, unchristian as it surely is.

•

We who are students of Calvin's tradition know that our ancestors in the tradition did not spare their lives or their fortunes. They were loyal to the will of God as they understood it at the most extreme cost to themselves—in worldly terms, that is. They also defended their faith militarily, with intelligence and great courage, but without ultimate success, except in the Low Countries. Therefore the migration of Pilgrims and Puritans, and Huguenots as well, and the great flourishing of Calvinist civilization in the New World. We might say that the oppressors meant it for evil, but God meant it for good, except this might lead us to forget a crucial thing, a factor not present in the story of Joseph and his brothers. Those oppressors were motivated by fear of us. We were heretics by their lights, and therefore a threat to the church, to Christian civilization, to every soul who felt our influence. We filled more or less the same place in the European imagination that Islam does now, one difference being that the Christianity now assumed to be under threat on that most secular continent is merely sociological and cultural, in effect racial, and another difference being that there was no ideal of tolerance and little concept of due process to mitigate the violence the presence of our ancestors inspired. Quite the opposite. To suppress our tradition however viciously was a pious act.

The terrible massacres of Protestants in France in the sixteenth century, whether official or popular in their origins, reflect the fear that is engendered by the thought that someone really might destroy one's soul, plunge one into eternal fire by corrupting true belief even inadvertently. If someone had asked a citizen of Lyon, on his way to help exterminate the Calvinists, to explain what he and his friends were doing, he would no doubt have said that he was taking back his city, taking back his culture, taking back his country, fighting for the soul of France. This kind of language was not invented in order to be used against Calvinists—Europe had been purging itself of heretics since the thirteenth century, so the pattern was already well established. These same terms had been used centuries before by the Roman emperor Julian, called the Apostate, when he tried to return Rome from its emerging Christianity to the old classical paganism. But it was applied to our case with notable rigor and persistence, and with great effect. I spoke not long ago at a homiletics conference in Wittenberg. There were people there from many distant parts of the world, and not a soul from France. I asked why there were no French people there, and was told that Catholics were not as focused on preaching as Protestants. I told them there are in fact Protestants in France. I told them how to find the Église Réformée on the Internet, preaching and music and all. I am aware of them myself because no Christian population anywhere has ever defended its beliefs with more courage against more entrenched persecution than the Protestants of France. These cultural erasures are almost always more apparent than real, and still they matter, because they assert the unique legitimacy of one descriptor, narrowly defined—Roman, or French, or Aryan, or Catholic, or Christian, or American.

It is difficult for any number of reasons to define a religion, to establish an essence and a circumference, and this is true not least because it always has its supernumeraries, often legions of them. I saw a cinema spectacular when I was growing up, *Demetrius and the Gladiators*. Demetrius, who bore an uncanny resemblance to Victor Mature, was a Christian convert, obliged therefore to turn the other cheek when taunted by a bully. A gladiator acquaintance of his, an enormous Nubian man, walloped the bully with a plated forearm, sending him sprawling, then growled after him, exultingly, "I am no Christian!" Needless to say, the theater audience erupted in cheers. There was popcorn all over the place. (Parenthetically: I watched this film and *The Robe* to see if I had been fair to Cecil B. DeMille and Delmer Daves, and I had not. Both represent the Christian community as gentle and serene, startlingly so by our standards. But then, in those early days Christians had only Caligula to worry about.)

Calvin had his supernumeraries, great French lords who were more than ready to take up arms in his cause, which was under severe persecution. He managed to restrain them while he lived, saying that the first drop of blood they shed would become a torrent that drowned Europe. And, after he died, Europe was indeed drenched in blood. So there is every reason to suppose that Calvin would have thought his movement had lost at least as much as it gained in these efforts to defend it, as he anticipated it would. Specifically, in some degree it lost its Christian character, as Christianity, or any branch of it, always does when its self-proclaimed supporters outnumber and outshout its actual adherents. What is true when there is warfare is just as true when the bonding around religious identity is militantly cultural or political.

At the core of all this is fear, real or pretended. What if these dissenters in our midst really are a threat to all we hold dear? Better to deal with the problem before their evil schemes are irreversible, before our country has lost its soul and the United Nations has invaded Texas. We might step back and say that there are hundreds of millions of people who love this nation's soul, who in fact are its soul, and patriotism should begin by acknowledging this fact. But there is not much fear to be enjoyed from this view of things. Why stockpile ammunition if the people over the horizon are no threat? If they would in fact grieve with your sorrows and help you through your troubles? At a lunch recently Lord Jonathan Sacks, then chief rabbi of the United Kingdom, said that the United States is the world's only covenant nation, that the phrase "We the People" has no equivalent in the political language of other nations, and that the State of the Union address should be called the renewal of the covenant. I have read that Americans are now buying Kalashnikovs in numbers sufficient to help subsidize Russian rearmament, to help their manufacturers achieve economies of scale. In the old days these famous weapons were made with the thought that they would be used in a land war between great powers, that is, that they would kill Americans. Now, since they are being brought into this country, the odds are great that they will indeed kill Americans. But only those scary ones who want to destroy all we hold dear. Or, more likely, assorted adolescents in a classroom or a movie theater.

I know there are any number of people who collect guns as sculpture, marvels of engineering. When we mount a cross on a wall, we don't do it with the thought that, in a pinch, we might crucify someone. This seems to be a little different when the icon in question is a gun. A "civilian" Kalashnikov can easily be modified into a weapon that would blast a deer to smithereens. That's illegal, of course, and unsportsmanlike. I have heard the asymmetry rationalized thus: deer can't shoot back. Neither can adolescents in a movie theater, of course. Neither can anyone not prepared for mayhem to break loose anywhere, at any time. And, imagining an extremely improbable best case, it is very hard to threaten or deter someone who is suicidal, as most of these assailants are. Gun sales stimulate gun sales—a splendid business model, no doubt about that. Fear operates as an appetite or an addiction. You can never be safe enough.

I know that hunting is sacrosanct in this country. This is beside the point, since hunting rifles are not the problem. And the conversation around this issue never stays long with hunting. It goes instead to the Second Amendment. Any literalist reading would notice the founders' words "well-regulated" on one hand, and on the other the alarm that arises among the pro-gun people at the slightest mention of anything that resembles regulation, and their constant efforts to erode what little regulation there is. The supposed neglect or abuse of this revered document, and the supposed "defense of the Second Amendment," is leveraged on that other fear, the fear that those bland blue helmets might be gathering even now, maybe in Canada, to commence their internationalist march into the heart of Texas. Will we wake to find ourselves betrayed by our own government? Maybe nothing has deterred them to this point but those Kalashnikovs. How fortunate that the factory in Russia is up and running. And how hard those Russians must be laughing, all the way to the bank. And all those homicidal insurgents and oppressors in the turbulent parts of the world, how pleased they must be that we cheapen these marvelous weapons for them. Oh, I know there are all sorts of reliable gun manufacturers, in Austria, for example. Our appetite for weapons is one of those vacuums nature hates, that is to say, fills.

The Second Amendment argument is brilliant in its way, because the Constitution is central to everything American. The president takes an oath to preserve, protect, and defend the Constitution—nothing more, nothing other. I took a rather similar oath myself once, when I accepted a generous fellowship of a kind established under President Eisenhower and continued under Presidents Kennedy and Johnson. But of course J. Edgar Hoover identified Dwight Eisenhower as a communist sympathizer. I guess he would cite me as proof, since I did indeed study Shakespeare with the sponsorship of the federal government, on a National Defense Education Act fellowship. I flatter myself that we are no worse for it. The government at that time felt that humanists also contributed to the well-being of the United States. How times change. I have in fact a number of credentials that would make me a driven leaf, as things are reckoned now. I have lived in Massachusetts and other foreign countries. My command of French is not absolutely minimal. I have degrees from elite institutions. I am a professor in a secular university. All in all I am a pretty good example of the sort who inspire fight-or-flight responses in certain segments of the population. I find myself musing over this from time to time.

Be that as it may. Our first loyalty in this country is to the Constitution, so if the case can be made that any part of the Bill of Rights, for heaven's sake, is under threat, then the whole edifice is imperiled. And what is a patriot to do in the face of such peril? Carry, as they say, just to assert the right. In the old movies a concealed weapon was the unfailing mark of a coward, but Clint Eastwood came along to rescue us from our scruples about such things. And besides, a visible weapon would not only spoil the lines of a business suit, it would also alarm and no doubt alienate anyone who watches the news. By pure coincidence, as I was writing these thoughts, sitting on my back porch in my quiet, crime-free neighborhood, I heard one man loudly lecturing another on the inappropriateness of going armed into a grocery store, telling him that if he did he could expect the manager to call the police, and that when the police ordered him to leave he was indeed obliged to leave. Do I feel safer in my neighborhood because this unknown man is wandering around with a gun, licensed though it seems to be? No, I don't. Since everything is economics these days, what would it cost a store in terms of trade if word got out that he frequented it, with his loyalty to the Second Amendment on display? Or possibly concealed? I'm betting he could put them out of business, because when people see weapons, they have every reason on earth to fear the worst. And what does it cost to police this sort of thing, in this time of budget cuts? If there is any argument for weapons from a public safety point of view, there is a much stronger argument for sparing the police the problem of dealing with such distractions, and for minimizing the risk of their killing or being killed by someone they must assume to be armed.

So, concealed carry. The gun lobby has made its product socially acceptable by putting it out of sight, issues of cowardice notwithstanding.

The next thing to do is to stockpile weapons. Buy gold from that man on TV, maybe some of that dried food, too. Prowl around in the woods with like-minded people. Some pretty intense bonding goes on, swapping fears around a campfire, as any Girl Scout can testify. And keep an eye out for traitors, active or passive, intentional or not. Who can say, after all, that the Christians did not turn the gods against Rome, that the Cathars did not kill souls, that witches did not cast spells, that Jews did not poison wells, that Gypsies did not steal infants, that a Republican president did not send English majors to graduate school as part of a scheme to soften the national resolve? It is notoriously impossible to prove a negative. I think the army of the United Nations is invoked in these contexts as a small and rare concession to standards of plausibility. No one would imagine such a thing of the United States Army. Other plausibility issues arise, of course. To the best of my knowledge, the forces of the United Nations exist primarily to be ineffectual in hopeless situations. Never mind. They are an ominous threat. We might need to shoot at them.

This is the point at which that supernumerary phenomenon I mentioned becomes a factor. There is a First Amendment, too, and it is directed toward, among other things, forbidding an establishment of religion. Yet among the self-declared constitutionalists, the word "Christian" has become the kind of test for electoral eligibility that the founders specifically meant to forbid. Is Mitt Romney a Christian? Mormonism has a pretty exotic theology, after all. Is Barack Obama a Christian? He joined a church as an adult and was unaffiliated with institutional religion before then. There was a time when we Calvinists felt the force of the terror and antagonism that can be raised against those who are not Christian in a sense other people are willing to accept. This doleful trait is being played upon in our current politics. Supernumeraries who strike out against the free exercise of religion might say, "I am no Christian." With equal truth they might also say, "I am no American." And a pretty large part of the crowd would probably cheer.

I defer to no one in my love for America and for Christianity. I have devoted my life to the study of both of them. I have tried to live up to my association with them. And I take very seriously Jesus' teachings, in this case his saying that those who live by the sword will also die by the sword. Something called Christianity has become entangled in exactly the strain of nationalism that is militaristic, ready to spend away the lives of our young, and that can only understand dissent from its views as a threat or a defection, a heresy in the most alienating and stigmatizing sense of the word. We are not the first country where this has happened. The fact that it was the usual thing in Europe, and had been for many centuries, was one great reason for attempting to separate church and state here. Jesus' aphorism may be taken to mean simply that those who deal in violence are especially liable to suffer violence. True enough. But death is no simple thing when Jesus speaks of it. His thoughts are not our thoughts, the limits of our perceptions are not limits he shares. We must imagine him seeing the whole of our existence, our being beyond mortality, beyond time. There is that other death he can foresee, the one that really matters. When Christians abandon Christian standards of behavior in the defense of Christianity, when Americans abandon American standards of conduct in the name of America, they inflict harm that would not be in the power of any enemy. As Christians they risk the kind of harm to themselves to which the Bible applies adjectives like "everlasting."

American exceptionalism is more imperiled in these moments than in any others, and so is organized religion. Try to persuade a skeptic of the value of religion, and he or she will mention some horror of European history carried out under the sign of the cross. They are innumerable. I have mentioned St. Bartholomew's Day. One hears of the secularization of Europe, often in the context of socialist economics, rarely in the context of a frankly terrifying history. We must be very careful not to defeat the safeguards our laws and traditions have put in place. Christian "establishment," the making of Christianity in effect the official religion, is the first thing its supernumeraries would try for, and the last thing its faithful should condone. As for America, the way we have of plunging into wars we weary of and abandon after a few years and a few thousand casualties, having forgotten what our object was, these wars demonstrate an overwhelming power to destroy without any comparable regard to life and liberty, to the responsibilities of power, that would be consistent with maintaining our good name. We throw away our status in the world at the urging of those who think it has nothing to do with our laws and institutions, impressed by the zeal of those supernumeraries who are convinced that it all comes down to shock and awe and boots on the ground. This notion of glory explains, I suppose, some part of the fantasizing, the make-believe wars against make-believe enemies, and a great many of the very real Kalashnikovs.

But to return to the problems of establishing the fact of decline and measuring the nature and degree of it. Astronomers use what they call "standard candles," celestial objects of known luminosity, to calculate celestial distances. Making estimates of the relative distances between phenomena afloat in time poses similar difficulties. Cultural history has its own version of the three-body problem, since it is composed of forces and influences that interact continuously in ways that can be neither predicted nor reconstructed. It occurred to me as I was looking again at those old movies on biblical subjects, notably *The Robe* and *Ben-Hur*, that they could function as standard candles for the purposes of this discussion. They date from a time many consider the golden age of religion in America. They are utterly Christian, and addressed to a very broad public they clearly take to be both receptive to the material and very knowledgeable about it. And they were successful, critically as well as commercially. So we may take them to be fairly reliable records of the religious sensibility they spoke from and to.

The first thing to be noted is that they are in no degree, in no smallest detail, anti-Semitic. Imperial Rome is the villain, the crucifier. It is striking, considering the overwhelming potency of its presence in the Mediterranean world of the first century, how Rome has dropped out of our contemporary conversation, scholarly and other, about the events of Jesus' life and death. The thought seems to be general now that the Passion and the Gospels as a whole are inevitably to be read as anti-Semitic, and that the Romans were, so to speak, mere spear-carriers. There is no need to consider this earlier interpretation to be revisionism brought on by postwar sensitivities, because the film genre of the Bible epic began in movie adaptations of the novel *Ben-Hur*, written by the former Union general and proud son of Indiana Lew Wallace, and published in 1880. *Ben-Hur* was the best-selling book after *Uncle Tom's Cabin* and before *Gone With the Wind*. Its Jewish title character is as robust a heroic figure as is to be found in literature, a man who is tenderly obsessive in his love for his mother and sister and utterly loyal to his people and his faith. The film versions are faithful to this vision of him. Furthermore, they are consistent in avoiding any suggestion that he undergoes anything like a conversion experience. In the films he encounters Jesus twice, once when he is being conveyed to the coast to be enslaved in the galleys and a young stranger gives him a drink of water, and a second time at the Crucifixion. His mother and sister are healed of leprosy by Christ but without direct contact with him. Christ brings an experience of sacred presence in the world that is perfectly consistent with the holiness to which Ben-Hur is devoted as a Jew. The princely Judah Ben-Hur is a gracious, pacific, and virtuous man at the beginning of the tale and, at the end, under the influence of Christ, he is once again a gracious, pacific, and virtuous man.

This is an instance of the cultural three-body problem. Beginning even with John Chrysostom there has been cultivated an antagonism against the Jews. I need hardly say it raged through the Middle Ages and into the modern period. So, is it inevitably part of Christianity, or did the universalistic impulses of a period in American religious culture actually allow us to escape it for a blessed while? Mel Gibson's work is not in this line of descent. In the truly miserable last movie of this line of Christian spectaculars, *King of Kings*, whose costume designer must have been Dr. Seuss with an enormous budget, and whose embroiderings on Scripture bring a blush to the cheek, there is nevertheless an exculpation of the crowds that shout, "Give us Barabbas." In this telling, Barabbas is a bold and effective resistance leader, whose life they value for good reason. He is also a foil for the figure of Christ, whose intervention in history is always treated as if it meant the fall of Rome in the relatively proximate future.

If the point of American yearnings for our past is to recover a religious culture that was uniquely ours, how do we deal with the many pasts that have come with immigration or that we have accepted as our share in a part of Western history? Must we not be a little careful about proceeding without inquiring into the emergence of our highly particular religious culture? It is a theological position no longer widely held that allows the narrative of Ben-Hur to be what it is. These days people read the Old Testament, or the Hebrew Scriptures, to condemn them, if they read them at all. This is a change from the days of Lew Wallace, and a return to the Middle Ages, in effect. A vast labor of scholarship and preaching, carried on over many generations, lay behind the reverence with which Americans in the nineteenth century regarded the Old Testament. All that has been put aside and forgotten. So the argument implicit in the novel and the films, that the Testaments are all one fabric, is no longer sustainable or even of much interest. These Christian artifacts, given to and received by a Christian culture, erase distinctions of a kind that many people now insist on, as if piety were a matter of delineation and exclusion. Once these delineations begin there is no end to them. They spill over into anxieties about who is really Christian, who is Christian enough, tests that, as I have said, the Reformed traditions failed persistently and catastrophically in most of Europe. For Lew Wallace and his immense readership on the other hand, and for his filmmaking heirs and successors, it would appear that a Jew is Christian enough. In nineteenth-century America and after, there was a strong strain of what was called even then Christian liberalism. In our day the very phrase is a driven leaf. All in all, with the loss of interest in our own actual past, the loss of interest in antiquity as well as in Scripture, nostalgia is most certainly a doomed enterprise. We can't get there from here. Any real attempt at return would mean more rigor in the seminaries, more depth and learning in the pulpits, and more meditation in the pews on the fact that God loves the world, not just the little islets of right thought we might hope he favors.

One more aspect of Lew Wallace's novel and the films is worth considering. The fascinations of Rome, its power and wealth, its self-worship and self-confidence, its discipline, are set over against the life and death of an obscure and powerless man in an occupied province. Power is brutal in this world, and the question is, What can stand against it? Since they are Christian films, the answer is familiar to us—gentleness, generosity, love, restraint, and, of course, the vision and faith that make these things possible. Under the new regime of Christ an army of resistance is disbanded though Rome still rules. The Roman tribune who is known to have been in charge at the Crucifixion is welcomed into the Christian community even before he acknowledges his role. Justifiable homicide is confessed as a sin. Vengeance is forgotten, and courage is expressed in the refusal to press advantage or to have recourse to violence.

All the weakness of Christ is to be understood as a great act of divine restraint, of course. If the reality of the moment were known, glorious Rome would be seen to flaunt mortal and trivial threats in the face of God Almighty. So do we all, insofar as any power we have as human beings transgresses the will of God. This great restraint has a lovelier name—grace. It is not the will of God that anyone should be lost. And if God loves those who hate him and despitefully use him—Jesus says we are to be like God in this—then we also had better be careful to show them the patience, the restraint, the grace that he wills for them. This is an instance in which for us the fear of God should cast out every other fear.

It is a moving thing to watch these vivid ghosts of iconic actors, most of whom we have seen to their graves long since. There they are, vivid with the beauty of youth, agile and deft and light on their feet. The lissome Jean Simmons dead at eighty, Charlton Heston at eighty-five. For all the art that lets us keep their images, it is as true as it ever was that "golden lads and girls all must, as chimney-sweepers, come to dust." At almost any earlier moment we would have taken a moral to heart from all this, that in good time absolutely everything will be pried from our cold, dead hands. And then, in the words of the parable, whose will it be? There is a little taunt in the fact that so much outlives us. Our very ignorance and neglect is carried on through time to impoverish later generations. Let us imagine that the most responsible gun owner on earth has a collection of beautiful weapons under lock and key, there only to be admired. He will die in due course, and his guns will be immune to time and change, on any future day brought to a high gleam with just a little polishing. And whose will they be? Let us imagine an estate sale. I've seen my neighbors' cherished souvenirs pass into the roadside economy of trinkets and oddments. Presumably by such routes guns show up at gun shows. Or let us imagine a nephew or grandson whose delusions might otherwise have been only his and his family's sorrow, but which become a disaster because one of those beautiful weapons comes into his hands. Whose will they be? In the nature of the case, because of the mortality of human beings and the immortality of these weapons, this same question will come down through generations. "Posterity" is a word we no longer use, though, according to the preamble, the Constitution was written with it in mind. And in fact America itself, and Christianity insofar as it is sustained by our mortal love and loyalty, can only be thought of as living if it can be passed on to other generations. We owe it to them to be calm and clear, to hold fast to what is good, and to hate the thought that we may leave behind an impoverished or a lethal heritage.

PROOFS

For a century and more we in the West have been told that our experience of life is deficient, lacking something truly essential, to our happiness and also to our humanity. Oddly, it is the privilege of advanced education that generally induces us to accept this impoverished condition as inescapably our own. Again, oddly, the interpretation of our condition, which quite invariably includes loss of religious belief, puts its apparent antidotes, notably religious belief, beyond the pale on grounds of naïveté, nostalgia, and so on. Those who might not otherwise suffer from this affliction are coaxed into acknowledging that God, however essential he has been proved to be, to our happiness and our humanity, was nevertheless a creature of historical circumstance.

None of this has ever seemed true to me, or even logical. Nor have I been persuaded that human life was or could be less a marvel than it was when it was felt to address and celebrate the sacred, being itself sacred. So I have studied Scripture and theology, and I have gone to church. My tradition places great importance on the sermon, and I go in hopes of hearing something that acknowledges this deep old human intuition, this sense of the sacred. Often I don't hear any such thing, but sometimes, more remarkably, I do. A good sermon is a pure, rare, strangely unworldly gift. How is the possibility of such a gift to be understood?

In his translation into Latin of the opening phrase of the Gospel of John, John Calvin followed Erasmus, and the earlier examples of Tertullian and Cyprian, in choosing the word *Sermo* rather than the word *Verbum*. It is clear from his Commentary that he found the more conventional translation lacking in substance and resonance, inadequate to the theological burden of John's *Logos*. The English, "In the beginning was the Word," is so familiar, so pleasingly straightforward, so sanctified by use, that it is hard now to think of it as insufficient, even though it is clearly a translation from the Latin, not from the Greek. Of course the whole world has changed, and Latin has receded so far in Western culture that associations that colored or burdened particular words in the sixteenth century are lost to us now. And over time the same words have acquired new resonances that elevate them.

Still, there is interest for me in the distinction Calvin insists on between *Sermo*, which he calls the *Sapientia Dei*, and *Verbum*, which is for him the temporal or transient utterance that is the human voice of Divine Wisdom, a thing to be sharply distinguished from its essence and its eternal source. He says, "When the Scripture speaks of *the Word of God*, it certainly were very absurd to imagine it to be only a transient and momentary sound, emitted into the air, and coming forth from God himself; of which nature were the oracles, given to the fathers, and all the prophecies. [The Word of God] is rather to be understood of the eternal wisdom residing in God, whence the oracles and all the prophecies proceeded." Christ for Calvin is the creative Wisdom expressed in the Being of all things. In his translation and Commentary his concern is to insist on the ontological meaning of 1 John. Christ, the Wisdom of God, is present in the order of Being itself, as he "upholds all things by the word of his power" and present as well in the testimony of the ancient prophets who "spake by the Spirit of Christ no less than the Apostles and all the succeeding ministers of the heavenly doctrine." For him the very sinews of reality are made of the wisdom proceeding from this source, whether implanted in materiality with all its aspects and conditions, or spoken by those "ministers of the heavenly doctrine" who have been its teachers through the whole of Christian time. The knowledge of God and the knowledge of ourselves are an aspect of this wisdom that is sacramental in its reciprocity.

This is consistent with a metaphysics, an ontology, that runs through the whole of Calvin's thought. It places humankind, and the most striking of human attributes, at the center of cosmic reality. The kind of thought that is often called modern forbids at least tacitly the acknowledgment of human exceptionalism, as if it were reasonable to exclude reality's most exotic expressions from an account of the nature of reality. Science itself tells us not to overlook the effect of the observer on any observation, an effect including but not limited to bias. Yet a very primary datum, ourselves in our undeniable distinctiveness, is folded into statements about primates in general, or about the wiles and aspirations of genes, human and other. Thought, that gorgeous blossoming of consciousness so deeply interesting to earlier civilization, dropped away as an object of thought as a consequence of the strange idea that we are not appropriately described by the qualities that are unique to us. This idea has eluded scrutiny, having created an environment friendly to its own flourishing.

Ontology creates a vast and liberating space. To propose that the order of the universe at every scale is, so to speak, of one substance with words preached—assuming that these words bear some relation to truth—may seem arbitrary. Contained in it is the assumption that human beings bear a privileged relation to truth, one that allows them to find it, however gradual and partial the discovery might be, and also to speak it, however imperfectly it is discerned and expressed by them.

Contained in it also is the assertion that the life proposed to us by faith, which is often said to run counter to the behests of our animal nature, actually finds its origins in a more absolute and essential reality, that is, in the Divine Wisdom that is the eternal source of all Being.

It would seem, objectively speaking, that human beings do indeed enjoy a privileged relation to truth. Science bears this out, to offer what is surely the least controversial instance. Calvin makes the relationship between Divine Wisdom and human knowledge explicit:

> Of [God's] wonderful wisdom, both heaven and earth contain innumerable proofs; not only those more abstruse things, which are the subjects of astronomy, medicine, and the whole science of physics, but those things which force themselves on the most illiterate of mankind, so that they cannot open their eyes without being constrained to witness them. Adepts, indeed, in those liberal arts, or persons just initiated into them, are thereby enabled to proceed much further in investigating the secrets of Divine Wisdom. Yet ignorance of those sciences prevents no man from such a survey of the workmanship of God, as is more than sufficient to excite his admiration of the Divine Architect.

For Calvin, Divine Wisdom has the character of revelation. As it emanates from God it also reveals him. And as we are able, within radical limits, to perceive and understand it as Wisdom, even to investigate it, we are participants in it. This ontology precludes all conflict among the varieties of knowledge. There is no devaluing of learnedness and inquiry on one hand and on the other no essential disability imputed to ignorance. The attributes of Wisdom are utter plenitude and perfect grace. It is justified in all its children.

My affinity for Calvin seems as remarkable to me as it has

seemed to certain of my readers and critics. And when I propose his metaphysics as a model for thought, I do so in full awareness that there are other excellent models. Calvin produced an extraordinary body of theology and scholarship, which is so broadly neglected as to seem new, and at the same time so deep an influence on my religious heritage and my civilization as to seem as I read it like the awakening of submerged memory. So its satisfactions for me are no doubt particularly deep. Lately I have been turning my thinking toward the ontological Christ, the Christ-presence in Creation. Calvin says, "Were it not that [Christ's] continued inspiration gives vigour to the world, every thing that *lives* would immediately decay, or be reduced to nothing." Emily Dickinson wrote,

All circumstances are the frame
In which His Face is set,
All Latitudes exist for His
Sufficient continent.
The light His Action and the dark
The Leisure of His Will,
In Him Existence serve, or set
A force illegible.

As is very often the case, I recognize that I have been more than anticipated in a thought that to me, for me, had seemed new. I was taught that the de-mythologizing of Christianity was a step forward, or at least such a deft strategic retreat that it came to the same thing. But since myth—never to be confused with fable—is ontology, since its terms attempt to describe the origins and nature of reality, Christianity was induced to excuse itself from explorations of this kind, to tend to its own truncated magisterium, or, to put the matter another way, to stumble forever at its own threshold, fretting over the issue of belief versus disbelief, having accepted garden variety credibility or plausibility as the appropriate standard to bring to bear on these reported intrusions of higher truth upon human experience. Calvin says, "All who are *not* regenerated [italics mine] by the Spirit of God possess some reason, and this is an undeniable proof that man was made not only to breathe, but to have understanding." Our strange, voracious brilliance is no less an anomaly on this planet than our propensity toward religious belief. Objectively speaking, there are no grounds for the tendency even in modern Christianity to make clean distinctions between these impulses, let alone to oppose them.

The great importance in Calvinist tradition of preaching makes the theology that gave rise to the practice of it a subject of interest. As a layperson who has spent a great many hours listening to sermons, I have an other than academic interest in preaching, an interest in the hope I, and so many others, bring into the extraordinary moment when someone attempts to speak in good faith, about something that matters, to people who attempt to listen in good faith. The circumstance is moving in itself, since we poor mortals are so far enmeshed in our frauds and shenanigans, not to mention our self-deceptions, that a serious attempt at meaning, spoken and heard, is quite exceptional. It has a very special character. My church is across the street from a university, where good souls teach with all sincerity—the factually true, insofar as this can really be known; the history of nations, insofar as this can be faithfully reported; the qualities of an art, insofar as they can be put into words. But to speak in one's own person and voice to others who listen from the thick of their endlessly various situations, about what truly are or ought to be matters of life and death, this is a singular thing. For this we come to church.

On my side of the ocean, at least, we have more or less let the word and the concept "wisdom" fall into disuse. Humanly speaking, this is an odd thing to have done. Wisdom literature seems to be as old a form as any there is. No doubt it is the record of an oral tradition much older than literacy. The Egyptians said, "Let not thy heart be puffed-up because of thy knowledge; be not confident because thou art a wise man. Take counsel with the ignorant as well as the wise . . . Good speech is more hidden than the emerald, but it may be found with maidservants at the grindstones . . . ," and "If thou findest a large debt against a poor man, / Make it into three parts, / Forgive two and let one stand. Thou wilt find it like the ways of life; / Thou wilt lie down and sleep (soundly)." Akkadian proverbs say, "You go and take the field of the enemy; the enemy comes and takes your field," and "Unto your opponent do no evil; / Your evildoer recompense with good; Unto your enemy let justice [be done]," and "A quarrel is a neglect of what is right." In Aramaic, "Many are [the st]ars of heaven [wh]ose names no man knows. By the same token, no man knows mankind."

Wisdom seems very often to correct against presumption and self-interest, to go against the grain of human nature as this is often represented to us. Its plain usefulness to us, if we could act on it with any consistency, argues for a higher order of understanding than immediate worldly interests, say survival and propagation, require, or, for that matter, endorse. Calvin interprets John's saying "The life was the light of men" this way: "[The Evangelist] speaks here, in my opinion, of that part of *life* in which men excel other animals; and informs us that *the life* which was bestowed on *men* was not of an ordinary description, but was united to *the light* of understanding. He separates man from the rank of other creatures; because we perceive [still] more readily the power of God by feeling it in us than by beholding it at a distance," that is, in the brilliance of the created order, which for Calvin is a revelation of the Divine Architect.

There is wisdom everywhere in Scripture. The grass withers and the flower fades, surely the people is grass. Our mortality radically undercuts the claims of power and prosperity, the claims of this world. And our very transience means that we partake of a reality infinitely greater than ourselves in the fact of our understanding. The grass withers, the flower fades; but the word of our God will stand forever.

The word of our God is surely that *Sapientia Dei* which speaks through time and order and instruction and prophecy, wisdom in which we participate first of all in the fact of understanding the brevity of our life and the beauty of it, and in the sense of recognition we share in hearing these words that were perhaps already ancient when Isaiah said them. All flesh is grass, and the beauty of it is like the flower of the field. In feeling the truth of such words we are seeing the world from a perspective like God's. In feeling our unlikeness to the eternal we are experiencing the very height of our humanity—experiencing, that is, our ability to know far beyond our needs, our immediate circumstance, and to ponder existence itself. As we humble ourselves we are exalted, a paradox familiar to Christians.

In saying this I am setting humankind within Calvin's ontology of Divine Wisdom. And I am proposing as well that our nature has an element in it that contravenes self-interest, and does so consistently and powerfully enough to be a demonstration of human exceptionalism. If the fierce old Akkadians could feel in their introspective moments that evil should be answered with good, this is certainly evidence that wisdom is indeed implanted in our nature, together with the thousand passions that make us sometimes harsh and meager, sometimes catastrophically unwise. Modern thought has tended to dismiss the pensive inclination in us, together with the conclusions our kind have come to in that mood, including the idea that ontology is meaningful, or at least that it is much more than a branch of physics.

In the absence of conceptual language that would allow us to elevate wisdom above foresight or discretion or practicality, what becomes of the sermon? If our humanity waits to be acknowledged in terms that make even the soundest instructions for leading the most respectable life seem trivial, and if it is deprived of this acknowledgment so long and so consistently that we forget what to hope for, what value can the sermon have for us? Yet wisdom can only mean insight, and so long as the dead level reality that is all contemporary thought admits to is the whole field upon which insight can be brought to bear, nothing nontrivial can result from it.

There is a word that fell like a curse on American religious culture—"relevance." Any number of assumptions are packed into this word, for example, that the substance and the boundaries of a life can be known, and that they should not be enriched or expanded beyond the circle of the familiar, the colloquial. We encouraged ourselves to believe that our own small, brief lives were the measure of all things. Wisdom would have told us that our lives are indeed small and brief, like the billions that preceded them and the billions that will follow, but this information was precisely not welcome. Wisdom would have told us, too, that, by grace of our extraordinary gifts, and theirs, we are heirs to the testimonies of unnumbered generations. But these gifts, of course, failed the test of relevance, which was a narrow and ungenerous standard, systematically unforgiving of anything that bore the marks of another age, or era, or decade.

It is always hard to know where these fads originate, but they do sweep through American culture, and they do conform it to whatever notion is having its moment. At first it seemed like an extravagant compliment to say that nothing mattered much if it did not address people where they were. But then it became clear that where people were, thus understood, was a very narrow place. The solution that was offered was to narrow it still further. I saw this as a writer having to defend against journalistic editing bent on purging from the pages of important publications any language not abjectly simple, even hackneyed. This ran its course. I saw it as a layperson, too. The same assumptions ravaged hymnals and made pabulum of Scripture in translation.

Day-old journalism is used for wrapping fish. But hymnals and Bibles are costly and durable. They can persist in the environment for a generation or more. Traditional language was expunged, making Christians less conversant in it and less aware of the philosophic and literary traditions that have made it so profound a presence in world culture. Theology was stripped out and replaced with fine sentiment—though never so fine as to startle the parishioner with any unreasonable demands. And scholarship, in its publicly accessible forms, the forms churches use for their classes and discussion groups, is a parody of itself. Karl Barth rightly said that Christianity that excludes the Old Testament has a cancer at its heart. So we have that to deal with.

But these are all only symptoms of a more profound problem. It is a canard among those who reject religion that it is essentially an attempt to dispel mystery, that it tells us how the leopard got his spots. These same despisers often speak of science as the proper and approved method for dispelling mystery. It tells us how the leopard *really* got his spots. In fact religion, like science, addresses and celebrates mystery—it explores and enacts wonder and wondering. It posits a vision of reality that incorporates into the nature of things the intuition that Being has a greater life than we see with our eyes and touch with our hands. The clutch of atheists who have been active lately, who claim to be defenders of science, discount physics as it has developed in the last one hundred years and more on the grounds of its strangeness, its exuberant indifference to common sense notions of how the world works. Whether rigorous thinkers would feel they had this option is a question for another time. But the fact that they feel free to exclude what they don't understand, even when its reality and importance are incontestable by their own standards, surely goes some way toward explaining the confidence with which they dismiss a profoundly human intuition they cannot share, that there is more to reality than their reductionist notions of science can comprehend. This is not to say that the existence of God is proved or disproved by the tractability of the next query science poses to itself. It is to say that no model of the universe of things can be descriptive that does not take into account the reality of human existence and nature, first of all in the fact that they are the sole lens or portal through which we know anything.

Our capacities and incapacities as creatures who know must be placed at the center of the universe, that is to say, the universe accessible to us—the only one we have, though not the only one there is. It may be that masses and forces forever "dark" to us support the reality we inhabit. Someday they may surge or fade, and the heavens will roll up like a scroll. Gravity, on which everything depends, may be a shadow phenomenon with its origins in a neighboring universe that happens to be approaching the end of its life. It is no criticism of human knowledge that it cannot know its own limits, or, for that matter, fully understand its own strategies, its own capacities. Moses Maimonides accepted Creation ex nihilo and Albert Einstein rejected it, until the implications of Edwin Hubble's observations became clear. Twelfth-century Maimonides took the idea from Genesis, from remote antiquity. The Genesis account is a most remarkable expression of an intuition found widely in ancient religion, that the universe did indeed have a beginning. We can never know what it is we only think we know, or what we know truly, intuitively, and cannot prove. Our circumstance is itself a very profound mystery.

There is a tendency, in the churches and in society as a whole, to push mystery aside as if it were a delusion of ignorance or fear that can have no relevance to people living in the real world. This is strange. Albert Einstein said, "The most beautiful thing we can experience is the mysterious. It is the source of all true art and science." Richard Feynman said, "Scientific views end in awe and mystery, lost at the edge in uncertainty, but they appear to be so deep and so impressive that the theory that it is all arranged as a stage for God to watch man's struggles for good and evil seems inadequate." Awe and mystery do not become simple, solvable puzzlement because they are encountered in a church, or because they are addressed in religious art or in the terms of religious thought. Feynman said something one hears often, "God was always invented to explain mystery. God is always invented to explain those things that you do not understand. Now when you finally discover how something works, you get some laws you're taking away from God; you don't need him anymore. But you need him for other mysteries." And so on. The mystery that compels science and the mystery that elevates religion seem very like one another. In neither case is there a reason to suppose that mystery will be exhausted or dispelled. In both cases the beauty of Being is acknowledged in its grand elusiveness. An ontology like Calvin's assumes that the boundaries between them are by no means clear, and that to set them in opposition is to misrepresent both science and religion. Presumably the results achieved by science are more quantifiable, though religion has inspired a very great share of that true art Einstein speaks of. There is an effort to supplant the kind of mystery celebrated by faith with a supposed "realism" that cuts us off from humankind, from the literature of thought, from the vast and weighty record we have of the brief history of our species. Simultaneous with this, perhaps identical with it, is the assumption that people will only be annoyed by references beyond the ever-contracting boundaries of the familiar.

Historically, Christianity has been a very great force behind the spread of learning. I have an old book I found in an antique store, a big volume that declares itself to be "the devotional and explanatory pictorial family Bible." It has a leather cover with scriptural scenes pressed into it. It was published in 1892 by the American Wringer Co. I looked this company up on the Web, and found it, of course. It was and is a manufacturer of minor household devices, notably wringers. The Bible it published is interesting in a number of ways. It presents the text in two columns, one the King James Version and the other the Revised Standard Version. It has a learned and judicious "Introductory," which explains that the verse divisions of the Old Testament were "adopted by Stephens in his edition of the Vulgate, 1555, and by Frellon in that of 1556 . . . It appeared for the first time in an English translation, in the Geneva Bible of 1560." The book is full of those soaring, hyperbolic engravings for which the nineteenth century was notable. It provides a history of every book; cityscapes of places where Paul preached; maps; very brightly colored and somehow gilded renderings of the furnishings of the tabernacle and the temple with a "comprehensive and critical description" of them in sixteen large and closely printed pages. It has pictures of every animal and plant mentioned in the Bible, most of them in color; pages of drawings of ancient coins; an essay on translators, reformers, and martyrs; all sorts of tables and chronologies of ancient history; an evenhanded and informative "history of the religious denominations of the world." (Mormons might take exception.) Then comes the "Complete and Practical Household Dictionary of the Bible," 112 pages long, also illustrated, showing an Assyrian plow, the Erechtheum, foreign captives making bricks at Thebes, the Ephesian Diana. This is just a part of the front matter. Someone pressed a four-leaf clover at the first page of Genesis.

I imagine a traveling salesman pulling up to a farmhouse in a wagon loaded with hand wringers to take the drudgery out of wash day, and Bibles to fill a whole family's educational and devotional needs. This is all very American, the unembarrassed mingling of religion and commerce. Something no longer American is that there is no condescension in it. A household in need of a hand wringer might also acquire a history of the

Scriptures as text. ("The Apocryphal books, to which, of course, no Masoretic division was applicable, did not receive a versicular division till the Latin edition of Pagininus, in 1528." That "of course" tells us worlds.) They would acquire not only a history of English translation but a thorough demonstration of its effects. And any child could dream forever over the fabulous cities of Egypt and Babylonia, the agonies of the prophets, the elegant vigor of angels. No doubt some of the scholarship is outdated. It appears rather free of tendentiousness, certainly by modern standards. It is a cliché of American cultural history that for generations many homes had no book except a Bible. If the Bible happened to be like this one, people in those homes might have been in many important ways more sophisticated than my graduate students. The book cost me only $50, because Bibles of its type are so common. I have a similar Bible in German, Luther's translation, also published in America. It tends to be forgotten that for a long time German was America's second language.

God is the God of history. Christianity is a creature and creator of history. On these grounds alone it is absurd to think history could possibly lack relevance. Then, too, if human beings are images of God, aware of it or not, and since they have been an extraordinary presence on earth for as long as they have been human, what they have thought and done cannot be irrelevant to very central questions about Being itself. We are grass, no doubt of it. But with a sense of history we can have a perspective that lifts us out of our very brief moment here. Certainly this is one purpose of biblical narrative and poetry. Then the fact is that we are made to know. It is in our nature. Einstein said that the most incomprehensible thing about the universe is that it is comprehensible. This can be looked at from another side—the most incomprehensible thing about humankind is that we want to understand the universe, and that we are, so to speak, sufficiently of one mind with it to find it in some degree accessible to our understanding. How to describe this fact, this experience? At the end of his Sixth Meditation, Descartes, always granting human fallibility, concludes that the reports his senses make of conscious experience can be taken by him as true. "For from the fact that God is not a deceiver it follows that in cases like this I am completely free from error." For him knowledge is a transaction with God, whose nature assures its integrity. It is not only his spending most of his life in the Low Countries and serving in a Calvinist army that makes me feel Descartes was open to Calvinist influences. To return to the distinction made by Calvin in his Commentary on 1 John, Christ, that is, God, is the essence of wisdom and its eternal source. "Astronomy, medicine, and the whole science of physics" are forms in which the knowledge of the grandeur of God, that is, human understanding of the universe, can be sought out and known by human beings. This kind of knowledge is at a long, qualitative remove from *Sermo*, Wisdom itself, and at the same time, as *Verbum* it is inexhaustibly revealing of that same Divine Wisdom.

We have made very separate categories of science and learning on one hand and reverence for the Creator on the other. Some people attempt theological proofs on the basis of what might be called the brilliance of the natural world, the intricacies of its interrelationships, their elegance. Arguments of this kind are generally persuasive to those who need no persuasion. This matter of proof, or of justifying faith in terms that might seem respectable to skeptics, has consumed a great deal of time and energy lately, and left those of us for whom God is a given without much help in contemplating a reality whose origins and subsistence are in God. It is surely appropriate to consider the implications for our understanding of reality of the character we ascribe to him. Let us say, first of all, that humankind is a true and appropriate object of his love. On its face this is an idea that runs counter to many things we know from experience and observation. But Christianity, like quantum physics, does not exist to affirm or rephrase common sense. Like quantum physics, it could not exist within the strictures imposed by common sense, supposing they were of a kind to be imposed on anything more substantive than our own thoughts. Let us say that atomic particles can be entangled at any remove in space and time. This is contrary to everything we thought we knew about space, time, and causality, but that's just how it is. The wisdom of common sense is the foolishness of subatomic reality. Let us say that human beings stand in a unique relationship with the Divine. Edwards's phrase, the "arbitrary constitution of the Creator," does seem increasingly useful in describing its physics. Then there is no justification for applying the test of common sense to what the religious must assume are reality's deeper structures, the orders and affinities that make human wisdom in its larger sense efficacious, beautiful, vital, and full of satisfactions.

MEMORY

It is interesting that this country could have transformed itself radically in the last one hundred years, and, after so much time and so much change, should still be divided along the same lines that divided us two centuries ago. The United States has drawn immigrants from the whole world, with all that has meant culturally and in terms of historical memory. It has rethought, and is still rethinking, the entire system of social relations as a consequence of the civil rights movement. It has entangled itself so deeply in the affairs of the world at large that its policies are as perplexed as the circumstances they are meant to address. Materially and technologically, it has outrun its own ability to appraise or to channel and discipline its transformations. We Americans are almost used to all this. We have phrases that go some way toward mitigating its centrifugal force, "dynamic equilibrium," "creative destruction." We have accepted it as an identity, and it works quite well as an identity. Scotland may sometimes drift out of Britain, the Flemish may divorce the Walloons. But, despite all the complexities of our economic and demographic life, the United States will still be the United States, in all likelihood. Should it fracture, as we have done once, and have seen other nations do, the fault line will lie along the old Mason–Dixon line.

Here is a hypothesis. Despite the fact of air-conditioning, of heavy industry and high technology, of the movement of Northerners south, of the redistribution to the South of Northern tax dollars, of the prosperity of the recent past, still the South as a region imagines itself to be an enclave in which the Good Old Ways persist, minus a few that have run afoul of judicial activism, of course. The threat to this enclave is the North, with its bad manners and godlessness and its materialism. Of course I exaggerate, I overgeneralize. But, like everyone else, I live with the consequences of there being a regional faction in Congress who will take needed help out of American hands, off American tables, no matter how disgusted I and my kind may be by what they do and the rationalizations they offer for doing it. Indeed, they seem to feel affirmed by our contempt. Populations are inevitably judged by the people they, or some plurality of them at least, choose as their representatives, and therefore as our government as well as theirs. Elections matter.

Other things matter, too, in much the same way. There is an implied religious rationale or impetus and obligation behind very deplorable trends in contemporary society. The arming of the fearful and resentful and unstable with military weapons, supported by the constant reiteration of tales that make mortal enemies of their fellow citizens and elected government, is pursued with a special passion in regions that claim to be profoundly and uniquely Christian, and well mannered, to boot. Biblicist that I am, I watch constantly for any least fragment of a Gospel that could, however obliquely, however remotely, cast all this in any but a satanically negative light. I am moving, reluctantly, toward the conclusion that these Christians, if they read their Bibles, are not much impressed by what they find here.

In any case, how is it possible, given this economics of dark grievance that has so benefited arms manufacturers, cable celebrities, gold mongers, and manufacturers of postapocalyptic grocery items, that they can not only claim Christianity but can also substantially empty the word of other meanings and associations? I'm a Christian, insofar as I can be. As a matter of demographics, of heritage, of acculturation, of affinity, identification, loyalty. I aspire, with uneven results, to satisfying its moral and spiritual standards, as I understand them. I have other loyalties that are important to me, to secularism, for example. To political democracy. These loyalties are either implied by my Christianity or are highly compatible with it. I am a Christian. There are any number of things a statement of this kind might mean and not mean, the tradition and its history being so complex. To my utter chagrin, at this moment in America it can be taken to mean that I look favorably on the death penalty, that I object to food stamps or Medicaid, that I expect marriage equality to unknit the social fabric and bring down wrath, even that I believe Christianity itself to be imperiled by a sinister media cabal. It pains me to have to say in many settings that these are all things I object to strenuously on religious grounds, having read those Gospels. Persons of my ilk, the old mainline, typically do object just as strenuously, and on these same grounds. But they are unaccountably quiet about it. And here we have a great part of the reason that these gun-toting resenters of the poor and of the stranger can claim and occupy a major citadel of the culture almost unchallenged.

Let's say the media are at fault. This is never entirely wrong. Reasonableness doesn't make anyone's pulse race. "The president is a crypto-Muslim" has so much more zing than "the president is not a crypto-Muslim." This is especially true if the question of religious affiliation is not of particular interest to the person making the denial. It is hard to know where to begin objecting to an agenda set by factions and interests whose conceptual universe is so alien, so opportunistically contrived.

Then again, I probably startled some here when I said, matter-of-factly, I'm a Christian. Even though I have been writing theologically influenced essays and novels for many years, I find that I startle people when I make this simple statement of fact. This is a gauge of the degree to which the right have colonized the word and also of the degree to which the center and left have capitulated, have surrendered the word and also the identity. A very close analogy is to be found in the strange history of the word "liberal," which erstwhile liberal people use to counsel earnestly against using. Asked what enormity liberals have been guilty of that made the very word opprobrious, they have no answer. Nevertheless, this was simply not a word one used. At the same time political liberalism more or less collapsed, with consequences that persist to this day. A movement that cannot acknowledge its name cannot acknowledge its history, its philosophy, or its achievements. Those who, so to speak, subscribe to the Consumer Report of Acceptable Language and Opinion knew that both word and concept were embarrassingly passé, a gaffe that marked one out as a nonsubscriber, the sort of person who bought suboptimal appliances.

The phenomenon is ridiculous and also truly grave. Look what has happened to us in the last fifteen or twenty years. Deeply held values and aspirations have been abandoned and betrayed. We have trouble now articulating a case for justice and opportunity. We have shrunk away from weighty controversies, shamed or intimidated by the suggestion that these things are un-American. The L-word, the detractors said, though it was introduced into our political vocabulary by John Winthrop before the Puritans had even landed. When it was used as an aspersion, we reacted as if it were one. We live in a moment when people say all sorts of self-revealing things and are admired for their courage, so it is interesting that taboos of a potent kind are still operative and can be brought to bear to such great effect. I was given to know once, quietly, in tones of the kindliest authority, that the world "ontology" could no longer be used. Well, one can say now "I am a liberal" without rousing that strange deflected scandal that once made well-wishers try to protect one from oneself. I believe *The New York Times* has announced that the word is rehabilitated. So all we have to do is figure out how to reinvest it with meaning.

Could my subject be cowardice? Let me say first that, in my view, true and utter cowardice is defined by the act of carrying a concealed weapon. Over against this, few varieties of fearfulness can seem absolutely disgraceful. Still, enniched as I am and have long been in a safe and comfortable life, am I in any position to raise this subject with reference to the generality of America's cryptoliberals? Be that as it may, I will have to nerve myself and run the risk of offending. If it were a small thing, only an adult equivalent to the adolescent dread of going to school in the wrong clothes, then it could be laid to anthropology, some subrational human need to affirm identity with one's tribe. But the analogy breaks down under the sheer weight of the good that has been done, and has since been ridiculed and abandoned, by generosity as a social and moral ethic, by openhandedness as a strategy of wealth creation, material as well as social and cultural. By liberalism.

As it happens, the capitulation I mentioned earlier, which has allowed Christianity to become a brand name for assorted trends and phenomena that have no more to do with its texts and traditions than mythical women warriors have to do with online retail, is the default of liberal Christianity. (My analogy is flawed in that these warriors are neither exploited nor traduced.) Perhaps the counterintuitive nature of certain of Christ's counsels, to cast bread on the waters in the confidence that it will be returned to you, for example, made it seem the weaker side of the argument. (I should note here that Jesus is quoting from Ecclesiastes in the Hebrew Bible, a section of the book for which the Puritan heading is "Liberalitie.") In any case, he was probably referring to those intangible returns that have become so suddenly and deeply unfashionable, that is, unmonetizable. Overcoming evil with good does not often yield results in the short term, and it lacks all the special satisfactions of revenge. The Consumer Report of Acceptable Language and Opinion was telling us that tough-mindedness was hot. In the face of all this, what to do but capitulate?

I wish I were joking. I wish I had better grounds for admitting that I have been unfair. Certainly I acknowledge that, through all this, persons of great integrity have been faithful to high ideals. But their integrity is underscored by their loneliness, and their heroic patience is proved by what can only be called their inefficacy. We live in a country with for-profit prisons, where the decency of treatment to be received by some hapless boy or girl can be weighed against the interests of stockholders. The gospel invoked in this case as in so many others is privatization, an addendum to Scripture greatly revered in those regions most inclined to call themselves Christian. Incarceration for profit. I would never have thought we could sink so low. I understand that marriage equality offends some people's religious sensibilities, and I know that denial of basic civic equality offends the religious sensibilities of others. My own, for example. Why does only one side of this question merit attention as an issue of religious freedom? My denomination blessed the unions of same-sex couples until the minute it could instead perform their marriages. Was not our religious freedom constrained by law until the state supreme court acted, and would it not be again if the Governor Jindals of the world had their way? Why is this controversy, insofar as it is conducted in the language of religion, so one-sided? I never feel more Christian than I do when I hear of some new scheme for depriving and humiliating the poor, and feel the shock of religious dread at these blatant contraventions of what I, as a Christian, take to be the will of God. And yes, I can quote chapter and verse.

We are all familiar with the assertion that America is a Christian nation. Obviously, I am not always sure what the people most inclined to say this actually mean by it. Those looking on from the outside are aware that we Christians have our factions, our rivalries, our quarrels. The fact is, however, that, demographically, we do preponderate. Demographically, America is Christian enough that what we do matters. We have a shared moral and ethical language that takes a particular authority from its origins—ideally, at least, or in principle. It has been pointed out many times that Christian morality is profoundly indebted to Judaism, and that it bears a strong likeness to the teachings of the other great religions. Well and good. This means that if we act as we ought to we will act consistently with the values of Americans at large, since even those Nones that show up in statistics now are alienated not by our ideals but by our hypocrisies. If an accident of history has made us a dominant presence here, the consonance of religions could make us worthy agents of values held in other terms and anchored in traditions other than our own. Conversely, as often as we fail to be their agents, every culture or faith with which we share these values suffers defeat.

The question of identification is interesting and important, too. There are any number of people who check the religion box based on whatever they think they ought to be, or intend to be at some unspecified later date. This can be true because they have an intuition of the good or the sacred which is embedded in that identity. Therefore it will have authority for them based on teaching and practice they do not feel they understand well enough to take exception to or to endorse, except passively. Very often, from this perspective, the harshest version of a religion seems the purest, the most serious and authentic. Those inclined to defer to "Christianity," however defined, can be persuaded by an apparent consensus that it is essentially a system of prohibitions meant to fortify believers' consciences against any doubt they might otherwise feel about behavior the Bible forbids—vilifying and condemning, for example, or about depriving and excluding. This might be what moral rigor looks like, after all. Those who identify as Christians but are dependent on the culture at large, or on the radio, to instruct them as to the particulars might reasonably have this impression. For their purposes, there is no countervailing view of it. Again, polemic on one side, virtual silence on the other.

One complicating factor is that Christianity is difficult. This is true because it is based on ancient texts and on a vast and diverse body of thought and interpretation, stretching back to antiquity. It is difficult because it is dependent on the kind of learning that occurs over time within community. And it is difficult in a much more important sense because it is contrary to our crudest instincts. Love your enemies. Yes. No sooner said than done. Throughout its history there have been many so moved by the beauty of its teachings that they have been willing even to murder those who seem to them to threaten it, whom they cast as Christianity's enemies, not their own, a useful bit of Gospel-chopping. We are seeing a version of this now, in all this talk about attack on religion. Such thinking serves well to sanctify exactly those crudest instincts. To encourage them is, as Hamlet would say, as easy as lying.

On the liberal side we have a long retreat from Scripture and tradition. Scripture so primitive, theology so elitist, everything between so middlebrow. Since the "higher" and very dubious criticism emerged in Germany in the middle of the nineteenth century, liberal American Christianity has been agonizing over mythic elements in Scripture, taking the crudest interpretations as the ones most liable to be correct, since "mythic" was thought in those days to mean "primitive"—if its origins were Hebrew, though certainly not if they were Greek. Out of all this has come trudging an ogre worthy of the Brothers Grimm—Jehovah has given place to Yahweh. Whether "Yahweh" is an improved rendering of the divine name is neither here nor there. The contexts in which the newer form occurs tend to be ones in which the deity is assumed to be patched together out of Baal and El, with a little Marduk thrown in. In other words, the ancient Hebrews were simply appropriating local narratives, not pondering a divine self-revelation, or, if this is too strong, a conception of divinity, of cosmic origins and human nature, that was unique to them. No one can read what remains of Canaanite or Babylonian myth—which is all these scholars have had to work from—and find this plausible, unless profound intellectual deference intervenes, as it does so often. Intellectual deference is in fact often prevenient, to use an old word. It can set in so instantly that these highly accessible Near Eastern remains are never looked at. A fair sense of them does emerge, however, where the transformation is made of the Hebrew God into this pagan amalgam. If I am blind to the complexity and profundity of Canaanite or Babylonian myth, these scholars are, too, because complexity and profundity are altogether lost from the conception of God when he is made a creature of that landscape. One beautiful psalm is often said to be adapted from an unspecified Canaanite hymn. I have looked for this hymn and have not found it. I suspect this bit of "information" is simply carried along on the tides of intellectual deference.

To work the New Testament free from the Old is an impulse that manifested itself very early in Christianity. Second-century Marcionism rejected the belief that the God of the Old Testament could be the father of Christ, and so posited another god in opposition to him. Very many people now who want their religion to be intellectually sound consider the Old Testament to have been debunked on the grounds of syncretism, and on the grounds that its primitivism makes it morally unacceptable, incompatible with whatever they choose to retain of Christianity. They cannot do as Marcion did and become dualists outright, but they are left with something like Marcion's problem. Say Yahweh is what the scholars say he is.

Then how is Christ to be understood in relation to him, when traditionally the holiness ascribed to Christ has a character that derives from the conception of the divine in the Hebrew Bible? Thou shall love the Lord thy God with all thy heart, thy soul, thy mind, and thy strength, Jesus said, quoting Moses. What happens to this greatest commandment when God is deconstructed into a set of beings who starve and sleep and cower and threaten to beat each other bloody? In order to discover Baal and El and Marduk in the God of the Old Testament it is necessary to strip away everything beautiful about him, his attention to humankind, first of all. To say he is the God of history is to say that he is the God of human history, there being no other kind. It is to say that he is bound to us, freely, out of love and faithfulness, and that he is in some sense defined by his relationship to us. Savior, Redeemer, Shepherd, Father. Even Judge and King bind him to us, since they imply equity and order. In their myths those other gods come near destroying the human race because they are so noisy that they literally prevent the gods from sleeping. The destruction ends when the gods realize they will starve if there are no humans to offer them sacrifices. Neither love nor faithfulness plays any part in their détente.

If some sort of evolution made the God of the Hebrew Bible unlike other gods, what pressures or influences would have brought about this change, this difference? Why is this a question of less than secondary interest? If there was a capacity within the culture to produce and elaborate a distinctive cosmic vision, when and how did this begin? And if the capacity was present, why propose that its god is essentially derivative? It is characteristic of evolutionary models of change that the germ from which anything is supposed to have had its origins is treated as its essence, and whatever departs from this assumed original character is treated as somehow not fully real. The Hebrew God is deprived of his character by the presumption of syncretism just as human beings are deprived of theirs when the beastly origins posited for them are taken to make guile or hypocrisy of compassion, generosity, creativity, and so on.

I have no idea what made Marcion determined to be rid of the Hebrew Bible. Why German scholarship in the nineteenth and twentieth centuries might wish to discredit it is a question that seems to answer itself. And why do we accept, even embrace, this project? Well, it seems intellectual. It creates a sphere of esoteric learning that lets us keep one foot in and one foot out of a tradition we are uneasy with but not ready to abandon. It excuses us from reading and pondering a difficult old book that looks squarely and at length at the problem of evil, which can seem to comfortable people to be more than a little impolite, and also primitive. Of course the vast majority of people who have lived on earth have had evil to deal with, and very, very few of them have been comfortable. We have no reason to expect the Bible to be addressed primarily to us.

I dwell on this because it is liberal Christianity that—very perversely, in my view—defers to this old German scholarship. It is meant to be an escape from literalism, but it is really an inverted literalism. Who was the Elohist? The Yahwist?—as if their existence, single or in troops, were more than the artifact of a questionable critical method. What interests were they serving? As if we could know. Two names must equal two gods, right? Then the primal abyss might be Tiamat the serpent, so that makes three. An ancient scrawl somewhere gave Yahweh a consort. Doesn't this prove an original polytheism? Syncretism? To quote Hamlet again, How if I answer no? In fact it proves nothing. It should be obvious that the word "proof" has no place in a discussion of this kind. To treat speculation as fact is no more sophisticated than to insist on a six-day Creation. We may sometime find the means to make dark matter and dark energy comprehensible, available to meaningful description. We will not know how or by whom the book of Genesis was made. Ever. Nor *The Iliad*, nor *Beowulf*, for that matter. Who wrote the plays of Shakespeare? Again, proof and disproof are not meaningful in many contexts. To proceed as if this were not the case is naive, unless it is tendentious.

The old positivist rejection of metaphysics has a part in this, no doubt. If God is Baal and El, Christian metaphysics is thoroughly incoherent, meaningless. For those who doubt the legitimacy of metaphysics this may be no loss. For many who have not been told that there ever was thought of this kind, or have been told that we have been wised up by a modernity that disallows such thoughts, it is a grave loss. In any case, the Incarnation, the Crucifixion, the Resurrection are all highly charged statements about the nature of Being and human being. They are profound, and, so far as I know, unique assertions of the transcendent value of human life, asserting most forcefully the value of the lives of the powerless and the obscure. Baptism, Communion, and worship are participations in this metaphysical, ontological vision.

Or they are pleasant customs. And Christianity is an ethical system that probably deserves to be taken seriously.

There has been a great collapse of the scale at which reality is to be conceived, which, remarkably, happened just at the time that science began to discover for us what a truly vast and astonishing system of Being we are a part of. Only think how the psalmists or the Job writer would have loved to see an issue of *Science News*. What actually happened at the events called Incarnation and Resurrection I do not know—that there was a crucifixion is far too plausible by historical standards to be at issue. Reality is subtle and free because its consistencies cannot be described as necessity or inevitability—this I do know. Whatever happened happened, and left to the world a statement that could not have been made otherwise. God so loved the world.

And here I return to the place where I began. One of the dominant canards in American culture is that the South is religious and the North is not, that this has been true time out of mind, and that the Bible offered justifications for the institution of slavery which the North answered with brute force. Of course there is slavery in the Old Testament, debt-bondage or indenture that bears very little relation to the industrialized chattel slavery that produced cotton for manufacture in Britain. On the grounds of this canard, however, biblical piety has long been made to seem mean, obscurantist, or sinister. I have been looking at the rhetoric, on the Southern as well as the Northern side, from before the Civil War, and I am interested to find that the Northerners allude to Scripture far more often, and use it far more essentially as the basis of their argument, than, say, Jefferson Davis and Alexander Stephens, who refer to it seldom, then only passingly and without particular awareness of context. Stephens famously referred to the institution of slavery as "the stone the builders [the founders] rejected." He said that through the Confederacy it was to become at long last the head of the corner. Remarkable. If there are Southern equivalents of Henry Ward Beecher or Lydia Maria Child, I haven't found them. Since American intellectual culture is an endless corridor of funhouse mirrors, we don't know what Karl Marx did know, that the cotton economy of the South was altogether the creature of British industrial capitalism. It was the greatest producer of wealth in the American economy, and its apologists foresaw a limitless expansion of it, into the North, and even into Central and South America. It was a great engine of wealth dependent on what Davis called, rather coolly, "this species of property," African slaves. One need not read far to see what our great experiment might have become. And the spirit behind it would have been Mammon, not Moses.

In a speech titled "The Conflict of Northern and Southern Theories of Man and Society," Henry Ward Beecher says,

> This relationship [that subsists between man and his Maker] begins in the fact that we are created in the divine image; that we are connected with God, therefore, not by Government alone, but by nature. This [initial] truth is made radiant with meaning, by the teaching of

> Christianity that every human being is dear to God: a teaching which stands upon that platform, built high above all human deeds and histories, the advent, the incarnation, passion, and death of Christ, as a Savior of men. The race is a brotherhood; God is the Father, Love is the law of this great human commonwealth, and Love knows no servitude. It is that which gilds with liberty whatever it touches . . . You cannot present man as a subject of Divine government, held responsible for results, compared with which the most momentous earthly deeds are insignificant, plied with influences accumulating from eternity, and by powers which though they begin on earth in the cradle, gentle as a mother's voice singing lullaby, go on upward, taking everything as they go, till they reach the whole power of God . . . you cannot present man as the center and subject of such an august and eternal drama, without giving him something of the grandeur which resides in God himself.

This is humanism articulated in the terms of Christian metaphysics, as it was, over the centuries, until somehow the notion took hold that the two of them are at odds. In any case, Beecher's terms being granted, there is no scriptural refutation to be made. Nor was any offered, so far as I can discover.

Where would we be if the Hebrew God had not said and insisted that human beings share his image and are sanctified by it? Do we have any other secure basis for belief in universal human dignity? There is no evidence at all that this is anything we know intuitively. We would not now have a sizable part of our own population walking around prepared to engage in homicidal violence if they truly believed that that young man in the hoodie was an image of God. If Christianity is thought of as a religion of personal salvation that allows one to sin now and repent at leisure, it is, one must say, almost limitlessly permissive. It virtually invites the flouting of Jesus' teachings. We can ignore what Jesus says and does, however we may admire it—with a few reservations—and love him most of all for the certainty that he will take us back, poor sinners, no matter what harm we may have done to those others he presumably loves just as much as he does us, or a little more. What protections he may have intended for them in his preachments he thoughtfully makes null and void in his ready forgiveness of those who violate these protections.

But if Christianity is instead a metaphysics that resolves all reality at every moment into holiness, whether honored or offended against, then its demands are of a higher order entirely. This second, utterly sacred cosmos is the splendid old home of liberal Christian thought. And we were the ones who once elevated the Hebrew Bible to a prominence unique in Christian history. It seems we have wearied of the demands our traditions made of us, perhaps of its emphasis on learning, perhaps of its mystery and beauty. At any rate, many of us, many in our pulpits and seminaries, have turned away from it. That strange verse in the first chapter of Genesis, "in the image of God he created him; male and female he created them," is meaningless by the standards of positivism or the higher criticism. It is unfalsifiable, undemonstrable, and dependent on terms for which we have no stable definitions. It is dependent as well on a conception of God that compels reverence and will make us reverent of one another. It tells us every essential thing about who we are and what we are, and what we are a part of. It is ontology. It is metaphysics.

VALUE

Dietrich Bonhoeffer gave us a beautiful model of Christian behavior over, against, and within, a terrible moment in history. Events in Germany in the last century have epitomized for us the deviancy of which a modern society is capable. It seems sometimes as if we feel we have put a period to evil at this scale, or as if the ocean and all the cultural difference it signifies isolates or immunizes us from the impulses behind a moral disaster of such proportions, or, again as though the severity of harm we know we do or permit is less grave intrinsically because it is so much exceeded in scale and ferocity by the events of the last century. Indeed, in some quarters it has been held that to suggest these events were not essentially unique is to minimize their gravity rather than to acknowledge that they tell us how very grave history can be.

In other quarters, of course, there are many who see moral collapse as imminent, brought on by big government, or by departures from whichever construction of religion they consider sufficient to stay divine wrath, or at least to deflect it onto others. These political and religious anxieties are frequently found together. The effect of such insistence that we are already turning on the event horizon of just such a vortex, or that we are already halfway down its throat, is to corrupt the data of contemporary history with frivolous panic.

Still, there are real grounds now for anxiety about the future of the West and the world. The effect of the insistence on the unique horror of the European midcentury should not be to distract us from a true recognition of our vulnerability to cascading error. Out of profound respect for Dietrich Bonhoeffer, and with deep faith in the clarifying power of Christian humility, I will look at our moment as he might have looked at his, before the forces that had been gathering strength in Europe at least since the late nineteenth century became irresistible. I will not be speaking here about skinheads or militias or survivalists or Klansmen, or even about the unashamed racism that has emerged in public life in recent years, not only in America. I will be speaking about a deeper tectonics that, in my opinion, produces the energy behind all these surface tremors and disruptions. If my remarks seem political, the whole of our life together is political, and to banish whatever sounds like politics from a conversation about where we are going and what we are doing is to trivialize and disable the conversation. Partisanism is another thing, of course, and so is ideology. Both of them begin with their conclusions and are loyal to them for reasons that are temperamental or circumstantial. I want to speculate, to ponder, to propose other ways of thinking.

•

I have read that the terrible destruction the German states suffered in the seventeenth century as the primary battleground of the Thirty Years' War created a potent will to recover a place within Europe, and that this accounted for the intensity of their devotion to national and cultural development. Whatever the impetus, the achievements of Germans (including, emphatically, the achievements of German Jews) in the centuries that followed are astonishing, unsurpassed in music, theology and philosophy, physics and mathematics, and distinguished in education, literature, and the visual arts. Dietrich Bonhoeffer was born into a stratum of German society where these high achievements were felt in daily life. A musician and theologian, he embodies them. There is a graciousness, a fine warmth, in his writing and in his life, that reflects his character, certainly, but which, before the midcentury, would also have been called German. When he thought about the direction things were taking, he may well have reassured himself by weighing the crudest impulses of the society, the passions of the streets and the press, against the great strength of its humanist traditions. Granting that his family seemed fairly aloof from the suffering of their country after World War I, and that he might not have made a good estimate of it, it is also seldom reasonable or prudent or even charitable to project from the excitements of any moment to their worst imaginable consequences. This seems only truer when they are the excitements of a culture one deeply loves, as Bonhoeffer did Germany. Perhaps at first he felt that in time there must be a correction, a return to equilibrium, and that he could wait out the interval in London or New York.

I know my account of historical circumstance is grossly inadequate. France benefited from the Versailles Treaty and its reparations as Germany suffered from them, yet fascism and anti-Semitism rose early and vigorously in France, and then in all of Europe and in the New World as well. I have mentioned violence in the streets, which implies the stirring of a rabble, but the early fascist movement Action Française, which engaged in murderous political violence, had as founder and guiding spirit the writer and Academician Charles Maurras. Indeed, there has seldom been an instance of more passionate and overt collaboration of the learned and privileged with plain thuggery. Intellectual work of the period is shot through with the theory and the worldview that stirred the mobs. To isolate Germany in any discussion of the events of the midcentury is to err dangerously—and it is also to repeat the narrative that has been dominant from the closing moments of the war. To locate their origins in the mobs and to exonerate intellectuals on the grounds that they were intellectuals is an equally dangerous error, with consequences for university curricula, among other things.

Well, my point is that the present, any present, is unreadable. Neither the best nor the worst propensities of a civilization can be thought of as predictive. This is largely true because we know too little about the past, and for this and other reasons we know too little about the energies that stir, or ebb, in this indefinable and transitory thing, the given moment. I think of Bonhoeffer trying to appraise the Germany of his time and of the near future, because I love a country, too, and am more bewildered by it at present than I would ever have thought I could be.

I do not wish to make the mistake again of isolating one culture with developments that are reinforced and amplified in many countries. If I could have one wish, it might well be that all contact between the economics department of the University of Chicago and the London School of Economics would instantly and forever be impossible. I recognize the unlikelihood of this.

But the wish is germane to my next point. I had always thought that the one thing I could assume about my country was that it was generous. Instinctively and reflexively generous. In our history, and with the power that has settled on us, largely because of the tendency of the old Western powers to burn themselves down and blow themselves up, we have demonstrated fallibilities that are highly recognizable as human sin and error, sometimes colossal in scale, magnified by our relative size and strength. But our saving grace was always generosity, material and, often, intellectual and spiritual. To the extent that we have realized or even aspired to democracy, we have made a generous estimate of the integrity and good will of people in general, and a generous reckoning of their just deserts.

I hate even to admit that I fear this might have begun to change. I do believe that we stand at a threshold, as Bonhoeffer did, and that the example of his life obliges me to speak about the gravity of our historical moment as I see it, in the knowledge that no society is at any time immune to moral catastrophe.

As a subcategory of the habit of generosity, Americans are very good at rescuing each other. Under all circumstances, however drastic, there are men and women who bring skill and training, life and limb, into our crises to do every bit of good that can be done. There is considerable drama in life in North America, from a meteorological point of view, and every calamity inspires an urgent civic festival of rescue and reparation, sandbags and pizza, bandages and backhoes and bratwurst. This is as true now as it ever was.

Recently America, along with much of the rest of the world, has been living through a grand-scale disaster that has cost families their homes, their savings, their livelihoods. It was an effect of practices at major national and international financial institutions. The response to it has been worse than meager. If error or malice had broken a dam or a levee, and George Bush was not president, the National Guard would be there overnight and alleviation would have begun by the next day. The losses to ordinary households, towns, and businesses that have resulted from this breach in the financial system are literally astronomical, and they are ongoing. How can this happen? And the losses are much more profound than they would have been if they were the result of a natural, rather than an unnatural, disaster.

There is a very tired but forever serviceable phrase, "blaming the victim." We have a new concept now—new or long suppressed, at least in polite company. We speak now, often implicitly, of the unworthy poor. If bankers wrecked the economy, what sense does it make to drug-test the unemployed who need help surviving the wreck? But this has been proposed here and there, in the tones of righteousness, or self-righteousness, to which we have lately become accustomed. It makes its own kind of sense. It would keep taxes down, since the proud, those who have always valued their self-sufficiency, will not seek help under these conditions. And who can deny the objective wonderfulness of low taxes? The Fabians, Beatrice and Sidney Webb and the rest of them, called themselves socialists. It is hard to believe they weren't joking, considering all the tedious little plots they spun to lower workers' already wretched wages, that is to say, their levels of consumption. It is embarrassing to see the questions these supposed socialists posed to themselves. What is to be done about the tendency of the poor to pool money against their own funeral expenses? About their preference for coffins with metal handles? These they said are proof of gross violations of the Iron Law of Wages, a venerable economic doctrine which taught that the effective wage of a worker must be as low as it could be, and still leave him or her standing. Subsistence was the word they used.

The Fabians can tell us important things, of course, for example that making public assistance "less eligible," a worse option than all but the worst destitution, really does winnow out a great many potential applicants at a great savings to the rate-paying public, though at severe but unmonetized, therefore negligible, cost in misery and humiliation. This kind of calculation goes back to the Poor Laws, in force in England from Edward VI through World War II. And now it has become fashionable among us, in certain quarters. Perhaps moral atavism is a little less ugly than moral degeneration. I find small comfort in the thought. Anti-Semitism in Germany and Europe was also atavistic.

I may be blaming the victim, too, when I note the strong tendency of victims to blame themselves. Again, this is the special affliction of the proud, those who have assigned great value to self-sufficiency, and to their roles as providers and contributors. I will even propose that they are participants in the great shifting of values that seems to me to be in progress. Many people feel that it is slovenly or dishonest to lay blame. They accept in principle that they can extricate themselves from their difficulties, and, what with the resourcefulness of the population in general, many do at least meliorate them. Much as such people are to be admired, they cloud the issue. They discourage a systematic understanding of a systemic failure—assuming that failure is what it was. I am not sure it was altogether a failure in the first place, and to the degree that it was one, it has been very much turned to the advantage of those who triggered it. Now the wealthy are, *eo ipso* and *q.e.d.*, superior to others. The relatively undamaged nonwealthy can be a little bit flattered, too, by this construction of things. I am moderately wealthy myself, and I hasten to add that many prosperous people find the preening of this vocal subgroup repulsive. Still, their influence has been enormous.

I have mentioned atavism as one source of the authority this narrative of fitness versus unworthiness has had for society. I know there is no such thing as a "reptilian brain," no part of the human sensorium that has persisted as we seemingly evolved away from our least pleasant ancestors. But if there is a collective sensorium, some part of it retains forever an impressive repertory of bad old impulses, called up by alarm or by tedium or simply at random. Here is an instance. The United States seems at last to be coming to the end of its dalliance with the death penalty. We had effectively given up capital punishment for decades, having proved how unjust, ineffectual, and demoralizing it was. Then the serpent stirred, and we were obliged to learn it all again. Reptilian memory is what makes things seem to make sense, despite reason, experience, compassion, morality, and a prudent fear of God. It nurses the oldest grudges and is proof against any change of mind. Its manifestations are often called fundamentalism, and, because it entails the reenacting of old errors, it is often experienced as traditionalism. It enjoys more or less authority on these grounds.

I confess I sometimes fail to distinguish theory from metaphor, even in my own thoughts. But things must be described before they can begin to be understood. The catastrophe in Germany and in Europe was the conscious and thoroughgoing accommodation of all that was best to all that was worst, corrupting science and philosophy to embrace notions like purity and authenticity and racial memory. And here we have the West, not America uniquely or primarily, but America, too, moving away from the social achievements of the modern past and toward restoring an old order that was and will be exploitive and destructive. There may well be little effective appeal against this restoration for some time, because a significant consensus has emerged around the notion that we cannot afford these provisions meant to create or sustain justice and individual dignity. Another consensus supports the idea that such provisions have created a deadweight of slackers and takers who imperil society by burdening the productive with the cost of their idleness or their fecklessness. This is the old Poor Law language again, the kind of law that required Shakespeare and his company to wear servants' livery so that they would not be branded as vagrants or sturdy beggars. It is impossible to read about the old social order without wondering how many million good and gifted people fell to its casual brutalities. Shakespeare ponders all this at some length in *King Lear.* But the Fabians would tell us that the poor were "demoralized" by charity, which in this context means they lost their morals, which in this context means they lost their willingness to work under often terrible conditions for the smallest wage any employer could manage to pay them. This while the disciplining effects of "surplus labor"—the pool of unemployed that sustained anxiety in the employed—were recognized and valued. The theory was that the national wealth was threatened by anything that brought the poor, for any length of time, in any measurable degree, above subsistence, very strictly defined. And "charity" was what kept them alive when work failed or when wages fell, provided they were deemed worthy of "charity." The meanness of the system was rationalized as moral supervision of the very many by the very few, wealth being the single qualification of those few. We see here the fate of the greatest of the theological virtues when it falls into Mammon's clutches. Understandably, there was controversy in the sixteenth century when scholars pointed out that the Greek word in question was better translated as "love."

The Poor Law system elaborated itself in Britain at the same time that Britain was establishing its colonial presence in the New World, notably, for my purposes, in the American South, which it filled with slaves. Slavery in the South was managed by methods very like those that controlled the great class of the poor in Britain, for example by pass laws. The plantation system was rationalized in the same terms that found poetry in the British system of landed aristocracy. So my references to atavism are not entirely offhand. Our recent economic disaster seems to have had its origins in New York and London, but, disproportionately, its peculiar social consequences have been shaped, one may almost say celebrated, in voices with the distinctive inflection of the South. How much kinder, really, to deny poor children a free lunch! How much better for them, morally speaking. It is because the old paradigm was there, waiting to float up to the surface, that unemployment, directly and spectacularly the result of malfeasance among a highly paid caste of financiers, could be turned almost overnight into idleness, shiftlessness, proof of the evil consequences of a culture of dependency. Of course there are those in the top 1 percent who understand the advantages of all this. Stigmatizing unemployment keeps wages down, because it makes those desperate to work who might otherwise have been only ready and willing. And wages have been a great issue since the first treatise on political economy was written in the seventeenth century, as they are a great issue now that Western workers have been thrown into a global labor market. As Mitt Romney pointed out, in remarks that became more famous than he might have wished, Chinese factories are full of young women who sleep in crowded dormitories.

The problem that confronts our economy, or so we have been told for decades, is competitiveness. In fact, Western and non-Western workers have been competing for Western capital, and Western products have competed in Western markets for consumers whose buying power has declined and who therefore opt for the goods produced by workers whose wages are yet lower than their own. Economists call this rational choice. And it is a good thing, from the point of view of those whose profits from foreign investment might be much less secure if they lost the advantages in the American market that come with the decline in real wages. In any case, "competitive" is a good choice of words. One might, just out of habit and optimism, think it meant something like "prosperous." But if it is based on depressed wages, it foresees only the creation of wealth in which most people cannot expect to share no matter how hard they work. This seems obvious enough.

The Poor Laws created and sustained a formidable oligarchy, and slavery did, too. Oligarchy is the new thing now. If it has ever had a basis in institutions that could bear a moment of moral scrutiny, I don't know when that was. No doubt this is why we apply the word almost exclusively to the economies of Russia and China. But the claims of wealth qua wealth have been asserted lately in America, with notable consequences for our electoral system among other things. Corporations are people. This means that the few who control the resources of a corporation can use them to overwhelm the political choices of their own employees, making these few a species of super-citizen. They have the economy in trust, and added to this a special stewardship of our political culture. So the theory goes. I will point out again that our economy is not managed well by the standards of our history, and add that our political culture is as dysfunctional as it has been since just before the Civil War.

•

One of our presidents, in bygone days, said that the only solution to the problems of democracy is more democracy. Things tend in another direction now. The word "capitalism" has replaced the word "democracy" as the banner under which we have flourished. This is as much the fault of the left as of the right, of the academics as of the business elite, a synergy a little like the one I mentioned above, where opportunistic judgmentalism in some inspired inappropriate shame in others. If we are to be blindsided by history, it will probably be the consequence not of unresolved disputes but of unexamined consensus.

In this case, academics have been as ready as any clutch of plutocrats to assert that capitalism has been the motive and impetus of all things American. It is very easy to interpret this to mean that any acknowledgment of the successes of American culture and society is a recognition of the benign effects of capitalism, indeed, to use capitalism as a standard to measure how truly American a given ethic or institution might be. I speak with all due respect for my academic brothers and sisters when I say I often doubt that they look deeply enough into the meanings of the words they use. From the cynicism of the classroom to the rage against the mailman there are only a few degrees of separation. And since our elites are educated, the rage among them against the whole public sector is come by very honestly. The anxiety caused by the financial crisis, and enhanced by those who have found moral and political advantage in prolonging it, have some people waving the banner of capitalism and many flocking to it, taking capitalism to have meant freedom and progress when the systems it stood for were unimpeded by—in fact—by social reforms meant to secure freedom and progress. So we see nationalism in the service of oligarchy, which really is the synonym we need here, the consolidation of wealth in quantities that make it an overwhelming, self-sustaining force in its own right, in its nature highly mobile and supranational. Which brings us to the present moment.

Sometimes I wonder if there is a strategy unfolding, older than the crisis but having the same agents. While I was paying attention to events in Britain, during the Thatcher years, the government announced a goal of making Britain an "ownership society." This means privatization, of course. People who had been living in public housing would be able to buy their apartments. Considerable fuss was made about this, the state having been so smotheringly overprotective, with consequences so "demoralizing." And a new day was a-dawning. But then the darnedest thing happened. In Britain all mortgage interest rates are variable, rates went up, and people lost their now-unaffordable homes, which were resold as second homes if they happened to be well located. The best-laid plans and so on.

Then I began to hear my own government talking about making America an "ownership society," which in fact it had been, at least relatively speaking, since the Homestead Act. And at the same time talk emerged about a "nanny state," which seemed a bit ill-suited to American experience, since the nanny as dominatrix has never been part of our culture. But the phrase has taken hold nevertheless, valued for its edge of contempt, I suppose. This importation of tendentious language interested me only more as events unfolded. The poor anywhere tend to be naive where finances are concerned, having little experience with them. And a great many Americans were persuaded that they could and should join the respectable circle of home owners. All sorts of bankerish razzle dazzle, with, as it happens, just the same effect as those variable interest rates in Britain, ended with mass foreclosures and a collapse in the value of homes all across the country. Since their homes are most Americans' primary asset, the relative wealth of Americans in general fell, often disastrously, and the relative wealth of those immune to such consequences rose dramatically. After all, wealth is measured in ease of access to goods and services. The broad distribution of wealth depresses its value in any individual instance, since the population at large can compete for goods, driving up their cost, and can exercise a degree of choice in their employment, driving up the cost of labor. When there emerge, in name, at least, job creators in the midst of a crisis of unemployment, their effective wealth is very much enhanced. Oligarchy is solidly founded in poverty. Every historical example demonstrates this fact.

This might very well seem right to those who benefit from it, and even to many of those who are harmed by it. When I was last in London, a prominent politician there was musing over the fact that IQs are arrayed along a bell curve, and that 15 percent of people fell in the bottom 15 percent, while only 2 percent were in the top 2 percent—as if in an ideal world there would be some way of squeezing the statistical balloon. Well, he concluded from this that a considerable fraction of society was not intellectually capable of anything better than poverty, so no point in trying to design policy around them. Good old social Darwinism. Its explanatory powers are endless, yet it is in itself so concise.

Losers lose.

Which of us with any experience of the world doesn't know better? I have known a great many people in no degree as well situated as this British politician who would get a good laugh from his thoughts on the bell curve. In my experience, given the chance, people want to be good at what they do, and, ideally, to have the quality of their work recognized. There are people who want to pile money on money, but they are takers, not makers. Easily half of the Bible by weight supports me on this point, and nine-tenths of cultural history. I believe it was Brahms who, like Shakespeare, wore servants' livery. And Mozart was expected to eat in the kitchen with the servants. How much have these three added to the wealth of the world, however measured?

But this raises an essential question, too important to be more than touched on here. What is wealth, after all? I will not bother with the sentimentalism we in the humanities are prone to. I will not say that Shakespeare has had a profound effect on the English language, sensitizing us to its beauty and subtlety and its great power, or that he has enriched our awareness that human life is charged with meaning. I will speak in the terms of the pragmatists.

For centuries Shakespeare has been a reliable and important contributor to Britain's gross national product. Much of this contribution comes through his attracting tourism, and also more generally in enhancing the prestige of British intellectual and cultural products. Then there are national identity and solidarity, which have indubitable value in difficult times. The positive economic effect of a "creative class" has been noted by economists. What is less often noted is that the word "value" can be paraphrased, or expanded, without any change of meaning, to "that which people value." The economic importance to the airline industry of Lourdes or Mecca is vast yet purely secondary to the fact that they are sacred places for a great many people. The intrinsic significance of one or the other or both can be rejected by skeptics, and this fact only underscores the economic importance of the possibly arbitrary assigning of significance to them. Americans travel en masse on a particular Thursday in November. I happened to be lecturing in London on that day last year and was asked from the audience what kind of American would not be home for Thanksgiving. These arbitrary valuations (I feel compelled to assure you that I had an excuse) are expected to override practical considerations, though it could certainly be argued that their importance makes them practical considerations in their own right. If there are, and surely there are, economists who find these intangibles as irksome as the Fabians found metal coffin handles, they are not attending to actual economics but to a privileging of materiality that takes no account of actual human experience and behavior. And it is as true of economics as of poetry that if it has no bearing on human experience it is simply nonsense and cliché. If the pillars of the modern world sometime tremble and fall, the hajj will continue. Does anyone doubt this? If half the Americans who exchange presents on Christmas gave them on Epiphany instead, the national economy would have to reconfigure itself around the change.

These supposed economic realists have an arbitrarily narrow conception of value. They promote on one hand toil whose primary purpose is to create relative advantage for the plutocracy, and on the other, wealth that exists in excess of any rational use that can be had for it or any satisfaction that can be taken from it. Are three yachts better than two? There are old men now who spend their twilight using imponderable wealth to overwhelm the political system. I am sure this is more exciting than keeping a stable of racehorses, or buying that fourth yacht. After a certain point there isn't much of real interest that can be done with yet more money. But imagine how great a boost to the aging ego would come with taking a nation's fate out of its own unworthy hands and shaping it to one's particular lights—which may not be, in fact, enlightened, even rational, and whose wisdom that same nation would never see or endorse if it were tested in the crude theater of actual politics.

I am proposing that the West is giving up its legal and cultural democracy, leaving it open to, or ceding it to, the oldest and worst temptations of unbridled power. Nowhere in all this is there a trace of respect for people in general—indeed, its energies seem to be fueled by contempt for them. Nowhere is there any hint of a better future foreseen for people in general than an economically coerced subordination to the treadmill of "competitiveness," mitigated by the knowledge that at least no poor child expects a free lunch. This is repulsive on its face, destructive of every conception of value. And it proceeds by the destruction of safeguards that would protect us from consequences yet more repulsive. At this moment, world civilization is being wrenched into conformity with a new and primitive order that has minimal sympathy at best with thought and art, with humanity itself as an object of reverence. If we are to try to live up to the challenges of our time, as Bonhoeffer did to his, we owe it to him to acknowledge a bitter lesson he learned before us, that these challenges can be understood too late.

METAPHYSICS

The debate between science and religion has been fundamentally misdirected. Physics has shown us a volatile, intricate, elusive substratum of reality that makes the great usefulness of the old nuts-and-bolts physics seem uncanny rather than obvious and inevitable. This new view of the cosmos does not supply or support a new Christian metaphysics, but it entirely discredits the antimetaphysics that has prevailed in Christian thought for some time, the huge and damaging concessions made to a crudely restricted notion of the possible. The basis for a new metaphysics is ready to hand in biblical and traditional theology. The terms that will make it Christian are established in passages like Colossians 1:15–20, notable for the collapsing of time and locus, which modern physics permits or requires us to respect as an ontological fact to be reckoned with.

My Christology is high, in that I take Christ to be with God, and to be God. And I take it to be true that without him nothing was made that was made. This opens on all being of every kind, including everything unknown to us still, and everything never to be known to us, for which our words and concepts may well be wholly inadequate. So, necessarily, I view cogency with considerable distrust. Pretty as it is in ordinary use, it breaks down at larger scales, and at smaller ones. And Christ as I understand him contains both of these absolutely. My favorite theologian at the moment is an Englishman named John Locke. In his *Essay Concerning Human Understanding* he notes "what a darkness we are involved in, how little it is of Being, and the things that are, that we are capable to know." He says that we must "sometime be content to be very ignorant." Amen and amen. I would add only that Locke evokes an extraordinarily beautiful, tantalizing darkness, full of fragments of experience that become luminous and singular, with something of the character of the astonishing that is in fact appropriate to them. Any faith I have I understand to be another given—William James would say another gift—of my experience.

From this perspective my faith does not differ qualitatively from anything else I know. I take the exalted view of experience. I believe that we do indeed inhabit the theater of God's glory. So I by no means intend to deprecate faith when I say that it is of a kind with our knowing of things in general. It raises profound questions, of course, as does everything else. I understand that this faith necessarily exceeds any account I can make of it, thank God, and will withstand every error I make in attempting to limn it out.

I am speaking here of Christ the Creator, the I AM Who exists, in the present tense, before Abraham. I am speaking of the Christ Who, in Paul's words, "is the image of the invisible God, the first-born of all creation; for in him all things were created, in heaven and on earth, visible and invisible . . . He is before all things, and in him all things hold together . . . For in him all the fullness of God was pleased to dwell, and through him to reconcile to himself all things." Good John Calvin was accused of unitarianism because often, in important contexts, he makes no distinction between Jesus Christ and God the Father. Like the New Testament writers, he uses the word "Lord" where either of them is intended, or, in effect, where both of them are. This is no doubt an inevitable consequence of his very high Christology. It acknowledges the Trinity as a mystery of the profoundest kind, one that eludes conceptualization. To me this seems entirely appropriate. And I am no more a unitarian than Calvin was.

Let us say that faith is given by God, and that it retains its character as given, as gift, despite the often bizarre and perverse transmutations it undergoes in the theater of human consciousness. On one hand this is to say that religion should always be subject to criticism, and that its accretions and distortions should be corrected against, granting the importance of acknowledging an equal human fallibility in the project of reform. It is to say also that such criticism can never finally be dismissive, because religion is always the encounter of a unique soul with a forgiving God. In any instance it is divine grace that is salient, first and last, and grace is the great variable that puts any reckoning of fault or merit very far beyond human competence. Ultimately a compassionate Lord must find our errors and insights to be of extremely limited interest in themselves, infinitesimally interesting at most, however fascinated we may be by the project of attempting to distinguish one from another, one mode of belief from another.

So it is with all respect for theologians and scholars of the modern period, my brothers and sisters in Christ, that I say the vision of Christ, of Jesus of Nazareth, they have retrieved out of the tempests and the droughts of their period is gravely impoverished. Metaphysics has been abandoned as if it were a mistake sophisticated people could no longer make, an indulgence an illusionless world would no longer entertain. I have seen this dire change laid to the influence of the Enlightenment, but I think this very common view of the matter is based on a misreading of basic Enlightenment texts. I have mentioned Locke's *Essay*, which is most certainly a Christian metaphysics. The Enlightenment's many critics have established a character for it, the lens through which it seems generally to be seen, offering nostalgia as an antidote for its supposed desolating effects on Western consciousness. These critics have themselves dismissed metaphysics by insisting that the Enlightenment with its barren rationalism has made metaphysics impossible. Once our eyes were opened there was no unbiting the apple, no way to reattach it to the bough.

In other words, the Enlightenment of the anti-Enlightenment imagination was right about everything factual, incisive in its methods, but wrong in thinking beyond certain conventions and boundaries within which a higher and precious but oddly fragile Truth once abided. This really is an updated version of the myth of the Fall, with the difference that it is, in this telling, we who banished God, reason and science being the flaming sword that makes the expulsion final. I know of no other way to construe this modern fable than as meaning that God is a human social construct whose existence, not to mention his power, is substantially dependent on what people think, and, crucially, dependent as well on authority and circumstance to preclude other kinds of thinking. This notion bears much less resemblance to piety than it does to anthropology of the type that claims to expound the primitive mind. Certainly it flies in the face of everything the Bible tells us about the nature of God.

Be that as it may. The modern predicament is apparently our fate, even though the assumptions it rests upon make no particular sense. They make no sense at all theologically or metaphysically. Of course their not answering to these standards cannot be understood as a fault in a worldview that disallows, however tearfully, both metaphysics and serious theology. Certainly, because they are metaphysical, therefore supposedly dispelled, the statements about absolute reality of the kind that are made by St. John and by St. Paul are not more possible for those who reject the Enlightenment on religious grounds than they would be in the terms of the crudest rationalism and scientism. That reality is sacred, and, as expressed in the being of Christ, is also profoundly human-centered, are statements that cannot be made if it has first been granted that it is possible for us to diminish God and diminish ourselves by thinking, and, within the limits of our capacities, by knowing, about this world. Paul speaks of "the knowledge of God's mystery, of Christ, in whom are hid all the treasures of wisdom and knowledge." This is a vision of the great Christ. There is a residual dualism in historic Christianity that has inclined many interpreters to take passages like this to have reference to a mystery more sacred than this shining Creation, a knowledge that looks past this world, that rejects it. Marcionism has never truly been overcome.

It ought to be. It blinds us. While, glorious as they are, the wonders we are shown as mortals will no doubt open on far greater glories, there are no grounds for supposing that they will differ altogether from those that dazzle us and move us in this life. We are told, after all, that God is love, and, based on what we have felt and yearned to feel, most of us have some sense of what this might mean.

When Locke dismisses the tendency to "let loose our thoughts into the vast ocean of Being; as if all that boundless extent were the natural and undoubted possession of our understandings, wherein there was nothing exempt from its decisions, or that escaped its comprehension," his purpose is to disencumber us of the false conclusions that have been reached through the application of inadequate resources to very great questions. Assumptions and certitudes imposed on matters that should in fact be conceded to ignorance warp and obstruct legitimate thought. Locke would free thinking of artificial constraints by acknowledging real and insuperable limits to the kinds of things we can think about fruitfully. I nominate the venerable doctrine of predestination as a classic instance of an inquiry beyond human capacity, which has multiplied disputes and confirmed skepticism, and has distorted Christianity as often as the doctrine is embraced or evaded. The difficulty of the issues it raises regarding justice and free will are intractable. The problem must be considered in light of the freestanding fact that we, I should say contemporary physicists, have no account to make of either time or causality. Nor has anyone in all the centuries that the problem has been pondered and disputed. In the absence of some comprehension of them we have nothing useful to say about how, cosmically speaking, events exist in time or in causal relation. In principle, this might change, sometime, in some degree. In fact, the extent of our ignorance is so vast and so germane to this question that it must figure decisively in our response to it. Therefore the only appropriate response is to put the question aside.

And I can propose no solution, however tentative, to the problem of evil. Attempts to exculpate God by putting evil beyond his control come at the very high cost of diminishing the power of God, and returning, again, to a version of Marcionism, since what we call evil is an important energy in the world, and to put it beyond God's power is to return to an implicit dualism. On the other hand, to attempt to assimilate evil to the nature of God leads to a temporizing with the great fact of human loss and suffering that does no credit to the divine nature or to the theological enterprise. Where there is no way to understand without compromising the nature of what is to be understood, I heed Locke's advice. I am content to "sit down in a quiet ignorance" of those things I take to be beyond the reach of my capacities.

•

Christ is a response to certain of these questions—a response, not an answer. To the fact of human suffering he says, "I was hungry and you fed me." There is gross and violent injustice, and he "took the form of a slave, and was obedient unto death, even death on a cross." I know the Bible interprets his passion as expiatory, the world's suffering as the consequence of sin, for which Christ is a guilt offering. I note as well that when God speaks through the prophets about sacrifice he treats it as the expression of a human need he tolerates rather than as anything he desires. It is remarkable how ferociously the prohibition against sacrificing one's child must be made and insisted upon by Moses and the prophets, and still there is the suggestion that such sacrifices have occurred even among Israelites. Certainly the death of Christ has been understood as expiation for human sin through the whole length of church history, and I defer with all possible sincerity to the central tenets of Christian tradition, but as for myself, I confess that I struggle to understand the phenomenon of ritual sacrifice, and the Crucifixion when explicated in its terms. The concept is so central to the tradition that I have no desire to take issue with it, and so difficult for me that I leave it for others to interpret. If it answered to a deep human need at other times, and if it answers now to other spirits than mine, then it is a great kindness of God toward them, and a great proof of God's attentive grace toward his creatures.

I do not by any means doubt the gravity of human sin or question our radical indebtedness to God. I suppose it is my high Christology, my Trinitarianism, that makes me falter at the idea that God could be in any sense repaid or satisfied by the death of his incarnate self. The tendency of some theologies to emphasize the attribution of sonship to Christ, and of others to see Jesus as a holy man but no more than a man, creates other problems around the concept of sacrifice or martyrdom—Christ as, in the ancient or the modern sense, the victim in an act that seems to epitomize the sinfulness of the world and nevertheless to be what God requires. Or else to be the exemplary death that has given Jesus of Nazareth an extraordinary place in history. Again, I defer to those who find these understandings right and moving. There is a richness of meaning overflowing from the text and the tradition and from experience itself, a glorious plenitude, that to my mind bears the mark of divine origins far more unmistakably than any scrupulously self-consistent teaching can do—with all respect to the gravity of attention that such teaching brings to bear on luminous particulars other doctrines minimize or overlook.

My Christology has awe as its first principle. It is a very generalized awe, since Creation is full of the glory of God. But it takes its essential quality from the belief that Christ was in the beginning with God, and without him nothing was made that was made. I take Christ in his eternal essence to have in some sense the character of humanity, since we are never encouraged to imagine him without this character. He is a beloved Son. The word "Christ" places him in the history of Israel, as the king or in any case the one to be anointed by God, anointed to be an actor in history, a Redeemer in the manner of the God who redeemed Israel from captivity in Egypt. Calvin integrates the testaments by seeing Christ in appearances of God in human form, in the visitors who come to Abraham, for example. To me this seems reasonable. Christians struggle to articulate a proper relationship with the Old Testament, but in their care to avoid supersession they alienate it inappropriately, refusing it continuity with the ingratiating, therefore "Christian," elements in the New Testament. This makes no sense theologically, putting to one side the implicit disparagement of the Hebrew Bible and Judaism that it entails.

In light of the unvarying solicitude of the Old Testament toward the poor, it might be metaphysically respectable to infer that Christ was in some sense present even in the least of them from the primordial moment when human circumstance began to call for justice and generosity. Nothing in the text forbids the idea. Tradition seems to have wrenched the Testaments apart, to have reserved compassion of this kind for the Christian era. But if the divine for our purposes is to be understood as a Trinity, this cleavage leaves the being of Christ unexpressed from the beginning until the Incarnation. This sounds like Marcionism. The obvious solution to the problem is to make Jesus of Nazareth simply a man who appears at a particular historical moment as the rest of us do. But this is not interesting. Metaphysics collapses around it. And it abandons that widow who must not be deprived of her garment, the laborer whose heart is set on his pay, all those wandering orphans and strangers, all those pagans who do not know their right hand from their left—to Sheol, I suppose, or its conceptual equivalent.

On the other hand, in them we can see an unacknowledged Christ-presence who has no form or majesty that we should look at him, a man of suffering and acquainted with infirmity. Anyone who reads the prophets or the newspapers knows who is wounded for the transgressions of their leaders, their notional betters, who bears chastisements in the place of the guilty. To my mind, the presence of Christ in nameless humanity, in all those images of God, Israelite or Scythian, would be a response to the problem of evil equal to the scale and gravity of the problem—not a solution, but a response. Jesus was not speaking to Christians or to the early church when he said "Blessed are you poor," or "Blessed are you who weep and mourn," since neither Christianity nor the church yet existed. He was simply speaking to a crowd whose attention he happened to have attracted. He is not teaching an ethic. He is giving assurance to those whose lives Moses and the prophets had seen as the objects of God's solicitude.

We learn John 3:16 as children—God so loved the world that he gave his only begotten son, that whosoever believeth in him should not perish but have everlasting life. This is that same Gospel whose Prologue I have alluded to, and which has nerved me to embrace the thought that the presence of Christ in the moment of Creation would have meant that the nature of Christ is intrinsic to Creation, and an aspect of the relation of God to the world from the very outset. The Trinity would seem conceptually unsustainable if this were not true. John's Gospel makes clear that, as surely as Christ's death was a redemption, his life was a theophany. John emphasizes the godlike character of Jesus' presence, and the other Gospel writers emphasize its human character, each of its aspects equally striking because the other is granted. If John's vision of the life is interpreted as showing the influence of Gnosticism, as merely the literary manner of a school of thought important at the time, then the statement implicit in it, that the word became flesh and dwelt among us, that the presence of the mortal man Jesus of Nazareth must be understood as theophany, is lost, though in light of his Prologue, and of Trinitarian belief, this can only be true.

So the question—if God loved the world so passionately, would this gift of his Son, "the Lamb slain from the foundation of the world," change the status only of those who lived after the Incarnation? The love would have long anticipated the gift. Calvin uses a beautiful phrase in his gloss on John 3:16. He says it is right for the gaze of faith "to be fixed on Christ, in whom it beholds the breast of God filled with love." He says also that "the secret love with which the Heavenly Father loved us in himself is higher than all other causes" of our salvation, though "the grace which he wishes to be made known to us, and by which we are excited to the hope of salvation, commences with the reconciliation which was procured through Christ," and "The death of Christ is the only pledge of that love," and a proof of its great "fervor." I understand Calvin to mean that the life and death of Jesus of Nazareth made manifest what was always true, that there was a love that could only be made known to us through a gesture of such unthinkable grandeur and generosity—over and above the grandeur and generosity of Creation itself. This is an interpretation I find more beautiful and more consistent with my understanding of the nature of God than the thought of Jesus' death as sacrifice. In the forty-third chapter of Isaiah, after verses that describe the failure of captive Israel to offer sacrifices and their having instead wearied the Lord with their iniquities, he declares, "I, I am He / who blots out your transgressions for my own sake, / and I will not remember your sins," a very godlike expression of power and grace.

How this secret love in the breast of God has existed in time is a question that always arises for me when I read the Old Testament. I know this may sound like the kind of question that has drawn the irritated dismissal of theologians down the ages—the "What was God doing before the Creation?" kind of question. But again, increasingly I seem to look past the kings and priests and prophets to the people who are its real subject, those nameless souls vulnerable to circumstance, liable to becoming "the poor," to drifting through the grain fields and the vineyards, taking and eating, because God has reserved to himself true ownership of the land in order to feed and comfort them, so that they will know of his care for them. Jesus fed his three thousand and his five thousand. Of course he did. I do not wish to imply that Christ as presence in Creation should be looked for only in human beings and human life—it could perfectly well have charmed a quark—but I do think that the neglect of Adam's children, their absence from "creation," as the word is commonly used, impoverishes our sense of both cosmos and humankind.

Once the "vast ocean of Being" Locke speaks of, which so far exceeds our understanding, is acknowledged as our most immediate experience of the mystery of God, then it is also acknowledged as a revelation of the grandeur of God. What we do not know should always function as a corrective to anything we think we do know. This depends, of course, on our diligently seeking out our ignorance. Science is the invaluable handmaiden of theology in that it tells us how astonishing and gigantically elusive are all the particulars of existence. And nothing is more unfathomable than ourselves, individually and collectively, at any given moment and from the earliest beginning of human time. Calvin characteristically speaks of a human encounter as "presented" or "offered" or "given" to us. A gift, William James would say, a datum. The kingdom of God is among us. Mystery waits upon ignorance—in the positive, Locke's sense of this word. Thinking that we know more than we do, therefore rejecting what we are given as experience, blinds us to our ignorance, which is the deep darkness where truth abides. And our wealth of ignorance grows and multiplies. Much more is known about the atom now than was known fifty years ago, and all the brilliant probing has brought on a cascade of new, more elegant, more pregnant mystery.

To be clear, I am not talking about the "black box" approach that reifies ignorance and makes it function as if it were fact, behave as another kind of erroneous certainty. It is always premature to say that something cannot be known or cannot be described or explained. In a dissertation, Houston Stewart Chamberlain pondered the fact that the rise of sap in trees was inexplicable by the fluid mechanics of his time. He asserted that a "vital force," not accessible to physical measure, must be at work. Clearly his worldview exploited this gap in understanding. A true and disciplined ignorance can never serve as pretext for giving ignorance itself an inappropriate meaning and authority, although in fairness to Houston Stewart Chamberlain, which he hardly deserves, the rise of sap is still a kind of conundrum.

The Bible seldom praises God without naming among his attributes his continuous, sometimes epochal, overturning of the existing order, especially of perceived righteousness or of power and wealth. When society seems to have an intrinsic order, it is an unjust order. And the justice of God disrupts it.

Hannah says, "Those who were full have hired themselves out for bread / But those who were hungry have ceased to hunger." Mary says, "He has put down the mighty from their thrones, / and exalted those of low degree; / he has filled the hungry with good things, /and the rich he has sent empty away." Jesus establishes the ethos that is to prevail among his followers in these terms: "Whoever exalts himself will be humbled; and whoever humbles himself will be exalted," a verse that can be read to mean that the estimation in which one is held within the Christian community is the inverse of one's claims or pretensions, and to mean at the same time that the divine tendency to cast down the proud and exalt the humble will be active in their case. One thing all this proves is that God is indeed attentive to the poor, the humble, the nameless, the hard-pressed and heavy-laden, and has been for as long as they have existed. In history as God sees it, they are the great potential who make his power in human affairs actual, and through whom his justice is vindicated. Granting a rather tenuous connection to the root of Jesse, Jesus of Nazareth is the great and culminating instance of the exaltation of the humble. He takes his place among them as one who is despised and betrayed. Christ humbled himself and took the form of a slave. He humbled himself not in the fact of being human, but to show us the meaning of making slaves of human beings. So if Christ is to be found as a presence in the world from the beginning, it is surely reasonable to suppose that he was to be found, so to speak, among the nameless and vulnerable, whether of Galilee or Babylon, whether of Egypt, God's people, or of Assyria, the work of God's hands. Again, I do not mean to relegate him to human things more than others, to divide the work of Creation among the divine Persons. I mean instead that Creation must have a quality at its center and in its substance to which we as human beings belong. I mean that God's first act of grace toward us was to make us worthy of his attention and loyalty and love.

If Christ's nature is in some high sense intrinsically human, then humankind by its nature must always have had a likeness or an affinity to Christ. Perhaps this is what is meant by our likeness to God. God names himself I AM. Christ in John's Gospel says "I AM" in contexts that make his statements atemporal—if he is the Truth, he was and will be the Truth. And, universally and alone in creation, in whatever state of weariness or weakness or bafflement or boredom, we mortals say and deeply feel, I am. Science finds consciousness, or mind, or the self, to be a mystery of the highest order. And that mystery has been replicated in every one of us, since the first creatures that were by any measure human understood themselves as themselves.

All this is by way of dealing with questions raised by Trinitarianism. If Christ was present at the Creation, and if existence was made with or through him, how is this manifest in Being as we know it? To put it another way, what do we fail to see or sense in Being if we exclude the role of Christ, the hypostatic Person of Christ in the Divine Creator, in the making and sustaining of it? For me a high Christology implies a high anthropology. To properly value this pledge of fervent love, the Incarnation, we must try to see the world as deserving of it—granting our almost perfect incapacity for seeing as God sees. Calvin constantly distinguishes between merit, a theological concept important in his time that he and the Reformation vehemently rejected, and the objective fact that we are made a little less than God and crowned with glory and honor. To worship God in the Creation is to celebrate as well the fact that we ourselves are created, and strangely and wonderfully made. Our honor and glory are not our own doing, and are only more precious, more to be enjoyed and explored, for this reason. Earlier interpreters took Psalm 8 to refer to Christ rather than to humankind. That the point could be debated is itself suggestive.

What is man? And the son of man? When the questions are rephrased inclusively—What is humankind? What is a human being, a mortal?—their power dissipates a little. The singularity of the human person in the uniqueness of his or her experience of being, and experience of God, is lost when we are thought of collectively, as the unspecific member of a species, or as defined by the fact that death will overtake us. "Man" is a stark, brave word, unaccommodated, solitary. Our recent struggles with gender have had strange effects on our use of language and unexamined consequences for our intellectual imagination. The word "soul" is feminine in Latin, and this seems not to have troubled anyone through all the centuries in which theologies were written in that language, even though in poetry and painting the soul is often represented as having the form of a woman. Pico della Mirandola, writing in Latin, speaks of the soul welcoming her bridegroom "in a golden gown as in a wedding dress." This is conventional. Perhaps our fastidiousness about gendered words is a consequence of the fact that they are much less common in English, and are fungible in theory.

In fact, however, since every life is stark and brave and singular, and God knows us by name, we are thrown back on the psalmist's question: What is it about us, each in himself or herself, that could, so to speak, reward God's mindfulness? The usual answers might be our piety, our suffering, or our sin. None of these seems to me to suggest a particular celebration of God's nature or our own. Piety very readily turns smug and even mean, as Jesus noted more than once. Suffering is usually the loss or destruction of better possibilities, and exactly the same may be said of sin, though more emphatically. There is little here to undergird the faith that God would break into history to secure eternal life for us, which will also be life with him. Yet this is the faith, that we should not perish but have everlasting life. When our sins are behind us and our tears have been wiped away, what will remain? Presumably some human essence we have no name for, and perhaps very little sense of, but which must be precious enough to make God take note of our disfiguring and disabling sorrows and sins, and free us of them. To assume this essence, even if we cannot define it, and to suppose a grander and in fact more profound and cosmic human nature that could answer to the fact of Christ's presence in the Creation, would honor God and exalt Christ, and give us reason to consider ourselves again.

I am not proposing anything new here.

Pico della Mirandola says, in his essay *On the Dignity of Man*, "I understood why man is the animal that is most happy, and is therefore worthy of all wonder; and lastly, what the state is that is allotted to man in the succession of things, and that is capable of arousing envy not only in the brutes but also in the stars and even in minds beyond the world. It is wonderful and beyond belief. For this is the reason why man is rightly said and thought to be a great marvel and the animal really worthy of wonder." This was written in the late fifteenth century, by a man overwhelmed by the splendor revealed to him by his learning in the languages and literatures of antiquity and tradition, a man of the early Renaissance, when all that was known to the preceding ages of European Christianity and all that was added to it by the recovery of other ancient texts and languages together created an abrupt awareness of the brilliance of human achievement. This "animal worthy of all wonder" is earthly and intellectual, an epitome of Creation, indefinable in himself in that he participates in the whole of it. Pico imagines God telling Adam, "I have placed thee at the center of the world, that from there thou mayest more conveniently look around and see whatsoever is in the world. Neither heavenly nor earthly, neither mortal nor immortal have We made thee. Thou, like a judge appointed for being honorable, art the molder and maker of thyself; thou mayest sculpt thyself into whatever shape thou dost prefer." His great exuberance cannot be dismissed as the privilege of a simpler age; the essay was written as preface to his defense against a charge of heresy.

If Pico were with us now, would he not be confirmed in his

astonishment at the human capacity to know? Have we not become the center of creation by making this speck of planet sensory, as if it were a hundred thousand eyes and a sleepless mind? There would be an element of the seraphic in this, if we could grant Pico his terms.

A generation earlier, Nicolaus Cusanus had said,

> Human nature it is that is raised above all the works of God and made a little lower than the angels. It contains in itself the intellectual and the sensible natures, and therefore, embracing within itself all things, has very reasonably been dubbed by the ancients the microcosm or world in miniature. Hence is it a nature that, raised to union with the maximum, would exhibit itself as the fullest perfection of the universe and of every individual in it, so that in this humanity itself all things would achieve their highest grade. But humanity has no real existence except in the limited existence of the individual. Wherefore it would not be possible for more than one real man to rise to union with the maximum; and this man assuredly would so be man as to be God, would so be God as to be man, the perfection of all things and in all things holding the primacy.

For Cusanus, human nature as microcosm implies the Incarnation. He goes on to say that this is "an order that by nature and perfection transcends time, so that he who exists with God above time and before all things, in the fullness of time and after many cycles of ages, appeared in the world." In other words, Christ in his humanity was in the beginning with God. The eternal Trinity includes a quintessential humanity which is expressed in Creation as the union of all things.

In quoting I do not mean to imply that I embrace his theology in general or even this aspect of it. For the most part it is remarkably disembodied and mathematical. And yet, paradoxically, it accepts the wholeness of things—Cusanus says, "the highest nature that comprises no inferior" is deficient, "for the union of inferior with superior is greater than is either separately," mathematics outflanking dualism. So we have humankind fully at home in the universe, anticipated in the nature of the Trinity itself and epitomized in Christ. This wholeness is achieved by acknowledging what he calls our intellectual nature as a part of our being that exists in its own right. The old association of knowledge with the divine made our participation in knowledge, warped and radically limited as it must be, a nimbus, a proof of godliness. And our exertions of intellect are another proof. Calvin, whose thought is full of the humanism of the Renaissance, interprets the verse in the Prologue to John "The life was the light of men" to mean that "Since this light, of which *the Speech* was the source, has been conveyed from him to us, it ought to serve as a mirror, in which we may clearly behold the divine power of *the Speech*." ("Speech" is the translator's uneuphonious attempt to render Calvin's Latin translation of *Logos* as *Sermo*, word as act, utterance. Presumably his choice of "Speech" over "Word" reflects Christ's creative presence in the beginning, by analogy with God's speaking the world into being in Genesis.) Again, we are Christlike and enjoy the effect of Christ's presence in the Creation in our possessing "the *light* of understanding." I hasten to add that this passage is an instance of Calvin's tendency to make no certain distinction between the Persons of Father and Son.

We moderns have accepted accounts of the human mind that make it a gratuitous compounding of the complexity potential in matter, not essentially specific to us, telling us nothing of the nature of God even where God is granted. There have been attempts at quantifying human intelligence that would effectively isolate it among a certain few of us. So it is refreshing to see intellect treated by Pico and Cusanus and Locke as well as a trait of our species, both Adamic and cosmic, by no means solely the gift of the privileged or the pretentious among us. Of course it is a very reduced conception of intelligence that has yielded such an idea.

I have read an article or two about the anthropic theory. I resist it because it is solidly based in our conventional model of reality. An argument in its favor, from a certain point of view, is that it does align with science as science is generally understood. My objection to it is that it does not lift the great issues of being out of the terms and limits of the physical universe as we know it. And I am not sure that it can be expanded to allow a reconception of human existence, a metaphysics, that would fully acknowledge the strangeness of our presence in the universe. The dust of which we are made has a cosmic origin and history. This can only mean that we were potential in the nature of the universe, the expression of possibilities inherent in it—an amazing thing to consider, enabling a kind of thinking different from the rather mechanistic and anthropomorphic language of design. I am no physicist, but when I read about phenomena like quantum entanglement that seem to discourage an excessively literal belief in space, time, and causality as we commonly understand them, I feel the need to establish a new ordering of priorities in inquiring into the nature of reality, by looking at its quintessential expressions, for example, those outliers relative to the implied norms of physical being that form the baseline of contemporary thought—norms that are arrived at by excluding outliers insofar as they are seen to differ qualitatively from the cosmic run of things. I take these to be the human mind, and the human soul as well, though the existence of the second is not so widely acknowledged. If reality is thought of in this way, then the sense of a bond of likeness between God and the whole of humankind, which can be understood as a Christ-presence in humankind, arises of itself.

I do not wish to be heterodox, and I do not wish to make a selective or tendentious use of Scripture. I do not wish to imply the kind of universalism that means nothing has really been at stake in this great storm of need and passion and beauty and brilliance that has swept and transformed the world in the few millennia of significant human presence. Leaving judgment to God, I do believe that we are capable of real evil, have proved this every day of those millennia and will prove it again tomorrow. The widow and the orphan will receive no justice, the laborer will be deprived of his pay, the man of sorrows will be crucified again. Revering Scripture as I do, I cannot doubt that these things matter absolutely.

At the same time, I feel a distinctly Christian dread at the thought that any good thing ultimate reality holds for the patient, the kind, the humble, the lovers of truth, the hopeful and enduring who are Christian will be denied to those excellent souls who are anything else. An ancient Egyptian aspired to be able to say, to the god who met him after his death, I never made anyone weep. This is a noble and gentle aspiration I can only imagine Christ would honor. All the people are grass, the grass withers and the flower fades. In Egypt and Greece and Assyria, in Gog and Magog. Such extravagance, such an outpouring, all of them living within the Providence of the Lord who forms light and creates darkness, and whose name they do not know, just as Cyrus, his shepherd, did not know his name. It is perhaps not irrelevant that Jacob was only one of the people Cyrus released, and Jerusalem was only one of the cities he helped to rebuild. We have no record of the joy these pagans felt at their rescue, but Isaiah lets us imagine it, the greatest probable difference being that the hosannahs would have been sung to other gods.

I feel strongly that Christians have misread the Old Testament out of some lingering Marcionist impulse to make it the opposite of the New Testament, for example, in their insistence on calling God "jealous" when the word could as well be translated "passionate," a translation thoroughly justified by context. On the basis of such interpretation we encourage ourselves to forget the implications of God's insistence that the whole world is his. If we broaden the ground of interpretation, taking into consideration the Book of Isaiah, for example, which is so important to Christianity that it is germane by any hermeneutical standard, we find the figure of the servant, who may be the people Israel and may be the promised Messiah, and we have the inspired generosity of the conquerer Cyrus, who is called God's anointed. Christ, the Son of Man, the King of Kings, who for us emerges so hauntingly in these oracles, might be thought of as promised or anticipated in the very fact that he is also implicit, present *in* humankind before he, in the Incarnation, became present among them. Granted it is often difficult to see Christ, to see the image of God, in ourselves and our kind. But, by the grace of God, we have God as our judge.

There is a beautiful sequence in the third chapter of the Gospel of Luke. This chapter is very much concerned with establishing the identity of Jesus as Christ. First, the calling of John the Baptist is described and his proclamation of the imminent coming of one much greater than he. Then, when Jesus has been baptized, the descent of the Holy Spirit in the form of a dove. "And a voice came from heaven, 'You are my Son, the Beloved; with you I am well pleased.'" Then the remarkable genealogy, moving backward through time from Jesus' putative father Joseph (Luke draws attention to the fact that Joseph was not really his father, therefore that the genealogy is not his in any ordinary sense), backward to Creation and the eponymous ancestor of the whole of humanity—"Enos, son of Seth, son of Adam, son of God."

THEOLOGY

I was slow in arriving at a Christology, at least in articulating one, because any account of Christ always seemed to me too narrow—however true in part, still false for all it excluded. This problem resolved itself for me in the Prologue to the Gospel of John, this reconception of the Creation narrative that places Christ at the center of the phenomenon of Creation even while it declares his earthly presence in Jesus of Nazareth. To me this implies that a quality which can be called human inheres in Creation, a quality in which we participate, which is manifested in us, which we epitomize. It implies that Jesus is the defining instance of this essential humanity. Christ is central ontologically, and what I have called humanity is ontological as well, profoundly intrinsic to Being because he was in the beginning with God and without him nothing was made that was made.

There is a very great imponderable at the center of Christian thought, the Trinity, which seems to me to forbid the attribution of any act or quality to any of its persons with even the passing implication that it is less the act or quality of the Others, or any less to be attributed to the Godhead altogether than to any of its persons. So, if I seem here to supplant God the Creator with Christ the Creator, this is the consequence of a distinction between God and Christ that is common but that I do not at all wish to make here. I should say at the outset that I am much impressed by the fact that the universe, so far as scientists and mathematicians have opened this mighty text, is not mindful of our mechanistic suppositions, which have made us so awkward in our conceptualizing of our profoundest intuitions. Is there any great Christian theology that does not have the Trinity at its center? Does the highest sense of the sacred abide where the Trinity as a concept is disallowed? Well, I think not, for what that is worth. The loftiest utterance of the holiness of Christ tells us that he was in the beginning, that he was with God, that he was God. And, of course, that he dwelt among us. Modern religious thought, with notable and distinguished exceptions, Karl Barth and Dietrich Bonhoeffer among them, has shied away from the unfathomable, as if grace could have other origins and truth another character. There has been a marked tendency to treat the commonplace as the standard by which the plausible, the credible, is to be gauged.

If anything we know about creation suggested that such metrics were appropriate to making judgments about the deeper levels of what we experience as physical reality, then there would be a stronger case for applying them to the deepest, most absolute reality John's language invokes. But anyone who has spent an hour with a book on the new physics knows that our old mechanistic thinking, useful as it is for so many purposes, bears about the same relation to deeper reality that frost on a windowpane bears to everything beyond it, including the night sky and everything beyond that. How very strange it all is. I have just read an article that begins this way: "Physicists have discovered a jewel-like geometric object that dramatically simplifies calculations of particle interactions and challenges the notion that space and time are fundamental components of reality."

It is never my point to make a theological argument based

on science—I wait for the day someone will lift a corner of quantum physics and find that it is underlain by a physics yet more bizarre. The point here is that religious thought is, persistently and inappropriately, influenced by a kind of scientific thought—which happens to be two or three hundred years out of date. This old science was very inclined to expose and denounce the impossible. It did much good service, and a good deal of harm as well. It set rationalistic limits to what could be believed which are still widely honored, though little we know now and little we do now would satisfy eighteenth-century notions of the possible. Of course it is still reasonable and necessary to say that there are effective impossibilities, vast categories of them. In their nature their numbers are hardly to be conceived of. But grander reality and deeper reality are volatile and fantastical. Our comfortable certainties—that if a thing is in one place it cannot be in other places at the same time, that the dimensions that are the architecture of our existence are all the dimensions there are, and so on—these certainties are the things to be marveled at. It is as if we were a quiet city in the heart of a raging sea, no foundation touching the seafloor, no spire rising out of the waves. Some gentle spell prevents us from grasping our situation, and this is all right because the same gentle spell shelters us from it. We know what we need to know to live in this city. Cows give milk, hammers drive nails, books should be returned to the library. But we know now that the overwhelmingly preponderant forms and theaters of existence are utterly alien to such business. Any reasonable standard of possibility would declare *us* to be impossible.

I saw a video of a physicist talking about the wonders that await us in the quantum computer. He said this computer would draw us closer to nature, to reality, because its processes would be the processes of reality. Fine. Then it seems to me that the great question is, What is this nonreality in which we live, this order of Being, endlessly confirmed to us by our senses, which seems to us to operate very differently from quantum reality though it must participate in that reality as deeply as everything else does? What is this nonreality that left us persuaded it was reality itself, the model, standard, test of all existence, until the start of the twentieth century? What is this nonreality that is orderly enough, thick enough, to be formed and manipulated by us, that in the ordinary course of things is to be trusted by us so absolutely that to ignore its rules and limits is insanity? This, by my lights, is a far deeper question than most. It is as if our senses and perceptions have fed us with milk rather than with meat. Why should our minds be at a remove, providential as it may be, from the processes of reality, until finally we are helped by a cunning device of our own creation? Is this not strange?

Well, let it be. I wish only to say one more time that the rationalistic arguments that claim to winnow out the implausible and the meaningless by applying the flail of common sense are the products of bad education. Religions are expressions of the sound human intuition that there is something beyond being as we experience it in this life. What is often described as a sense of the transcendent might in some cases be the intuition of the actual. So the religions are quite right to conceptualize it in terms that exceed the language of common sense. The rationalists are like travelers in a non-English-speaking country who think they can make themselves understood by shouting. Sadly, too many religious have abandoned their own language, its beauty and subtlety and power, accommodating to the utilitarian expectations of these demanding outsiders who have no understanding of the language or culture and refuse on principle to acquire any. But the unfathomable has a most legitimate place in any conceptualization of an ultimate reality. Paradoxically, I suppose, it is only our limited understanding that keeps the unfathomable from being more unfathomable still. For these reasons I am grateful to science for freeing me to consider essential elements of Christianity without bringing the prejudices of what is still called modern thought to bear on them.

Christ as Creator implies to me that his role as Christ is intrinsic to Creation—that in that first moment creatures were foreseen whose nature and course of life he could take on altogether without in any way diminishing his high holiness. It was foreseen that these creatures would need him to restore them by an epochal act—of love, forgiveness, loyalty, grace, friendship, brotherliness—all of them human things, whose names we have learned from our own capacities, and in every good human bond, perhaps for as long as we have walked upright. They are things we know from our own experience, our own hearts, souls, and minds. Then in this profounder sense we are not aliens in the universe, taking the word in the largest sense, but are singularly rooted in it. If Providence is reflected in this arbitrary construction, this beautiful and orderly, knowable and manipulable delusion we share, then our privileged place is very evident.

The objection will be made that if Creation from its beginnings anticipated, that is to say made inevitable, our need for such intercession and rescue, then what the theologians and philosophers call evil was also made a constituent part of Creation, whence all the familiar arguments about human culpability on one hand and the nature of God on the other. This is a grave objection. I know of no better response than to consider the history of our species, and the future it appears to be preparing for itself. It is a truism that humanity is deficient in humanity, but who would dispute it? In the privacy of our thoughts does not any one of us feel the difference between our best impulses and our actual behavior? Does not any one of us feel the difference between the thought and work we are capable of and the thinking and working we let ourselves get by with? Freedom comes to mind—we are not termites who have been honed over the eons to be state-of-the-art, infallible termites. Maybe something that feels like courage and loyalty floods the bodies of bees that swarm to defend hive and queen, but these stimuli fall something short of virtue since bees cannot do otherwise. We wander the terrain of a very remarkable freedom—to default, to betray, to habituate ourselves to mediocrity, to turn away from the emergencies that strike our nearest neighbors, or to profit from their misfortune. We are unique in nature for our ability to be consistently, even catastrophically, wrong. I received a letter a while ago from an economist, a very polite rebuke for my having impugned the wisdom of the market, or, more precisely, its inerrancy. His defense, which flabbergasted me a little, was that the market is merely a reflection of human choices—which of course I am ready to concede, stipulating only that it may be a small and particular clutch of humans whose choices are reflected in it. In any case, his account of the market by my lights lands the whole phenomenon solidly on the terrain of our peculiar fallibility. No economist myself, I have for proof only recent and ongoing global catastrophe, which, for whatever reason, he did not mention.

Then the capacity for evil is the price of our freedom? No, this is a conclusion I choose not to draw. It has the look of gross oversimplification, of having the same clear legitimacy of derivation as any reductio ad absurdum. But thinking ought not to be balked by the fear of undesired implications. A thousand things can go wrong in any slightly ambitious thinking, and correctives must be ready when the mind recoils, even without an articulate objection. This statement regarding evil does not acknowledge its terrible cost, the fact that freedom on one side is so often the worst kind of grief and affliction and bondage on another. If the only possible response to the gravity of the question is to let it stand, so be it. I have not intended to offer an answer to it, only to draw attention once again to the great strangeness of the human situation. The features and dimensions of the moral universe we inhabit are as particular to us as is the simulacrum of physical reality given to us by our senses and perceptions.

Jonathan Edwards was a metaphysician and abreast of the best science of his period. He pondered problems that are still current, having to do with time and causality. These anomalies, selfhood among them, he took as proofs of the active, present, unfolding will of God. To my theistic mind, this seems an elegant response to the givenness of things. I find myself too often reaching for analogies—and here is another one. If time and gravity answered to the expectations of scientific theory, if time were symmetrical and ran backward as well as forward, if gravity were as strong as its kindred forces imply it should be, then the whole human narrative could not have happened. Say a different universe might have entertained a different kind of narrative. Yes, and this is what defines the word "arbitrary." Finally, no necessity we can describe requires that the universe should be thus and not otherwise. This is one implication of the theory of multiple universes. If we take the question from the other side and say accident made the conditions that eventuated in our existence, with all its strangenesses, then we are left with the problem of explaining the accidental or the random in a system that seems, in rationalist theory, to be driven by necessity. If necessity needs to be reconsidered so fundamentally that it is at the point of becoming another thing, then the rationalist argument seems to me to be in need of very radical criticism indeed. Let us grant the reality of chance or accident, or of quantum phenomena that are the same in effect. If there are constraints on possibility, which our experience tells us is the case, and which the rationalists certainly assume to be the case, then those constraints are arbitrary. Analogies are available: language of every kind, culture at every scale.

I do not wish to seem to be reasoning, nor even theologizing, my way to an apologia for the Christian mythos. It is simply time to put down the burden of bad and assertive thought that has induced us to compromise or abandon it. This kind of thinking is so profoundly engrained in us in the West that it is no easy thing to see past it. Then again, I am certainly not proposing that we make way for those consumer-friendly mysticisms that have contributed so largely to the banality of our time. I wish to explore the questions of Being within the terms of Christian orthodoxy. I know "Christian orthodoxy" is a problematic phrase in itself. For me it is expressed succinctly in the Apostles' Creed. I am aware that my interpretation of the Creed may not square with others'.

Be that as it may. I have concluded that only a radical Christocentricity can address the problem of Christian exclusivism, which has gone against the grain of Jesus' teaching these two thousand years. If his presence in the Creation asserts the human as a uniquely sacred and intrinsic aspect of Being, and his presence on earth underscores this, then how are we to believe that he, call him Christ, call him God, would sweep almost the whole of our species out of existence, or into some sort of abyss, because of historical accident, or because of the terrible and persistent failures of our churches and of those who have been smug or cruel or criminal in his name. Granting all complexities, is it conceivable that the God of the Bible would shackle himself to the worst consequences of our worst behavior? Reverence forbids. Is it conceivable that the reach of Christ's mercy would honor the narrow limits of human differences? It might be that the Christ I place at the origin and source of Being would be called by another name and would show another face to all those hundreds of billions who are or were not Scots Presbyterians or American Congregationalists or anything remotely like them. This is my devoutest hope, not least because it promises our salvation, too. Maybe his constant blessing falls on those great multitudes who lived and died without any name for him, for those multitudes who know his name and believe they have only contempt for him. The philosopher

C. S. Peirce says somewhere that it would be most Godlike of God to love those least like himself. Most Godlike, most Christlike. I know the refutation. If salvation is universal, what about Hitler, Stalin? Well, hard cases make bad law. I am not willing to open an abyss, conceptually speaking, just to accommodate Hitler and Stalin. It is surely perverse to construct a whole cosmology around them. Thus begins the casuistry, as it used to be called, that provides hell with so many other tenants. My thoughts on the ultimate disposition of the great villains and monsters of history might incline me to curtail my conception of grace. The cost would be too high.

•

Here my argument takes a turn that might be unexpected, though all the foregoing was meant as preparation for it. The human self has been clapped into the durance vile of rationalist thought these many years, as it is now. If it is true, as I propose, that human nature enjoys likeness in kind with deep reality, if it has the means to see beyond the limits of the quasireality in which it also of necessity participates, then anyone is, indeed, a microcosm, just as the old philosophers said. Every one of us has privileged access to the unique source of insight on this question, a living mind. I will report briefly on my own consciousness, which is no doubt somewhat singular, but then so are they all.

In a month I will be seventy. I recognize the privilege of living in an age and a culture where this is not a significant attainment. I have the whole cohort of my friends around me. I could almost choose not to give a thought to my age. But something surprising has happened, some ticking upward of pleasure and intensity that is really not what I had been led to expect. My pleasures are the same—books and plays, church and teaching—and my feelings about them are changed only in degree. It must be obvious that my life has circled these fascinations and taken their rewards for decades. Now they are all refreshed. This has nothing to do with any intention of mine. It is not that I have changed my mind. Rather, my mind, quite abruptly, seems to have changed me.

I thought these fevers ended with adolescence, and here they are, back again and raging. This time I know how to give them welcome. This time I know my life is drawing to an end. The strangeness of life on earth first of all, and then of everything that takes my attention, is very moving to me now. It feels freshly seen, like a morning that is exceptional only for the atmosphere it has of utter, unimpeachable newness, no matter how many times old Earth has tottered around the sun. Sometimes I am so struck by an image or an idea that I cannot sleep nights. Now my mind has begun to appraise its own state at inconvenient moments, to bring me back from the brink of sleep by noticing when its own activity has become—hypnagogic.

I'm frankly surprised it knows the word. Where did that come from? Why was it stored up all these years to tease me now? In writing I have always felt as though I am my mind's amanuensis, in reading its researcher, in repose its slightly dull companion. I feel a novel begin to cohere in my mind before I know much more about it than that it has the heft of a long narrative. This heft is a physical sensation. A forming novel is a dense atmosphere more than it is a concept or an idea. I find my way into it by finding a voice that can tell it, and then it unfolds within the constraints of its own nature, which seem arbitrary to me but are inviolable by me. When I lose the sense of them everything goes wrong. I suppose it is inevitable that I should think of a fiction as a small model of the simulacrum of reality that is given to us by sense and perception, and as a way to probe anomalies that emerge in the assumed world when it is under scrutiny. But this is only a hypothesis, an attempt to account for a phenomenon I cannot will and, in an important degree, do not control.

Then what am I? Or, to put the matter more generally, what is *I*? It is a seemingly complete and knowable self always vulnerable to startling intrusions and disruptions that can only have their origins in that same self—impulse, inspiration, sudden access of memory. The sense of self is as necessary to us as our physical bodies. But it is incommensurate with the nature and potentialities of the mind with which it would seem to be synonymous. By what is it constrained? Why do we have so little experience of our mind's actual working? Why do we never really know what we know? A great deal has been written about the mind/brain, though little about its brilliance, which has everything to do with these intrusions, this mental overplus that asserts itself as it will, when it will. At seventy years of age, I know myself as I eventuate, as I happen. Rationalistic accounts of mind and self do not suit their subject any better than a mechanistic physics suits a quantum universe. What I do or feel, however it may surprise me, will of course be retrojected to become a part of my definition, a part of who I, so to speak, am. This does not mean that I can repeat what I have done or that any emotional state I experience will persist, even in accessible memory. It is entirely reasonable to assume that there are limits to what I am capable of, what generosity, what perfidy, though my experience has not been of a kind to test these boundaries. It is also reasonable to assume that these boundaries could be remarkably broad, or porous. In this sense I will never know myself, nor will anyone else know me.

Let us say, then, that the world of ordinary experience that is the world of rationalism is inexplicably unlike other systems of being in which it is immersed, including our own subjectivity. I emphasize the word "experience," because its claims to objectivity are by no means so straightforward as they have been made to seem. While we as subjects can hardly venture a tentative conclusion about who we are, our species has reached a remarkably solid consensus about the nature of time, space, and causality. This model of the world, which seems to be the product of our peculiar limitations—and powers—stands up to endless tests of its reality. Then what is improbable, or impossible? Again, the most scientific answer would seem to be: We are.

This is not an anthropic argument in the usual sense. I am not interested in making the case that the universe as we know it seems to be extraordinarily well suited to our emergence in it. While this is apparently true, the argument can be reversed easily—only in such a universe could we have emerged. My point is very different—that we are somehow a little enclave of qualitative unlikeness, an enclave not to be thought of as spatial, but as experiential. When we fling some ingenious mock sensorium out into the cosmos so that it can report back what it finds there, inevitably it provides human answers, data addressed to notions of relevance that, however sophisticated, are human notions. We will never know what we don't know how to ask, which is probably almost everything.

Then the reality we experience is a matter of mind, but not to be called illusory, because it is profoundly shared, and because, within very broad limits, it works. It works so well that, over the millennia, though philosophy, poetry, and religion have expressed restlessness with its strictures, these strictures have been taken increasingly to define and limit reality itself. To oversimplify greatly, the argument in Western civilization has been about whether the sense of an Other, an order of Being that exists in meaningful relationship with humankind, or that at least can be described in human terms, is or is not a meaningful intuition. The rejection of this intuition has always been, and is to this day, based on a scaling upward to infinity of the properties of what I have called our simulacrum, this quasireality that holds us at a remove from the world's true workings. In other words, the criticism of religion that derides its central intuition as a projection of human fears and desires onto a universe that is alien to such things is itself a projection of human inferences, deductions, and expectations onto a universe that is wholly incommensurate with them.

•

Let us say that we live in a small model of reality, providentially scaled and ordered to serve us and content us for most purposes, beautiful enough to sustain our spirits endlessly, transparent enough to help us learn to see beyond it, and wrapped in a quiet of its own that lets us leave the roar of its origins to mathematics and its wild eons of unfolding to physics and cosmology. If this is not Providence, or miracle, it altogether awaits explanation in any other terms. It is wholly unsuited to the extrapolations rationalism has made from it, which leave it mechanistic or algorithmic and in any case oddly or tendentiously inhuman, though it is a product of a reciprocal relationship between limited human consciousness on one hand, and, on the other, whatever it is that sustains this model and makes it, as I have said, stable, usable, testable, and thick. When I introduce the word "providential" I am changing the character of the discussion, of course.

Providential is fairly exactly what Jonathan Edwards meant by arbitrary. He argued that the aspects of experience that seemed then and seem so far to be inexplicable, for example, the persistence of identity over time, express no intrinsic necessity but, instead, the active intention of God. A discipline of modern thinking is the assumption that if a thing is not explained, then in good time science will explain it. Therefore the thing, the self, for example is, for all purposes, explained, insofar as its complexity or elusiveness might otherwise reflect on the nature of existence. The phenomenon of consciousness is no different in this regard from the attractive power of amber. The triumphalist tone of people who speak as if from the posture of science comes from the notion that if the imperium of science has not yet spread to every aspect of existence it might as well have, taming and enlightening every corner where superstition might lurk. I do not, by the way, find this attitude among actual scientists. The word "explain" is typically used in scientistic contexts as a synonym for the much more tentative word "describe." It is a triumph of science to have, in some degree, described the electron, and preposterous to suggest it has been explained.

I have spent all this time clearing the ground so that I can say, and be understood to mean, without reservation, that I believe in a divine Creation, and in the Incarnation, the Crucifixion, the Resurrection, the Holy Spirit, and the life to come. I take the Christian mythos to be a special revelation of a general truth, that truth being the ontological centrality of humankind in the created order, with its theological corollary, the profound and unique sacredness of human beings as such. The arbitrariness of our circumstance frees me to say that the Arbiter of our being might well act toward us freely, break in on us, present us with radical Truth in forms and figures we can radically comprehend.

I have mentioned my recent bout of obsessions and intensities. Shakespeare has been very much on my mind, to my surprise. I studied him in graduate school, then put him aside entirely for decades until something stirred in my brain a few months ago. This happened as I was finishing a novel, writing the end of it, which ought to have been obsession enough. But it is very tiring to write, and naps and walks are an important part of my working life. Now that I have acquired every respectable video I can find of productions of Shakespeare, I watch them when I am tired, and they refresh me more satisfyingly than sleep. I am predisposed to attend to the plays as theology, among other things. I have found this kind of attention to them spectacularly fruitful. *The Tempest* takes us as far into the thinnest upper atmosphere as anything I know, whether art, metaphysics, or theology. Since Shakespeare was active during a period of sectarian turmoil and controversy, attention to the religious element in his plays tends to focus on the question of his loyalty to one side or the other, Catholic, Anglican, or Protestant. But his history plays are proof of his awareness that England was entirely capable of violent turmoil without there being anything so interesting as religious controversy involved in it. The great central concepts of Christianity were in dispute while he lived, and this would have been interesting in itself, putting aside the question of his alignment with positions articulated by others. Out of it all, I propose, he drew a powerful vision and aesthetic, of a grace that transcends even the most embittered differences. The great scenes of reconciliation that conclude so many of his plays are moments of Shakespearean grace.

For my purposes here I wish to draw attention to the scenes of recognition that are the prelude to reconciliation. When Lear is reunited with Cordelia, Leontes with Hermione, Posthumus with Imogen, the qualities of the despised and lost, which are constant from the beginning, are only truly perceived and valued after the terrible alienation has ended. The contrivances of plot that bring these reunions about are treated as providential and the scenes themselves have a religious radiance and intensity, though the worlds of all these plays are non-Christian. Again and again they tell us really to see the people we thought we knew, and really to feel the sanctity of the bonds we think we cherish. They open onto the inarticulable richness concealed in the garments of the ordinary—in the manner of Christianity, properly understood. Death has a very similar effect in Shakespeare. His characters question the reality of the whole world of experience, but not of their own souls. Beyond the accidents of hate and harm that distract and corrupt us, there is grace, reality indeed, in whose light all such things simply fall away. The plays make a distinction between mercy, which is given in despite of faults, and grace, for whom no fault exists. When

Lear tells Cordelia she has reasons not to love him, she says, "No cause, no cause." When the villain Iachimo kneels to Posthumus for forgiveness, Posthumus says, "Kneel not to me; The power that I have on you is, to spare you; The malice towards you to forgive you: live, and deal with others better." In the great age of the revenge play, this visionary aloofness to the very thought of revenge is striking, certainly. So it would be now. If the world is indeed arbitrary, temporal in this sense, then an absolute reality would have no traffic with its accidents, our errors and confusions. Heaven make us free of them.

I find Shakespeare confirming that late, vivid sense of mine that everything is much more than itself, as commonly reckoned, and that this imaginary island is the haunt of real souls, sacred as they will ever be, though now we hardly know what this means. Paul says we may take the created order as a revelation of God's nature. We know now that there is another reality, beyond the grasp of our comprehension yet wholly immanent in all of Being, powerful in every sense of the word, invisible to our sight, silent to our hearing, foolish to our wisdom, yet somehow steadfast, allowing us our days and years. This is more than metaphor. It is a clear-eyed look at our circumstance. Let us say that this quasireality is accommodated to our limitations in ways that allow us an extraordinary efficacy. To me this would imply a vast solicitude, and a divine delight in us as well.

The Prologue to the strange play *Pericles, Prince of Tyre* says the tale it tells is an old song, sung, among its other benign effects, "to make men glorious." Again, this tale ends in recognition and restoration. Pericles is stirred from his trance of grief by the voice of a daughter he has not known, whose voice he has never heard. Thinking her dead, he has given way to utter sorrow. So her being restored to him is like resurrection. He sees her as he might never have seen her—miraculously herself. The tale "makes men glorious" by allowing plausibility to drop away in profound deference to human particularity, human love and loyalty and worth. I take these pious pagans to be living out a meditation on the meeting in the Garden, the supper at Emmaus. Our love and hope are sacred, and existence honors and will honor them though the heavens finally roll up like a scroll.

EXPERIENCE

All the great Christians have said we must be humble. This should be easier for us moderns, knowing what we know. Of course we have been anticipated, by the psalmist, by the Job writer. Where were you when I laid the foundations of the world? Here we stand staring beyond the great mysteries we have opened, having stepped to the threshold of still profounder mysteries. We can look far back in time. This is remarkable. Indeed, where the cosmos is concerned we can only look back in time. This is also remarkable. We don't know what time is, of course, but we do know that it is not symmetrical. It goes in one direction. We look into the deep past, a maelstrom of sorts, in which time changes its nature, then perhaps disappears altogether. We can only conclude that we have our origins in this unfathomable storm, mundane creatures that we are, rumpled, trivial, tedious, our minds full of flotsam and small grudges, yet creatures somehow profound enough to have made our way nearly to the verge of creation, even as we fly farther from it into a future governed by forces that are dark to us. I have read that there was a moment well into cosmic history when the expansion of the universe abruptly accelerated. I have read that its rate of acceleration continues to accelerate. This is at odds with expectation. Now we have antigravity to account for it, an explanation that would be more satisfying if we had any understanding of the nature of gravity. If over time the universe can change radically, then it can change again. The conditions now friendly to life on earth, since they seem to be rather finely calibrated, could shift a little and then the universe would be done with us, our vanishing no event at all as things are reckoned at these scales. There would be no one to attempt a reckoning, no one to speak the word "event." Light would be darkness without eyes to see it, I suppose, but, in the nature of the case, this would be a matter of no consequence. Our brilliance has shown us grounds for utter humility. We could vanish into the ether like a breath, leaving nothing behind to say who we were, even that we were. No doubt we will vanish in fact, mere transients in a cosmos that will realize itself over eons.

How astonishing that we know this.

My particular saint, John Calvin, says that our brilliance, our inventiveness, our imagination, our need to understand the movements of the stars and the planets, are unmistakable proofs of the existence of the soul. He says that in descending into ourselves we find God, we being the products of such exquisite workmanship. In his praise of humankind, of God therefore, he makes no distinction between the body's intricacy and adeptness and the mind's or soul's agility and fluency. He treats them as one thing. Then there is the other side, of course, our thoroughgoing sinfulness. Some people are shocked by this. I am ready to grant an overwhelming bias toward error in human affairs, though most of what I know about human fecklessness and brutality I have learned from the newspaper and from history books. Calvin's sense of human depravity, however honestly come by, is by far the most conventional aspect of his thought. He is unique, so far as I can tell, in rescuing out of the general ruin the whole human being, body, mind, and spirit. He is unique in evoking a sense of the soul that is more than a better self, more than a diaphanous second presence that will enjoy or endure the eternal consequences of our temporal life. He describes an embodied soul realizing itself in human thoughts, even in dreams. He sanctifies the best pleasures of existence, from the work of our hands to our dazzling senses to the heroic aspirations of our sciences, our learning and inquiring. For him the spiritual is intrinsic to the temporal, a present pleasure, most felt when we do anything that amazes us as an exercise of the God-given brilliance that we take for granted or that we might have left untried. And the concept "soul" allows us to acknowledge the richness and variety of the experience of the self. Robust old Martin Luther wrote, "My conscience is a lady and a queen."

This is the soul as experience. It is also for Calvin the place or mode of encounter of the soul with God, sanctification of another order. All this is relevant to current debates about the soul, which are based on that notion of the diaphanous second self which really cannot be discovered in any special region of the brain, just as all the skeptics tell us. I remember reading an article once about starfish. They were thought to have no eyes. Then it was discovered that they were all eyes, that their bodies were entirely covered with visual receptors, and that the simple-looking creature somehow integrates a mass of sensation. A more considered understanding of the soul, as an experience that I think we do share, would put an end to these mystifications about its physical locus.

I'm often surprised by the literalism of rationalist and even scientific belief in the physical as a unique category, and as one whose norms and predictabilities, however localized, have an authority out of all proportion to their place even in the cosmos we know. And this is apparently about 4 percent of the cosmos we may reasonably infer. I will not pause here over unexpressed dimensions and multiple and successive universes, though the possibility of their existence only reinforces my point. What we experience as physical reality is profoundly untypical of physical reality. Human experience is the central factor here. We can know that we are part and parcel of the universe at large, that great storm of energy. From the soles of our feet to our worst idea, from a Beethoven sonata to Yankee Stadium, nothing can be accounted for in any other terms. Yet we can never really believe it. We could all go to school to Heraclitus.

I have called it a storm, but there is a profound order or predictability in the whole fabric of it. Whatever atoms are, certain of their properties and combinations can be described. There are other constancies, which we call laws and forces. I take the Jamesian view, that what we know about anything is determined by the way we encounter it, and therefore we should never assume that our knowledge of anything is more than partial. If this principle applies to reality at the smallest scales that are so far accessible to us, it most emphatically applies to the stratum of reality that we consider familiar. A number of times I have read or heard from the scientists and the rationalists that the brain is a piece of meat. This being true of the brain, then the brain/mind, the mind/soul, are degraded or dismissed by their being revealed in their actual, brutish nature. But why limit this insight to the brain? The entire human person is meat, except where it is bone, no enhancement. If it is reasonable to say the brain is meat, it is reasonable on the same grounds, the next time you look into a baby carriage, to compliment the mother on her lovely little piece of meat. I could as reasonably say that pieces of meat come to my classes, sit in the chairs, and gaze at me with something that looks for all the world like interest or indifference. Whatever else might be said of these living hams and chops and ribs, they seem to bore easily. Speak this way a few times, and your dearest friends might start whispering words like "sociopathic" and "psychopathic." There might be murmurs about intervention. My point is simply that there is nothing reasonable about speaking of the brain as meat when it is equally and in the same way true of the whole person. Abraham Lincoln was meat, and so was John Wilkes Booth. If it is meaningless to say this, if nothing that distinguishes them is conveyed when it is said, and the brain/mind is already disqualified from making the difference between them, then by my lights the whole notion is reduced to absurdity.

More to the point, what is meat? Complex life. And what is that? The universe's greatest mystery. It is meat that sings and flies and fledges, meat that makes civilizations and pulls them down. It is probably an error to localize intelligence in the brain too exclusively, but it is no more reasonable to doubt what it does on the grounds that it is an organ than to doubt that the lungs oxygenate the blood or that the eyes see. And what does the brain do? It orchestrates the functioning of the body, and it learns, weighs, imagines, designs, devises theories and rationalizes them, among other things. But the mother of the baby to whom you paid your rationalistic compliment would not be offended because you seemed to undervalue meat. My students would not defend themselves from my scientific view of them by insisting on the complexity of the nervous system. What is weirdly absent from all this is a sense of the human, and even, for that matter, of the animal. It is a pointed exclusion of what we simply know, of what is manifestly true. Reductionist definitions of humankind are radically inadequate. They are not made scientific by the putting out of account of the very qualities that make our inquiries into ourselves interesting, or even possible.

Calvin's approach is more scientific. He says we should be amazed by our very toenails, should find them a synecdoche for a brilliance in which we participate, which in the mere functioning of our bodies and minds we express and enact. Einstein said that time is man's most persistent illusion. With all respect, I would suggest that our great illusion is in fact stasis, solidity. Time flows one way, gravity is much weaker than it ought to be—existence as we know it depends entirely on these anomalies. And why does the reality that contains us cohere as it does, given that it is and can only be of one substance with that primal storm I mentioned earlier? What strange nexus is this that has let us feel becalmed? We look out at the collisions of galaxies and are amazed. We should be more amazed that our cities stand, our bodies pass through maturity and aging, our selves are rooted in and derive from a past that cannot be evaded and is nowhere to be found.

Look at Mars, a planet that is at present dead. Once water flowed there, apparently. But now it seems fair enough to call it a lump of stasis. It falls decisively within the range of things our perceptions tell us are solid. Then look at Earth, teeming and swarming, full of embodied life that, yes, we can see and touch, nourish, injure. Everything that exists or happens within our cocoon of atmosphere is altogether physical, if we give the word "physical" its proper meaning. As the word is used casually, ordinarily, inexactly, it means only what is accessible to our senses. But our senses select arbitrarily. Is space a void or a substance? This is debated. If antimatter should cross the little margin of relative scarcity that allows matter to exist, Being would be gone in the blink of an eye, solid Mars extinct as the dream I might have had the next night. But who has any conception of antimatter? These are conditions for the existence of everything we call physical, and we don't know what they are. Like the word "human," the word "physical" carries an implicit modifier that conditions its meaning—"merely" human, "merely" physical. It is absolutely medieval, downright pre-Copernican, to isolate the world we know from the heavens as we know them to be. Creation can only be altogether one phenomenon, ourselves included. Taken down to its essence, it is energy, whatever that is.

The brain as an object is less readily conceived of in these essential terms than is perception or thought, which are swift and transactional. Patient matter accommodates them, so to speak, and that is the marvel here. Renaissance writers argued that we human beings participate in the universe profoundly, precisely in our thinking, knowing, imagining. Certainly there can be no grounds for isolating these phenomena, which are almost the whole of our experience, from any model of reality. This is especially true if the isolating is done on the basis of a strikingly primitive conception of reality, one which is itself in service to a conclusion that precludes the kind of data that would call it into question. This refusal to be alive to the character of manifest life produces all sorts of absurdities. Where did an idea come from? Someone else had it first. Where did he get it? From someone else. And he? Maybe from Persia, which is another way of saying, from someone else. It seems that the genealogy of ideas must go back to Adam. Or might it be that ideas arise in living brains, meaty things that they are? Thought, memory, language, art, mores are all subtle, fluid within imperceptible and mutable constraints. We can no more generate ideas that are strictly our own than we can acquire ideas without making them our own. These complexities more nearly resemble the volatile and orderly substance of Being than they do the fortuitous accretions of matter that present themselves to the capacities of our senses.

My point is simply that the distinction, which is still very sharply drawn, between the physical and the nonphysical, is an important error, understandable in 1400 but inexcusable now. It has spiritualized the soul out of meaningful existence and de-spiritualized the world into an object of contempt at worst, or, more typically, a thing defined by its difference from anything called spiritual, which includes, as I have said, almost everything that is distinctively human. It is usual to blame Descartes for mind-body dualism, which is odd, since he identifies thought, the experience of consciousness, as the one thing that can be proved to be real. Beginning there, the reality of any other thing can be proved or disproved. His object is to find a sound starting place for scientific inquiry at large. And where else do we begin in fact? Disliking subjectivity will never make it go away.

Here is an idea that would make Descartes blanch. Apparently, there are scientists who believe that at some point fairly soon we will be able to upload our minds to computers, freeing ourselves from our bodies, being, therefore, immortal. I suppose they will program in the virtual experience of taking the uploaded dog on a walk to the virtual park, through the rain on randomly assorted virtual days adjusted to reflect prevailing weather patterns in some selected place and season. These immortals would at last be free of the thousand natural shocks that flesh is heir to, and with them no doubt of all urgent reflection on what we are and what we mean. I can't help imagining that, given the sterility of it all, the sullens would set in and these uploaded minds would do what many of their creators do—devise ingenious viruses, spy on one another, refine resentments, contrive schemes to dupe the mortals. Then physical reality, let us say a great solar storm, the impact of a meteor, even a major war, would sweep them all away, making the always necessary point that, for our purposes, the physical is not to be transcended. In any case, an uploaded mind would be as void of soul as a cryogenically frozen body. We know this intuitively.

If we think of the human person with all her senses and faculties participating in reality equally—and isn't the reality of a thing an absolute, yes or no judgment about it, which sets everything to which it is granted on an equal ontological footing?—then we cannot put anything out of account in our attempt to define or explain her. Is error real? We all feel its effects every day. What about malice, ignorance, falsehood? They are mighty powers in this world. And, as it happens, we, humankind, have a monopoly where such things are concerned. Our brilliance can go very wrong. The old intuition that every life is or ought to be a moral contest is sound, given that the so-called real-world consequences of our thoughts and actions can be very grave. And, in a wholly real way, they accumulate, and they compound themselves. We can be trapped for generations in a frightful misapprehension, or we can be swept up in a terrible lie. Prisons and pogroms are secondary consequences of these potent untruths. So a great reality must be conceded to these anomalies of human thought and behavior, if we are to understand ourselves at all. There may be other intelligent life in the universe. If there is, I wish it well. If there was, we may have had a great deal in common with it. But for now we must assume that we are unique, the quintessence of cosmic dust. Our self-love and our humility are two sides, or many sides, of one fact: We are in a very great degree the creators of the reality we inhabit.

Calvin has little to say about eternity. For him it is continuous with mortal time because the glory of God is shown to us here, and because God confronts us in our thoughts and circumstances and in every image of God that we encounter, fallen as we are, and they are. This perspective is useful to me, a good discipline. There is much talk of judgment in Western tradition, and little acknowledgment of the primary character of judgment, that is, revelation. It is no departure from tradition or orthodoxy, only a shift of emphasis, to say that, granting a Day of the Lord, we will learn what we have been and what we are, against the standard of grace and true righteousness, of which we have had no more than inklings, and in the light of a fullness of Being from which it has been our nature to withhold ourselves. Surely no skeptic could doubt that a sound intuition lies behind the recognition of a profounder moral reality than any we have attained to. Grant it reality in an ontological sense—is there another one?—and there are important interpretive consequences, cosmologically speaking.

In any case, a great deal depends, perhaps our humanity depends, on our sensing and acknowledging that quality in our kind we call the soul. The soul is a universal and unalienable sacredness. It confers the dignity of a great competence that reaches far beyond the self and its necessities. There is a poem by Vachel Lindsay I memorized as a schoolgirl—"Let not young souls be smothered out before / They do quaint deeds and fully flaunt their pride. / It is the world's one crime." No, it isn't. But it is one of our gravest crimes, massing now to impoverish the future in ways we will never know to name. But the souls we let our theories and our penuries frustrate are souls still, and, if Jesus is to be trusted, they will be our judges, they are now our judges. Clearly I am very much influenced by the parable of the great judgment in the twenty-fifth chapter of Matthew.

•

Lately I have been watching ghosts—the ghost of the young Olivier playing a wistful and inward and elegant Hamlet, the ghost of the old Olivier playing a Lear mightily bemused by mortality. And, most movingly, I have seen the ghost of the lithe young prince in the eyes of the age-ruined king. How remarkable it is that we can summon these spirits, head to foot as they lived, perfect in every gesture and inflection. All our best art is the art of conjurers, calling up likenesses, inviting recognition, their praise and vindication being that they may have made something true to life. The actor playing an actor weeps for Hecuba. And we will weep for Hamlet, for everything we recognize in Hamlet. So slight a thing as a thought can assume weight and dimension through so slight a thing as a word. Great meaning can be contoured by a glance. This in the earthy atmosphere we all breathe, the here and now. It is elusive to us, like other great realities, like time and space and gravity. And it is the haunt of souls. We know who might look up at us from any injury we do or allow to be done. A soul, in its untouchable authority. It is an authority made good, Jesus tells us, when the Son of Man appears in his glory—that same son of man who has appeared to each of us a thousand times in the raiment of sorrow and need. The same son of man who has done us ten thousand kindnesses we have not noticed to acknowledge. The same son of man who moves our hearts to kindness, when we are moved.

Some of us have believed that a treasury of merit, in the gift of a church, can compensate for our failures and our deficiencies, our sins. Some of us have believed that only divine grace, in the gift of God, can make good our shortcomings. But what does any of this mean? Does it mean that the grand cosmos is so ordered that in the best case some of us might 'scape whipping? This does not seem to me to reflect well on the Creator. And granting the magnificence of Creation, which we have hardly begun to comprehend, and our extraordinary place in it, surely it is all about more than these traditional preoccupations encourage us to think. I do believe we blaspheme when we wrong or offend another human being. And I understand that, over the millennia, this continuous, often outrageous blaspheming has put a vast, unspent stress on the order of things. But the other side of this same reality is the great fact that human beings *are* sacred things whom it is *indeed* blasphemy to wrong. Only think what we are, *then* why God might have a fondness for us. Think that God is loyal to us, and then what, in ultimate terms, we must be. I have no problem with the word "sin." I think it is one of our most brilliant evasions to have associated sin so strongly with sexuality that we can be coy about it, or narrowly obsessed with it, or we can dismiss it as a synonym for prudery, as we go on hating and reviling, as we go on grinding the faces of the poor. We alone among the animals can sin—one of our truly notable distinctions. Or, to put it another way—we are the only creatures who are, in principle if seldom in fact, morally competent. Responsible, or at least answerable.

•

There is a sense in which the life of Jesus reiterates the implication of God in Creation. So when I read about apocalypse I cannot think of it otherwise than as an epochal moment in the life of the living God. I know this statement is full of problems. In the nature of things there is an awkwardness in applying time-bound language to the eternal, and yet that is the problem God gives us in making himself known to us, if we assume that there is a God and that he is indeed mindful of us. The word "time" is a problem in itself. Creation did not exist and then it did, emerging out of and into what greater reality God knows. At a particular moment Jesus came into the world. And at some particular hour when we least expect it, a veil will be lifted and there will be an ending and a beginning, creation purged, healed, and renewed, afterward forever in a new and right relationship to God, who so loves the world. The clocks will stop, and we will find ourselves on the threshold of the everlasting. There is an ambiguous relationship between judgment and revelation, which has caused us to put the emphasis in the wrong place, that is, on judgment. Divine judgment implies a true and absolute understanding of the nature of transgression, which would be a great revelation, certainly. Grace itself, if it is nontrivial, must also have its meaning with a final recognition of what has been at stake here. For this reason Jesus is, from birth to death, a figure of judgment, an apocalyptic figure. And, therefore, so, by the grace of God, are we all.

Here is a question: If the soul is embodied, how does it survive the death of the body? Well, if the human self is information, as the talk of computer-mediated immortality seems to assume, and if information cannot pass out of the universe, as I read elsewhere, then presto! we have a theory—which I do not credit for a moment. My point is simply that finding the true boundaries of credibility is not nearly so easy for us moderns as it has been thought to be by previous generations. For myself, I have no more to say on the subject than that the resurrected Jesus let Thomas touch his wounds. If substance is only energy in a particular state, then the opposition of soul and body is a false opposition, and our passing through nature to eternity a different thing than we imagine. Suppose that the body is more wonderful than it is frail or flawed or full of appetites. The hairs on our heads are numbered, after all. We might be tempted to think of Paradise as a place where language would be unneeded since everything would be known. Doubt would be extinct, goodness would lack the shading of darker possibilities. We know ourselves in struggles and temptations, and what would remain of our selves if these were no longer the terms of our existence? Something more interesting, no doubt, some purer discovery of what a self might be. Perhaps we could trust God that far—to give us a heaven better than earth—if we really did value human beings enough to believe *he* values them.

I share Calvin's view, that this world is what God gives us to know, that our thoughts about eternity can never rise above speculation. So we are certain to distract and mislead ourselves. The rest really *is* silence. If we think of the other potentialities for Being we are aware of now, and the degree to which our present reality is arbitrarily constituted, first in itself and then because of the limits of our knowledge and our means of knowing, it is not hard to imagine that another reality might be, for our purposes, inarticulable. I am speaking metaphorically here. I do not want to saddle science with theology. My meaning is simply that while science has shown us our powers, it has also shown us our limitations. Try to find a book on quantum theory that does not begin with a confession of bewilderment. And quantum theory is an account of the ways of the reality we inhabit and feel we know. My point is not that our thinking should be formed by contemporary science, but that it should *not* be formed, as it has been, by primitive and discredited ideas, whether scientific or commonsensical. Cynics mock the notions that hover around immortality, and as usual they have a point.

Speculation about the afterlife has had a very long history. It has in some cases become dogma, or else commonplace, which is more fixed than dogma. Pagan sky gods would feel at home in some precincts of it. Understandably, it has been a projection of this world minus time, earthly grandeur much aggrandized. Rest and plenty and companionship with Jesus and with those one has loved—however these might be changed in new circumstances, in essence we might recognize them because God loves and God provides and God has put his particular blessing on rest. These graces are elements of present life, or they can be. If we construct beyond this point, we have impossibilities to deal with. How can the dead live again? We will see. Why should they live again, motley and cantankerous as they have been for the most part? Because God values them. And he is the God not of the dead but of the living.

Still loyal, even to our dust? What is there to conclude, then, but that in ways we cannot conceive, we are very wonderful? Imagine that we find ourselves restored, and our friends, and our enemies, and those so blighted and neglected that all their beauty had been only God's to enjoy. Souls. A heaven of souls. We know something of what this might mean if we have ever loved anyone, and we would know more if we loved more. The kingdom of God is among us.

SON OF ADAM, SON OF MAN

Existence is remarkable, actually incredible. At least tacitly, awareness of this fact is as prevalent in contemporary science as it is in the Book of Psalms, the Book of Job. Those who follow such things will be aware, for example, that reputable scientists can hypothesize other universes where beings precisely ourselves live out other lives, or where our consciousness subsists immortally. Our reality might in fact be a hologram. Contemporary physics permits and indulges extravagant notions of the possible, many of them quite beautiful. There is no need to credit any of these theories in order to reject the claims of the old commonsensical science to have discredited the Christian mythos, which is actually rather restrained by comparison with them, loyal as it is to what might be called a sacred thesis concerning the origins and the nature of things. Implausibility, a word that needs looking into, no longer affords reasonable grounds for rejecting this grand statement about the place of humankind in the cosmos, this account of a grand enactment of human value. So I have returned to the original language of my faith, crediting its Word as meaningful in the very fact that it is aloof from paraphrase. I accept it as one among the great givens to be encountered in experience, that is, as a thing that presents itself, reveals itself, always partially and circumstantially, accessible to only tentative apprehension, which means that it is always newly meaningful. In this it is like everything else, but much more so.

The human sense of the sacred is a fact. Like mathematics or human selfhood, its existence is not to be reasoned to by way of positivist or materialist premises. It is a given, a powerful presence, whose reality it is perverse to deny on the basis of a model of reality constructed around its exclusion. Granted, a million complications follow from giving primacy to Christianity, even assuming there is reasonable consensus around the meaning of that word. A million complications follow from imputing value to religion indiscriminately. Nevertheless, to avoid these problems is to close off the possibility of exploring any religion, here Christianity, deeply, in its own terms. In what follows I propose that certain Christian tenets that have been challenged and devalued should be considered again.

I have taken my title from the genealogy in the Book of Luke. Son of Adam, that is, of man, and Son of God are profoundly resonant phrases for Christianity, which have become over time virtual synonyms for each other and for the figure we call the Christ. Their appearance here, in Luke's genealogy, should remind us that they address the matter of sonship, literal descent, which was central to messianic tradition before Jesus. And they transform it.

Both Matthew and Luke acknowledge the difficulties involved in satisfying the expectations of their culture that the Messiah should be identified by, among other things, his having a place in a particular line of human descent.

(Perhaps I should say here that when I say "Matthew," "Mark," or "Luke" I mean the text that goes by that name. I adapt the *sola scriptura* to my own purposes, assuming nothing beyond the meaningfulness of forms, recurrences, and coherences within and among the Gospels, at the same time acknowledging that different passions and temperaments distinguish one text from another. I have solemnly forbidden myself all the forms of evidence tampering and deck stacking otherwise known as the identification of interpolations, omissions, doublets, scribal errors, et alia, on the grounds that they are speculation at best, and distract the credulous, including their practitioners, with the trappings and flourishes of esotericism. I hope my own inevitable speculations are clearly identified as such.)

When Christianity made dogma of the virgin birth, it seems to me, with all respect, to have put the emphasis in the wrong place. In the matter of improbability, conception in the Virgin Mary is not categorically different from conception in ninety-year-old Sarah. Is anything too hard for God? The astounding claim, from a scriptural point of view, and the claim that is secured by the virginity of Mary, is that God is indeed, in some literal sense, Jesus' father. The circumstances of his birth have an importance to early writers far beyond any credibility the Christian narrative is assumed to derive from their miraculous character, especially weighed against the skepticism they aroused even in antiquity, and beyond their placing Jesus in the series of improbable births that recur in Scripture, from Isaac to John the Baptist. Throughout biblical history, epochal lives had begun from two parents as well. So to be a second and greater Moses or David or Elijah would not require this singular, extraordinary birth. While Luke draws attention to God's fatherhood of the whole of humankind, the special case of the divine paternity of Jesus means for these writers that he is himself God, and that he participates profoundly in human life without any compromise of his divine nature. This is an extraordinary statement about the nature of human life. The role of Mary, notably her virginity, has been interpreted in ways that have caused anxieties about the flesh, and reifications and disparagements of it. These are anxieties the Incarnation, to my arch-Protestant mind, should properly allay. Granting that our physical life is fragile and easily abused, precisely on these grounds it craves and should not be denied the whole blessing of Jesus' participation in it.

•

Incarnation, Resurrection—where do these ideas come from? It is almost a commonplace that Paul invented Christianity. Paul is often said to have imposed a massive conceptual superstructure on the life and death of a good man, perhaps a holy man, who would not himself have dealt in these daunting abstractions. Then what was the character of the movement that was already active before the Gospels were written, even before Paul's conversion? We can catch some glimpses of it. In his Letter to the Philippians, Paul is generally taken to have been quoting a hymn when he holds up to them the example of Christ, who surrendered "equality with God" and "emptied himself, taking the form of a servant, being born in the likeness of men." To be able to allude to a hymn implies a community that knows and values the hymn, which in turn implies a stable culture, however small. The Gospel writers might have known this hymn, or one like it. From Jesus' birth to his exaltation it tells the story they tell. The Gospel writers can evoke at the same time a figure so persuasively human that his life seems sufficient in itself, without any reference to his transcendence. This means that his Incarnation, his life on earth, was real. Theologically speaking, this is a crucial point.

The "messianic secret," concealed by the veil of flesh that obscured Jesus' character and meaning from his contemporaries and followers, was of course no secret at all to the Gospel writers or to the primitive church. The truth of Jesus' nature and role was the point of the telling, withheld in the narrative, to the extent that it is, because Jesus would not have been understood even by his disciples if he had revealed it earlier than he did. His reticence permitted him in his life and his death to give new content to an expectation that had been mulled for generations. The story is so familiar to us now that we can forget how strange it would have sounded in anticipation of Resurrection and Pentecost, before the meaning of death was transformed, and while the emergence in the larger world of the movement to be called Christianity was hardly to be imagined.

It would be interesting to know when or by what means these writers came into possession of the stories of his birth. It is an extraordinary achievement on the part of the writers that they make the full revelation of his epochal meaning simultaneous with his rejection and death. To the extent that there was secrecy involved—yes, Jesus forbids even the fact of his healings to be revealed, though they clearly became widely known, and yes, he forbids the disciples to reveal who he is, as they finally begin to understand—still, it is hard not to hear rueful amusement in his reply, when John sends messengers to Jesus to find out whether he is the one who is to come, or they must wait for another. The blind see, the lame walk, good news is preached to the poor. Jesus seems to have been healing people in meaningful numbers. Yet he remained among them as a son of man in the usual sense, someone to be betrayed for a little money, denied by friends, abused by authorities, and killed with approval of a mob. This seems remarkable, objectively speaking. But it is consistent with his being merely a man. His "secrecy," which he intends but which still seems largely the effect of the blindness of human eyes and hardness of human hearts, appears meant to cast off all the protections and immunities that might come with his claiming special status. Everyone abused and martyred since the world began should have been able to claim special status, of course, if there is anything to the idea that we are children of God. In his life the man Jesus shows us what we are, sacred and terrible.

•

What did the ancient church take from these earliest teachings, those reflected by the hymn in Philippians? In his homilies on the letters of Paul to the Corinthians, expounding on Jesus' saying "the Son of man came not to be served but to serve," John Chrysostom says that if this service of love "were everywhere in abundance, how great benefits would ensue: how there were no need then of laws, or tribunals or punishments, or avenging, or any other such things since if all loved and were beloved, no man would injure another. Yea, murders, and strifes, and wars, and divisions, and rapines, and frauds, and all evils would be removed, and vice unknown even in name." And "if this were duly observed, there would be neither slave nor free, neither ruler nor ruled, neither rich nor poor, neither small nor great." There is a tendency, I think, to suppose that the earliest Christians were drawn primarily by this new cult's seeming to offer a charm against death. That this idea is taken seriously is an effect of the ebbing away of Christian thought properly so called, together with the anthropologizing of religion. There is no doubt some justice in the fact that condescensions once projected onto distant cultures are now brought home to discredit the historic center of Western civilization. It is important to remember the beauty in the old dream of a world reconciled to God and itself, here through the figure of the selfless servant. Chrysostom had Christian Scriptures, of course, as Paul did not. But he would have been speaking to congregations more like Paul's than any we can imagine, people who would have known the stigma of servitude and poverty, and the harshness and turbulence of ancient life. In their best moments such people were clearly worthy to shape the faith. It is moving to think how servants and slaves must have felt, hearing their lot and their labors proposed as the pattern of a sacred life, and as a force that could transform the world. It is moving as well that others, free, prosperous, even aristocratic, were drawn by such preaching.

•

Certain expectations needed to be addressed if Jesus was to be understood as Messiah, this is to say, if he was to be understood as the fulfillment of God's promises to his people. The Gospel writers' claims for Jesus of Nazareth are based on or expressed in the faith that he did not proceed from any paternal line. This complicates the matter of conventional patrilineal genealogy, which would be assumed to trace the Messiah's origins to David. They address the matter boldly, argumentatively, making no concessions, and in terms that are full of radical meaning. Matthew begins with "an account of the genealogy of Jesus the Messiah, the son of David, the son of Abraham." But what we find, if the word is given its conventional sense, is a genealogy of Joseph, who, as Matthew points out immediately and establishes at length, is not the father of Jesus. The genealogy might be read as a claim of royal descent which has passed into obscurity after the monarchy itself is destroyed, so that an ordinary carpenter might share the blood of kings. But again, except by a kind of ascribed status, no claim made through Joseph is presented as bearing on Jesus. This might mean that, though the argument by lineage for his being Messiah could be made if it were simply conceded that Joseph was indeed his father, the truth of Jesus' origins, and therefore of his nature, is too essential to permit recourse to this very available expedient.

Matthew's genealogy might be considered a history of Israel itself, as it bears the marks of divine Providence, in the equivalence in human generations of the time that passes between the great events signified by the names Abraham and David and by the deportation to Babylon and, after them, by Jesus. Understood in this way, it does not defend the claims made for Jesus, but instead asserts them. Rather than arguing for an unbroken ancestral line, the writer punctuates the series by drawing attention to its signal moments, including the exile, which would be extraneous if the point were to document ancestry, but which is very relevant indeed if the point is to present Jesus as the next defining act of God toward Israel. Matthew transforms the biblical convention of genealogy, making explicit what had before been implicit, that these names and generations were not primarily significant for fixing the identities and claims and obligations of those who found a place in them, but as preserving a record of God's mindfulness of Israel over time, and of his acting toward them decisively through the lives of particular human beings. The otherwise rather surprising appearance in the list of Rahab and Tamar, both Canaanite women, of the Moabite Ruth, and of Bathsheba as "the wife of Uriah," is consistent with this reading, since each of them had a crucial part in the history of Israel.

It should be taken as an important consequence of Matthew's setting Jesus in this context that his humanity and his place in the history of Israel are both affirmed. At the same time, John the Baptist is quoted in Matthew as saying, "Do not presume to say to yourselves, 'We have Abraham as our father'; for I tell you, God is able from these stones to raise up children to Abraham." Luke contains very similar language: "Do not begin to say to yourselves, 'We have Abraham as our father'; for I tell you, God is able from these stones to raise up children to Abraham." In other words, so much for genealogy. If it is true no necessity makes it true that God acts in history in the ways recorded in these narratives of descent. This again addresses questions raised by the claim made by Jesus' followers that he had no human father, that he did not in any ordinary sense have a place in the line that proceeded from David. In Jesus God brushed away this web of contingency.

Luke famously departs in another way from conventional genealogy, moving from Jesus in the near term back through the generations to Adam, whom he calls "son of God." Like Matthew he traces the line of Joseph, though again like Matthew he is careful to stipulate that Joseph was only the putative father of Jesus, his father "as was thought." Luke's play on genealogy could be taken to dismiss altogether the practice of counting off the generations, except when the counting is exhaustive enough to acknowledge that all humankind are the children of Adam, therefore "made in the likeness of God," as in the preface to the first list of human generations in Genesis 5:2. This is so primary an article of faith that no tracing back through time would be needed on one hand or sufficient on the other to establish it. Again, so much for genealogy.

A saying that recurs in all three of the Synoptics is Jesus' quotation and interpretation of Psalm 110. In verse 4 this psalm invokes Melchizedek, the mysterious pagan priest who appears in Genesis to bless Abraham and receive a tithe from him. The text in Genesis gives Melchizedek no paternity and no age at death, departures that are taken to set him outside the mortal run of things, to make him, as the psalm says, "a priest forever." Jesus draws attention to the first words of the psalm, "The Lord says to my lord: 'Sit at my right hand, till I make your enemies your footstool,'" and asks, "If David thus calls him Lord, how is he his son?" In Matthew, this is his response to the reply of the Pharisees, whom he has asked, "What do you think of the Christ? Whose son is he?" If Jesus' meaning is that the Christ is greater than and other than even the great kings of Israel, it is notable that he makes this argument by rejecting the concept of messianic sonship, despite the attenuated claim made through Joseph in the two genealogies, and for Jesus, though only as he, like Abraham and David, has a place in the sacred history of Israel, or as he is a son of Adam.

•

Jesus' origin as son of God, shared, as Luke says, by Adam, makes ancestry moot and opens the way to universalism, the movement of the knowledge of God beyond the ethnic, cultural, and historical boundaries of its first revelation, to all those other children of Adam, to humankind. This movement was already taking place through the efforts of Paul and others before the Gospels were written. If this expansion into the world, epitomized in an astounding event at Pentecost and by the conversion and mission of Paul, seemed to the Evangelists to be a realization of Jesus' purpose and an expression of his nature, then it would follow that the teachings of Jesus in which it was anticipated would receive special emphasis in their recounting. The Gospels were written in light of the emergence of what came to be called Christianity, and subsequent to the events recounted in the Acts of the Apostles. If their writers took the spread of the faith to be the presence and work of the resurrected Christ—"Wherever two or three are gathered in my name, there am I also"—then of course every foreshadowing of it during his lifetime would seem essential to an understanding of him. Any account made of him before they had witness of his impact on the larger world would have been entirely premature.

There are those who worry because the Gospels were probably written decades after the death of Jesus, as if his mortal life were all that was relevant to questions of his nature and his meaning, which the passage of time could only obscure. But for his early followers, a flood of new meaning would have become apparent in the aftermath of his death. They would have other bases for interpreting what he did and said, and what his resurrection meant, which would, very reasonably, shape their telling of it. The Incarnation is, by itself, the great fact that gives every act and saying of Jesus the character of revelation. With the Resurrection, it is the grand and unique statement of the bond between history and cosmos. The disciples, the Temple authorities, and the general population can have had no notion of what was transpiring among them, unprecedented as it was. The Gospel writers and readers would know much more. They might know, for example, that people in distant cities were moved and changed by the vision expressed in the hymn in

Philippians, and might take it to be true that the Holy Spirit is at work in the emergence of the faith, and in its forming character. In light of such knowledge it would seem appropriate to assume, as they did, that the words and actions attributed to Jesus have a meaning unlike and in excess of virtue or wisdom or morality, chastisement or consolation, all of which would be the marks of teacher and prophet, all of which are temporal and will pass away.

•

We can assume, at a minimum, that there was indeed a historical Jesus of Nazareth, as there were a Thales of Miletus and a Pythagoras of Samos. Ancient teachers whose disciples attested to their teachings are numerous. We are in the habit of assuming the fragments that survive give us these philosophers, to the extent the accidents of transmission and loss will allow, granting that this extent cannot be reckoned. We have four accounts of the teachings and the life and death of Jesus, three of them largely consistent with one another. Their differences should surely be taken as evidence that they were the work of very human witnesses, receivers of the tradition and interpreters of it. God honors us with important work. And where they are similar, this might be taken as evidence of a particular emphasis and centrality in the teaching, whether explicit or implicit. If Karl Barth and Dietrich Bonhoeffer had been put in separate rooms and told to write from memory a fifty-page summary of the Gospels, their two versions would be alike in important respects and different in important respects. And both would be sound and valuable.

Many have questioned the reliability of the biblical narrative as history, therefore its credibility as the basis of belief. Like the genealogies in Matthew and Luke which dismiss genealogy, the Gospels might be said to testify against themselves in the fact of their unreconciled differences, at least when they are judged by the standards of the literary forms to which they are presumably compared. This kind of comparison itself raises questions, of course. The accounts of the life and death of the Persian Cyrus the Great vary markedly, and the tales of his abandonment in infancy and adoption by a herdsman certainly have the character of myth or folklore. Yet no one questions that there was indeed a Cyrus. He left a wake of consequence the mighty do leave, and records, and relics. Jesus, of course, had little status while he lived. Obscure as he was, it is notable, perhaps miraculous, that his life is attested at all. If we knew Cyrus only by ancient accounts of his life, there would be as good grounds for doubting his historical reality as for questioning the historicity of Jesus. The mythic elements in the tale of Cyrus' infancy are conventions that mark him out as no ordinary man, reflecting his historical importance. If the circumstances said to surround Jesus' birth are in fact retrojections of the same kind, they cannot reasonably be taken as casting doubt on his existence, though they very often are.

There are great differences between the accounts of origins of the Persian conqueror and the Jewish carpenter, one being that Jesus' birth and the circumstances of his life were of his own choosing. As Chrysostom says, "He took to himself a mother of low estate"—ironically, a prerogative no mere emperor could dream of. He fulfilled an exalted purpose in living and dying an obscure figure in a minor province. His birth was indeed humble, consecrated by the sacrifice of two pigeons. As a boy he impressed the elders in the Temple, but this did not bring him to a more elevated condition, as youthful kingliness is said to have done for Cyrus. He did not, like Oedipus, find his way to a destined role at odds with his apparent origins. If Jesus had become king of the Jews in the ordinary sense, his narrative would indeed follow this ancient paradigm very closely. Instead, in his truest nature, human and divine, he really was to be found among those who hungered and thirsted and were sick and in prison. If all the tales and myths and histories of greatness obscured and greatness revealed hover behind the Gospels, they are there to be overturned, with all the assumptions that give them currency in the human imagination. It is not alien to the divine nature to be aware of the stories we tell ourselves and to be articulate in their terms. After all, we live by stories, as God knows, and the books of Moses tell us. If we say Jesus explicitly and purposefully rejected the expectations, that is, the anticipated narrative, that had grown up around the promised Messiah, then against the background of these expectations his life takes on particular meaning. His self-characterization as a, as well as the, Son of Man, speaks precisely to this point.

In the Gospels the phrase "Son of Man" is spoken only by Jesus himself or is directly attributed to him as speech, in contexts that imply, whatever else, complex reference to himself. It is notable that, as often as he uses these words, no one else uses them to speak of Jesus or to him, not even the Gospel writers in passages of exposition. The Gospels also record as exclusive to Jesus the prefacing of statements with the word "amen." Together the preservation of these usages suggest care on the part of the writers and the tradition to respect the particularity of his speech and therefore, so far as possible, of his meaning as well. That is to say, the phrase "Son of Man" is retained without paraphrase or interpretation. Another pattern appears to me to have been remembered and preserved. In response to mention of God, the Son of God, or the Christ, Jesus replies with reference to the Son of Man, as if this image should always figure in any conception of holiness. In the nature of the case this occurs most frequently when recognition of Jesus as Christ begins to emerge as a question, later in the Gospels. So its context tends to be called apocalyptic, as if this adjective, without definition, by itself gave a sufficient account of his meaning. The richness of the phrase "Son of Man," the thousand suggestions in the fact that Jesus adopts it for himself, are lost if he is taken simply to be identifying himself with the anticipated figure of the Messiah.

It is notable also that the sayings of Jesus in which the phrase "Son of Man" appears are reported with a high degree of consistency from one Gospel to the next, though the sequence and the immediate contexts in which these sayings occur can differ markedly. I take this to suggest that they are something ipsissima verba, remembered as teachings with special authority, of greater interest to his tradition than the particulars of circumstance, perhaps even tacitly interpreted by the context in which they are placed by individual writers. A documentary theory that implies dependency on written texts to account for their stability within these significant variations would require a good deal of inelegant splicing. If there were sayings collections behind the Gospels that were written as well as oral, as I assume there were, it would still be remarkable that only Jesus uses this phrase, which is, in its ordinary meaning, perfectly commonplace, meaning simply a man, a human being. He spoke the language of his time and people, in awareness of the associations particular words and phrases acquired, through scriptural contexts and their elaborations, and in the streets as well. In the ordinary course of things, embedded as they were in centuries of use, their senses would interact. It is surely among the mysteries of Incarnation that Jesus could take on human language as well as human flesh, and that he could find it suited to his uses. The problem, if that is the word, of putting divine utterance into plain language gives particular interest to a phrase he turned to frequently, as he did to the phrase "Son of Man." If we grant that it is Christ we are speaking of, then we must be struck by his insistence on just this phrase.

The phrase had, of course, an extraordinary meaning, drawn from Ezekiel and Daniel, later elaborated in the extrabiblical 1 Enoch. I note here that this is a slender basis for establishing its meaning when Jesus used it. It is usual to say that in apocalyptic writings the Son of Man, or "one like a son of man," appears in the last days. But this seems not to be what disciples hear when Jesus says these words. Seemingly they would be readier, if not better able, to interpret his presence and his teaching if they did hear it. Or they would have taken it up as a title, or at least have pondered it, asked him about it, if the apocalyptic associations of the phrase seemed to be important from the perspective of Jesus' contemporaries. Scholarship tends to see in the Gospels the appropriation of this language by their writers or the early church for messianic uses. I suppose this could account for its being unassimilated into the narrative. But the fact that the phrase is so distinctively Jesus' could as well mean that it is Jesus himself who makes the appropriation, from vernacular speech as much as from Scripture, giving the phrase a meaning that is in fact not wholly prepared in Scripture or apocalyptic. This reading is no more speculative than others. I assume that Jesus was, at very least, a man of unusual gifts. If Shakespeare's language is not exhaustively anticipated by his precursors and contemporaries, there is no reason to assume that the language of Jesus must be.

•

It is striking that the writer of the Letter to the Hebrews interprets the phrase not in the context usually called apocalyptic, but as it occurs in Psalm 8, "What is man that Thou art mindful of him, and the son of man [here *Adam*] that thou visitest him?" The writer of Hebrews says, "It has been testified somewhere," then quotes the psalm at length. About the writer's suppression of the name of David as the psalmist, Calvin says, "Doubtless he says *one*, or some one, not in contempt but for honour's sake, designating him as one of the prophets or a renowned writer." If this is an instance of tact, it is consistent with the fact that discretion in Scripture can reflect a special veneration, as for example in respecting usages unique to Jesus. Calvin says that for various reasons in Hebrews, Psalm 8 "seems to be unfitly applied to Christ." He concludes, "The meaning of David is this,—'O Lord, thou hast raised man to such dignity, that it differs but little from divine or angelic honour; for he is set a ruler over the whole world.' This meaning the Apostle did not intend to overthrow, nor to turn to something else; but he only bids us to consider the abasement of Christ, which appeared for a short time, and then the glory with which he is perpetually crowned; and this he does more by alluding to expressions than by explaining what David understood." The writer of Hebrews says, "He who sanctifies and those who are sanctified have all one origin. That is why he is not ashamed to call them brethren." This comes shortly after an extraordinarily exalted account of the nature of Jesus, "through whom also he [God] created the world," and who "reflects the glory of God and bears the very stamp of his nature, upholding the universe by his word of power." If the psalm is considered as being helpful to an understanding of Christ in his humanity then human nature and circumstance are its primary subject. This makes it only more fitly applied to Christ, whose humanity gives extraordinary power to the question "What is man?"

It is at this point that this discussion has meaning beyond *explication de texte*. "What is man?" can be translated without loss into certain other questions—What are we? What am I? In order to broach the matter in the plainest terms, let us say for just a moment that in our addressing it God is not a given. There is no disputing the fact that we human beings have abilities not found in other animals, for example, the ability to split atoms. While this is factually true of very few of us, generations of thought and experiment, and the material wealth we create as civilizations, have enabled those few. So their achievements are in a sense communal. We can preserve and transmit learning and technique with amazing efficiency, for weal and woe. Our brilliance manifests itself in forms that are moving and beautiful, which does not alter the fact that we are a clear and present danger to ourselves, and to every creeping thing that creepeth on the face of the earth. This is an inversion of the dominion over the earth celebrated in the psalm, but dominion nevertheless, in its most radical sense. In other words, we are fully as exceptional as the psalmist would have us believe. There is something inversely godlike in our potential de-creation of the biosphere.

The fact, or at least the degree, of human exceptionalism is often disputed. In some quarters it is considered modest and seemly for us to take our place among the animals, conceptually speaking—to acknowledge finally the bonds of kinship evolution implies. Yet, in view of our history with regard to the animals, not to mention our history with one another, it seems fair to wonder if the beasts, given a voice in the matter, would not feel a bit insulted by our intrusion. History is the great unfinished portrait of old Adam. In the very fact of having a history we are unique. And when we look at it we are astonished. Only in myth or nightmare could another such creature be found. What a thing is man.

Say, however, that God *is* a given, the God of the psalmist and of Jesus. Then it is possible to claim a dignity for humankind that is assured because it is bestowed on us, that is, because it is beyond even our formidable powers to besmirch and destroy. Say that the one earthly thing God did not put under our feet was our own essential nature. The one great corrective to our tendency toward depredation would be a recognition of our abiding sacredness, since we are both, and often simultaneously, victim and villain. The divine image in us, despite all, is an act of God, immune to our sacrilege, apparent in the loveliness that never ceases to shine out in incalculable instances of beauty and love and imagination that make the dire assessment of our character, however solidly grounded in our history and our prospects, radically untrue.

It is not uncommon for those who are respectful of Christianity and eager to rescue some part of it from the assaults of rational skepticism to say Jesus was a great man, and no more than a man. A teacher, a martyr to intolerance, from whom we might learn compassion. He is defined in terms of an equivalence, his mystery anchored to what is assumed to be a known value. But what *is* man? What does it mean to say, as the Gospel writers say and insist, that Jesus was indeed a human being? What we are remains a very open question. Perhaps some part of the divine purpose in the Incarnation of this Son of Man was and is to help us to a true definition.

LIMITATION

There is an element of the arbitrary in our experience of life on earth—nonsymmetrical time, weak gravity, and the physical properties of matter that are artifacts of the scale at which we perceive. Out of such things is constructed a reality sufficient to our flourishing, even while we are immersed in a greater reality whose warp and woof are profoundly unlike anything we experience. I am drawn to Calvin's description of this world as a theater, with the implication that a strong and particular intention is expressed in it, that its limits, its boundedness, are meant to let meaning be isolated out of the indecipherable weather of the universe at large. A flicker of energy in the great void may dissipate in those oceans, but a flicker of energy in the small space of a human brain interacts with a mind's history, expresses and changes a human self. It can mean insight or delusion, and they in turn can mean compassion or hostility, with consequences well beyond that self. Old John Locke understood the power that comes with constraint. Having proposed that all thought or perception is based on four simple ideas, he said,

> Nor let anyone think these [simple ideas] too narrow bounds for the capacious mind of man to expatiate in,

> which takes its flight further than the stars, and cannot be confined by the limits of the world; that extends its thoughts often even beyond the utmost expansion of Matter, and makes excursion into that incomprehensible Inane . . . Nor will it be so strange to think these few simple ideas sufficient to employ the quickest thought, or largest capacity; and to furnish the materials of all that various knowledge, and more various fancies and opinions of all mankind, if we consider how many words may be made out of the various composition of twenty-four letters . . .

Reading the thought of the seventeenth and eighteenth centuries makes one aware of the detour the next centuries took away from the true path of modern thought. Locke would be interested to know what we can do with 0 and 1, what nature does with A, C, G, and T. Locke makes the point beautifully that our limits are entirely consistent with our transcending them, and so it is with limitation itself wherever it occurs in this strangely constructed world. In effect limitation could be understood as leverage, a highly efficient multiplier of possibility that creates and gives access to our largest capacities. This would no doubt seem a mighty paradox, if we were not so thoroughly accustomed to the truth of it.

Here is another paradox. Positivist assumptions and methods, which seem to bring stringent standards to bear on every question, actually obliterate the kind of boundaries that are necessary to meaningful inquiry into any but the most rudimentary questions. The great and ancient axiom that a negative cannot be proved has no standing with them, because it is at odds with a notion of proof that arises out of their model of reality and reinforces it. They can say, for example, that a historical Jesus did not exist. They can say that, though he may have existed, he did not teach the things attributed to him. They can say that the whole phenomenon of Christianity was the invention of St. Paul and had little or nothing to do with Jesus. The odd power of these assertions comes from the fact that they assume the possibility of proof and interpret the absence of proof as determining, a classic error. In fact we live in a world where there is seldom anything deserving the name "proof," where we must be content with evidence. We read the *Commentaries on the Gallic Wars* as the work of Julius Caesar, but who can prove that he wrote it? He had a good many officers with him, no doubt some of them highly literate. A general who has undertaken such a vast campaign and set his political hopes on its outcome would hardly be blamed for signing his name to the work of a lieutenant. We attribute the Latin Vulgate to St. Jerome, but who can prove that it was not the work of Paula and Eustochium? If Anonymous was a woman, was not Pseudonymous her mother? It is absurd to pretend that such things can be known, or that their negative corollaries—the Vulgate was not the work of Jerome, Caesar did not write the *Commentaries*—should be treated as true or even meaningful on the basis of the fact that they cannot be proved false. Bertrand Russell and others have made just this critique of certain arguments for the existence of God, reasonably enough. There is an interesting insight to be had here—that a very great part of what we think we know is and can only be hypothesis. Most of our beliefs about the world are unscrutinized because not much is at stake. Shakespeare is paid the great compliment of being suspected of not being who we think he was, to the glory of the seventeenth Earl of Oxford. Moses has been called an Egyptian, a worshipper of the solar disk. But Jesus is unique in the energy that has been put into reducing or nullifying him by one means or another. This is understandable as a polemical strategy, but the fact is that it has had great impact on Christian thought for a century and more. It has put it awkwardly on the defensive—awkwardly, because it is difficult to make a reasonable response to an illogical challenge, especially when the intellectual high ground is uncritically conceded to the challenger.

The life of Jesus is very well attested by the standards of antiquity. How he is to be understood is a question of another kind. The essential point is that the demand for proof as the positivists understand the word, if it were made rigorously and consistently, would be disappointed in the vast percentage of cases. This would by no means justify the conclusions that whatever cannot be proved is therefore meaningless or false. And it most emphatically would not legitimize the burgeoning of fundamentalist truth claims that are themselves totally unprovable and that flourish in contempt of evidence, as a slow walk past the religion shelves in any bookstore will demonstrate. I take what comfort I can from the fact that this kind of thinking is pandemic in contemporary society, and that members of Congress participate in it or defer to it. This is the coldest of all possible comfort. Be that as it may. In light of all this, I feel free to return to the traditional vocabulary of my faith.

•

Calvin said the world is a school that draws us on always to know more. It is true that this has been a large part of our business as a species. Christian tradition tells us that we have a history of error, and a predisposition to err not at all diminished by the endless grief we have caused ourselves. So let us say Christ entered the world as essential truth, cosmic truth mediated to us in a form presumably most accessible to us, a human presence, a human life. That he should have done so is an absolute statement of our value, which we have always done so much to obscure.

If I am justified in proposing that the human is intrinsic to infinite creation, then the finitude by which we are constrained is providential, adapted to our genius—for meaning, thought, the treasuring up of art and knowledge—all of them things cultures have called god-given or godlike. Here is an analogy. Old John Locke wrote this about the self:

> I suppose nobody will make identity of persons to consist in the soul's being united to the very same numerical particles of matter. For if that be necessary to identity, it will be impossible, in that constant flux of the particles of our bodies, that any man should be the same person two days, or two moments, together.

Richard Feynman, the great twentieth-century physicist, wrote this:

> [Atoms in the brain] can remember what was going on in my mind a year ago—a mind which has long since been replaced. To note that the thing I call my individuality is only a pattern or dance, *that* is what it means when one discovers how long it takes for the atoms of the brain to be replaced by other atoms. The atoms come into my brain, dance a dance and then go out—there are always new atoms, but always doing the same dance, remembering what the dance was yesterday.

So the self would seem to be another arbitrary constraint. If there is at root no physical reason for individuality to be self-identical from one day to the next, then the self, like the world of our experience, is of great interest in the fact that it abides within and despite constant flux. There are times when selfhood feels like exasperating captivity, times when it feels alone with its ghosts, times when it feels confident in its particular resources, times when it is deeply disappointed with itself, distrustful of itself. Yet it is a constant in experience. And, within it, a history of life, a coherency of thought, a system of persisting loyalties, language, culture, habit, learnedness, even wisdom, accumulate and enrich themselves for all the world as if the self were a shelter from the storms of change. It isn't, and it is. Vulnerable to influence of every kind, recidivist, intractable, through all its variations it is an indubitable presence. The wealth we can make of our capacities and perceptions we have entirely by grace of our selfhood. It is our part in the drama we all live out in this theater—of God's glory, Calvin would say. But, unmodified by the language of theology, there is plain truth in the fact of its special character, as an enclosed place, so to speak, where what we say and do and feel, our birth and death, can be said to matter. Think how languages and cultures free and shape—and limit—expression and understanding. The pattern is so strongly recurrent that it ought not to be set aside simply because it does not reward interpretation in positivist terms.

We might turn to the mystery of a divine self. Certain attributes have always been ascribed to God and claimed by him—love, faithfulness, justice, compassion, all of these expressing but also certainly constraining an infinite power. The paradox of the Incarnation is already implicit in the divine nature. A boundless freedom is in effect limited by gracious intent toward our world and our kind. Calvin makes a beautiful integration of cosmic power with intimate solicitude. He says: "The whole world is preserved, and every part of it keeps its place, by the will and decree of Him, whose power, above and below, is everywhere diffused. Though we live on *bread*, we must not ascribe the support of life to the power of *bread*, but to the secret kindness, by which God imparts to bread the quality of nourishing our bodies." Within the closed system of the world we are nourished, life sustaining life. Language like Calvin's expresses the sense that, within this world, God is articulate in our terms, terms we share because he created us to share them. Kindness is uttered again in everything that nourishes. The attributes of the divine self are not merely theological, but present and intentional, as they would be if the bread were from Christ's own hand. Calvin would say, And it is.

Christian theology must always be tested against its consequences for the interpretation of text. This is the vocabulary we have been given, to sound it as well as we can. I will turn to the Gospel of Mark. If my primary argument is that the experience we inhabit is an arbitrarily constructed, special reality relative to which God, Creator of the universe and whatever else besides, remains free, limited only by his own nature and will, then certain historical contingencies that are respected and sustained before the Incarnation can be put aside after it, without any negative reflection on the brilliance with which they also serve as carriers of sacred meaning. If I am correct that the genealogies in Matthew and Luke are both in some degree ironic, critiques of the assumptions that lie behind all genealogy, then there should be no surprise in the fact that laconic Mark altogether omits any mention of Jesus' descent, and even of his parentage.

If the writer of Mark was John Mark, in Rome with Peter, he might have been writing for Gentile hearers who would not care much about blood ties to Abraham and David, and might even be misled or alienated by the mention of them. In any case, the conventions Matthew and Luke test and transform, changing the question of the meaning of the Messiah's origins, Mark passes over entirely. That his Gospel was addressed to Gentiles is suggested by the explanations of Jewish practices that occur in it. In 1 Timothy, Paul cautions against those who "occupy themselves with myths and endless genealogies which promote speculations rather than the divine training that is in faith." Paul says, "The aim of our charge is love that issues from a pure heart and a good conscience and sincere faith." These defining attributes of those who identify with the God of the Bible are not new. They depart from earlier tradition in the degree to which they are freestanding, sufficient by themselves. They define and constrain without appeal to the historical identity of a people, the community to which Paul writes being newly created, self-selected, heterogeneous, polyglot. The writer of Mark, whoever he was, might simply have felt that the case for Jesus was strongest if Jesus himself, his healing and preaching and his Passion, were made the sole focus of the Gospel, with the story of his baptism and his acclamation by John and by the voice from heaven to establish his identity.

It is in order to find a broader base of interpretation that I discuss the three Synoptic Gospels together, no more than touching on any of them, but taking there to have been a community behind them, and a brief but striking and unfolding history as well. Never assuming anything as tactile as the dependence of one document on another, I do assume that the major business of the early church was to tell a sacred narrative again and again, to ponder it, to refine it to its essence, and that this would be as true for apostles and evangelists among themselves as it would be when they spoke in congregations. This is to say that refinement is no doubt to be expected even in very early writings. Paul's epistles are sufficient to make the point.

Whether or not Mark was the first Gospel to be written, I assume there was conversation and correspondence among the leaders of the congregations and a sharing of experience among them that would yield differences in approach to the work of making their good news accessible and faithful to its meaning as they understood it. A hypothetical Mark might say, If the Holy Spirit is carrying the Gospel into the whole world, then why recite these genealogies even to dismiss them? If the Annunciation sounds to pagans like stories they have heard all their lives, why start there, when the very life of Christ can justify every claim made for his birth? I venture my hypothesis on the grounds that the Gospel of Mark is impressively strong and self-consistent, not crude or tentative or fragmentary.

•

All three Gospels contain some account of Jesus' forty days in the wilderness. Matthew deals with it in eleven verses, Luke in thirteen, Mark in only two. In each case, the testing of Jesus comes after his baptism by John. Matthew and Luke have made the case for Jesus' divinity or his identity as Messiah and dealt with arguments against it that would arise among people who were aware of the nature of the expectation within Israel. Mark begins with the baptism, profoundly meaningful in itself but no part of the expectation. He omits the teaching of John reported in the other Gospels, which is in the tradition of the Hebrew prophets, and retains only his acclamation of Jesus as the Christ.

If the birth narratives and the genealogies of Matthew and Luke establish who Jesus is not—that is, not the inheritor of an identity foreseen and defined in the expectations of his people—and if at the same time they establish who he is—that is, the Son of God—then a question arises very naturally: How does such a being live in the world? If his divine nature is granted, what shape and content will it impart to his singular, mortal life? The Adversary taunts Jesus the Son of God with the fact of his own power. He need not be hungry; he could instantly seize all earthly station and wealth; he need not die. Jesus answers, "It is written," quoting Deuteronomy in response to every temptation the Devil offers. According to the Gospels the devils are knowing, and here we have, in effect, the testimony of Satan that Jesus possesses the power and authority he has also put aside, that his humanity is both real and a chosen restraint. This dialogue between the Devil and the Son of God might be thought of, so soon after the spectacle of his baptism, as a cosmic rather than a historic moment in which Jesus assumes, so to speak, the full panoply of the mortal condition. Milton's *Paradise Regained* is simply a retelling of the Temptation, reasonably enough.

I have spent too many years reading manuscripts not to wonder from whose point of view this story in Matthew and Luke is told. Jesus had no disciples, no companions, during those forty days. I think of the story as a sort of epitome of Jesus' teaching about himself, explicit and implicit. It has a folkloric quality that is not typical of Gospel narrative. I think it should be thought of as a kind of midrash. By "midrash" I mean a proposed interpretation of a text or a tradition that takes the form of narrative. That this passage is interpretation seems to me to be supported by the fact that no speech is attributed to Jesus except the language of the Torah, and these might very probably be laws he was heard to quote. In other words, presumption is avoided. There is no invention of Jesus, as there is of Satan.

His going into the wilderness, as Mark agrees that he did do, is a very human act. Fasting and solitude are extraordinarily human experiences. In accepting them, "driven by the Spirit," Mark says, Jesus is following the discipline of the prophets. So, taking those forty days as its frame, the midrash, if it is one, establishes and elaborates a meaning already implicit in his time in the wilderness. It has great relevance to questions the disciples must have asked themselves—Why did he sometimes suffer hunger or thirst? Why did he not calm the world's turbulence as he did the sea's, with a rebuke? Why did he have to die? And, what enlightenment could come to him by fasting in the wilderness, he being the Son of God? The answer is that he chose to relate to reality in the way of a pious man, honoring God, and at the same time honoring the laws of Moses by accepting the obedience that identified him as a Jew, a son of Abraham. More than all this is the fact that in this passage he dismisses the promises of power and preeminence that were thought to have been made to biblical kings and to the Christ—of which this Satan is clearly well aware, and the writers of Matthew and Luke and the audience they addressed were aware also. Instead Jesus identifies with generic "man"—"Man does not live by bread alone." Presumably nearly every word the tempter says is true. Jesus could indeed have done any of the things Satan proposes—except, no doubt, to worship him. Then again, to have done any of these things would have been to abandon his meaning and intent. So an old-fashioned theological question arises, whether God could indeed act against his own nature, which in the Christian narrative is expressed in this embrace of servanthood. Clearly, if God cannot act against his own nature, then his nature is expressed in Christ. "And being found in human form he humbled himself and became obedient unto death, even death on a cross." So a profound theological assertion is made here.

These mysteries were perhaps raised and answered more directly when they were new. What could it mean to say that God might be tempted to act like God, to assert the power that is intrinsic to his nature? "Though he was in the form of God, [he] did not count equality with God a thing to be grasped, but emptied himself, taking the form of a servant, being born in the likeness of men." This encounter with the Devil refers beyond itself to a very great question—If God is God, why does he permit evil and suffering and death? The response of the Christian narrative, that God has not exempted himself from these things, is not an answer to the question. It is, however, a vision of the nature of God that is the fullest assurance one could imagine of his loyalty to humankind and his love and respect for it. There is much that is thrilling and telling in the thought that true divinity can assume the place of a human being and yet remain an ordinary man to every mortal eye.

In any case, never mentioning the phrase, this story of the Temptation gives content to Jesus' self-characterization as a, and the, Son of Man. Luke's telling of it differs from Matthew's in the order though not the substance of the temptations. The laws or instructions of Moses by which Jesus defines the place he will take in the world are the same in both. It seems reasonable to suppose these laws are the mnemonic that stabilizes the story, since it would seem to have less claim to authority than teaching attributed to Jesus directly. Luke does draw an available conclusion from Satan's offering Jesus the glory and authority of all the kingdoms of the world. "For it has been delivered to me," says the Devil, "and I give it to whom I will."

What in all this might my hypothetical Mark have thought it best to exclude? As a form of reasoning, midrash would have been alien to Gentile hearers. It may bear some resemblance to the "myths" or "fables" Paul warns against in 1 Timothy. And even if it had currency among the holiest and profoundest Christian teachers in Jerusalem, it is not and does not offer itself as witness. Like the genealogies, which are also theological statements, not witness, it does seem to address the doubts of the skeptical. Granting miracles and healings, why was Jesus not more godlike? The character he takes on in this story is indeed his character in life. The Temple authorities might have questioned his piety and his humility. But by the standards of the great prophets, say, he led a mild and quiet life, invisible to the world until his thirtieth year. Why should this have been true? Why no grandeur, why no show of power? How could he have been vulnerable to death? The story of the Temptation means that he chose to live within the limits of humanity—thus are the skeptics answered. In Mark we have a forceful Christ who seems to be moving always, impatiently, toward Jerusalem and his culminating death. It is as if Mark would say, with all emphasis, that Jesus did not suffer death but sought it. No need to rationalize apparent weakness when the Crucifixion was an act of divine power, both in the Son who passed through death and in the Father who transformed creation by means of this death. I do not intend by this Trinitarian language to create a distinction between the will and act of Christ on one hand and of God on the other, or to invoke the idea of expiatory sacrifice,

Christ dying to mollify God. The Christ of Mark reminds me of the Old English poem "The Dream of the Rood." In it the poet, speaking in the person of the cross, sees "the Lord of men, hasting with mighty, steadfast heart," to mount the cross. He says, "The Hero young—He was Almighty God."

This vision puts aside some very disturbing interpretations of the Crucifixion that have had the effect of transforming an act of infinite mercy and grace into a piece of pure vindictiveness. Realist or positivist readings and the concessions made to them have much aggravated this effect. The wider the difference between Christ and God is taken to be, the more inevitably this invidious understanding will follow. The trouble here, and trouble of every kind, conceptually speaking, comes from the fact that Jesus was indeed a man, flesh and blood, living in mortal time. As a man he was as vulnerable as we all are.

If he was a carpenter, we may imagine that his hands were calloused and sinewed with the long practice of difficult skills, and that they would have shown the marks of injury long before his Crucifixion. Perhaps Calvin was right, that his appearance was much marred by poverty and hardship. This would have been true of generic humankind at any time in history. So also for the Son of Man, perhaps. Reluctance to accept this view of him can only arise from the difficulty of relinquishing our biases against those who have no comeliness that we should look at them, who are held in no estimation. Yet if God did become a human being, then it seems reasonable to suppose that the word "human" must be understood in the largest sense. Our ancient habit of celebrating the glory of God has tended to obscure the fact that, in the Incarnation, it was not glory he chose, except as it is inherent in all humanity. This again raises the question: What is man? Jesus' role, according to the ancient hymn, is not only humble relative to his divine nature, but humble among men, death on a cross being the great fact and proof. To put the matter another way, in what human form can the divine be wholly present without violating the conditions of human existence? A very ordinary life, it would seem. Isn't this carpenter the son of Joseph? Jesus' humanity is indeed the stone of stumbling. If he is truly man and truly God, he is the profoundest praise of humankind the cosmos could utter—in the very fact that he could and would walk among us, feeling the heat of the day, and—bearing the suffering for our oldest crime—be rejected and killed by us, as the unvalued were and are. This is another meaning of the prayer "They know not what they do."

On the other hand, if the irrefutable truth (irrefutable in terms of the testimony of the Gospels) that Jesus of Nazareth was a man is modified, as it often is, to mean that Jesus of Nazareth was *only* a man, then the chasm between God and humankind opens in the minds of the faithful despite the Incarnation and all that followed, and the great gesture is refused. The pagans of Mark's time and ours might understandably reject the Gospel out of hand, given Jesus' hunger and thirst, sorrow, suffering, death, and all the rest that meant he was one of us. The knife edge, belief and disbelief ready to be rationalized in exactly the same terms, is very much a subject of the Synoptics, although we have the Epistles to assure us that it was not their innovation. What would tip the balance toward accepting the truth of the Gospel? What would make the Incarnation with all it implies credible, even necessary? Reverence toward humankind. The hardest question Jesus puts to us is really whether we believe in Man.

Son of Adam, Son of God. How is this to be understood?

"Foxes have holes, and birds of the air have nests; but the Son of man has nowhere to lay his head." This is the bare, forked animal, unaccommodated man, the one creature that must find, contrive, create the minimal circumstances of existence, unhelped by instinct or by adaptation. This is humankind as anomalous presence on earth, singularly vulnerable to deprivation. Calvin remarks, charmingly, "It is strange that Christ should say, that he had not a foot of earth on which he could lay his head, while there were many godly and benevolent persons, who would willingly receive him into their houses." He says Jesus is simply warning the scribe that he could not expect more than "a precarious subsistence."

This is no doubt true, and it is also consistent with the idea that the saying is proverbial, therefore not precisely suited to Jesus' situation. It does suit the situation of those who hunger and thirst and are naked and sick and in prison—many of us actually and all of us potentially—those with whom Jesus specifically identifies the Son of Man in the parable of the great judgment. Let us say, tentatively, that for Matthew the phrase is defined in this proverb.

Yet we are told twice in Matthew and once in Mark that human faith could move a mountain. These are sayings of Jesus, and who am I to venture the word "hyperbole"? A general regime of forgiveness, like the reign of love imagined by Chrysostom, could have unforeseen benefits, more epochal than the moving of mountains. It might revoke, or have precluded, the infernal possibilities we have created for ourselves, which would be a momentous transformation of our circumstance. There seem to be assurances here of a great unrealized power in humankind, not power of a Promethean sort but one aligned with the spirit of God, in faith and in forgiveness. Our sacred dignity and our extreme vulnerability are the basis of a profound ethical obligation to weigh our actions in the scales of grace, not by our corrupted notions of justice and retribution. This is consistent with the return of the Son of Man as apocalyptic judge in Matthew 25, a parable that brilliantly unifies the ordinary with the prophetic meaning of the phrase. I consider it consistent also with an intended transformation of humanity's conception of itself, an intent to persuade us to believe in our ontological worthiness to be in relationship with God.

REALISM

"Grace" is a word without synonyms, a concept without paraphrase. It might seem to have distinct meanings, aesthetic and theological, but these are aspects of one thing—an alleviation, whether of guilt, of self-interest, or of limitation. I have chosen the word "alleviation" with some care. It means the lifting or easing of a burdensome weight. I suppose the moon, when it raises the tide, can be said to alleviate the imponderably burdensome mass of the sea. This is an uncanny phenomenon certainly. I have begun to think of reality, strange and arbitrary as it is, as a kind of parable. Primordial water mantled a young planet—this is true though particulars are lacking. The sun that had made the planet was younger than the water it shone on—also true. In its new light the seas could slide and slap and shine. All very well. Then somehow—again no particulars—a moon appeared, cool and demure but with pull enough to countervail gravity and lift the sea above the constraints of its own vastnesses.

Like most parables this one might as well be called a metaphor. It is meant to suggest the feeling all of us have who try something difficult and find that, for a moment or two perhaps, we succeed beyond our aspirations. The character on the page speaks in her own voice, goes her own way. The paintbrush takes life in the painter's hand, the violin plays itself. There is no honest answer to the inevitable questions: Where did that idea come from? How did you get that effect? Again, particulars are lacking. We have no language to describe the sense of a second order of reality that comes with these assertions of higher insights and will override even very settled intentions, when we are fortunate.

It might seem pedantic to allude to the classics, or simply arbitrary, though the old convention of invoking the muses is relevant here. The ancient Greek poet Pindar has come down to us only in the many odes he wrote to celebrate victories in athletic competitions, notably the Olympic games. His poems are themselves amazing achievements, so the scholars say, and are therefore basically untranslatable beyond crude approximation. Their subject is always the intervention of the divine in lifting an athlete beyond merely human strength or skill, an experience the poet could claim for himself, mutatis mutandis. Pindar says, "One born to prowess / May be whetted and stirred / To win huge glory / If a god be his helper." This is another way of describing the kind of experience I am attempting to evoke, which is no doubt encountered across the range of human skill and effort. Our own athletes may deserve a more respectful hearing when they, like Pindar, attribute a magnificent throw or catch to a moment of divine favor. This second order of reality, the feeling that one's own capacities are somehow transcended in one's own person, seems to find no expression among us in terms that can be understood as descriptive rather than as merely pietistic. We have YouTube to measure the nation's pleasure in a spectacular athletic instant or two. In Pindar's ode, great acts of prowess exalted and sanctified experience on one particular ancient evening "lit / By the lovely light of the fair-faced moon." And they might well do as much for us, since they can only mean that we are more than we are.

We moderns have defenses against notions like this one, defenses that in effect preclude our looking without prejudice at what we might as well call reality, since so many of us can attest to it. Now that I find myself elderly, I am impatient with the artificial limits we put on our sense of things—in the name of reason, I suppose, or in any case in deference to what consensus will support as reasonable. Out of this rather narrow consensus is extruded from time to time an interest in mysticism or spirituality. By my lights this is a siphoning away of attention, a distraction from a quality intrinsic to brute fact, not to mention the numberless categories of fact available to being described in far gentler terms. Our realism distracts us from reality, that most remarkable phenomenon. I feel that I have been impoverished in the degree that I have allowed myself to be persuaded of the inevitability of a definition of the real that is so arbitrarily exclusive, leaving much of what I intuited and even what I knew in the limbo of the unarticulated and the unacknowledged. I wish I had experienced my earthly life more deeply. It is my fault that I didn't. I could have been a better scholar of Walt Whitman.

I can't find excuses in statements that begin "American society" or "American culture," because in my lifetime there has been a brilliant explosion of knowledge and of access to knowledge. A Martian might think this has been the highest priority of our civilization. And she/he/it might be right. We are groping around on Mars today, piecing together its geology. But if the Martian proposed to an American that all this implied a civilization that is intellectually voracious and highly disciplined, to boot, is there anyone who would not dismiss the notion out of hand? The whole impatience I feel with this constricted awareness I have lived with, and that I see around me, comes from the dazzling universe of contemporary science on one hand and the impressive and moving and terrible record of the deep human past on the other. How many people who have lived on earth could dream of such access? It is a heaven for the pensive and the curious, if they happen to wander into it. (Being who we are, we have an invidious term for all this—we call it information and claim that it somehow displaces knowledge.)

I am speaking again of an odd sort of doubleness. We are archcapitalists, so we tell ourselves and everyone else at every opportunity. We publish hundreds of thousands of books each year. Being archcapitalists, we must proceed always and only in search of profit. So what are we to conclude, except that there must be a voracious market for books not only to sustain this vast output but to make it profitable? But this can't be true, since another conviction universal among us is that Americans don't read books. A conundrum, certainly. The objection will be made that publishing in this country is a risky business, by no means reliably profitable. Then a new problem arises: How does this industry persist on such a scale if there is not a lot of money to be made in it? Is this consistent with the disciplining effects of the profit motive? Unscrutinized comparisons are implied in generalizations about the state of the culture. Was there an era in which publishers did not often struggle and fail? Not that I am aware of. Are things different and better in other countries? I don't know, and I don't know anyone who does. Government subsidies should not be allowed to blur the issue. If, as a last-ditch defense of the right to weltschmerz, the argument is made that our literary culture is provincial and middlebrow, Philip Roth recently listed seventy formidable and gifted American writers of postwar fiction and called the list incomplete. Any student of literature knows that this is an extraordinary flourishing of a difficult art. For such a thing to have happened, many people have to have been doing many things right. It is characteristic of Americans that they think of the ideal as the norm, at least among the polished civilizations, and feel their shortfall relative to this imaginary standard as a great humiliation. We are so loyal to these formulae of self-contempt that there is no interest in or tolerance for doubt as to their basis in fact. To question is jingoism. That these good writers are read all over the world is called cultural imperialism, though, if the same were happening in another time or place, we would say without hesitation that people then or there were living in a golden age. Yes, we are struggling in a swamp of dysfunction and malicious factionalism. But by the standards of, let us say, Renaissance England and Europe, we're really not doing too badly.

I may seem to have strayed from my subject. In fact I am offering another illustration of the difference between what we think we are doing and what we do in fact. On one hand we scold and scorn the mass of the populace for what we choose to see as their intellectual laziness and their borderline illiteracy. On the other hand we have a flourishing literature and an educational system that, at the level of college and above, is unique in the world and also in history. I have traveled widely in undergraduate America, as many of you have, too, and I have found the experience touching and impressive, especially as it is found in little-known institutions that will never be ranked nationally for anything at all, since there is no way to measure good faith or intellectual seriousness. These colleges are supported by taxpayers, sometimes grudgingly, and by donors, sometimes opulently, and they go on about their quiet work for generations, groves of academe.

Our literature and our colleges are only two instances of the fact that, culturally speaking, often to our great good fortune, we don't know who we are or what we are doing. Something intervenes between cynicism and vulgarism on one hand—these are the two poles of our public discourse at the moment—and, on the other hand, what transpires in the study and in the classroom. This is not to say that the effects of both these postures are not felt and that they are not corrosive. Their impact on our political system is obvious and frightening, and inevitable, according to them both. It is to say that the two of them are equally the consequence of an insistently pejorative tone in our discourse, if it deserves the name, as it interprets, or assumes, the nature and tendencies of our culture. Cynicism and vulgarism are cheek and jowl. One teaches us helplessness in the face of the abuses and atavisms the other encourages us to embrace. And still the civilization as a whole is sounder, smarter, and vastly more interesting than it is itself able to acknowledge. How does this happen? And why does it happen?

This pejorative stance bothers me because it is so unreflecting, because it is unshakable in the way of moralistic judgments, because it supplies an adequate intellectual posture in the minds of its many adherents and is therefore doubly unshakable. Uninformed deference to a handful of cultures—all European—is an entirely sufficient definition of sophistication for virtually the whole of our educated class, no matter how much authentic sophistication they should have attained in their own right, no matter how immovably such deference enshrines our prejudices in favor of those who are, in a word, white. Still, our towns and cities build great libraries, love them, and people them. Still, the good and generous work of teaching goes on, much of it unpaid and much, underpaid. There are legislatures and institutions who exploit the willingness of many people to teach despite meager salaries, overwork, and insecurity, and this is disgraceful. But it should not obscure the fact that there are indeed people teaching for the love of it. They are the ones sustaining civilization, not the exploiters of their good faith, or, better, their good grace. Therefore it seems right to me that they should have an important place in any definition of the civilization, though they are invisible to cynicism and to vulgarism. They are, of course, a synecdoche for millions of people who work without recognition or adequate pay and contribute vastly more to the common life than the vulgarians who exploit them or the cynics who dismiss them.

Again, there is the issue of respect for reality. It is odd to treat the country, by which I and commentators in general mean its population, as grasping capitalists on the basis of the fact that 1 percent or fewer control 40 percent of the national wealth. Which is to say that 99 percent, or more, control, per capita, a very small share of it. Why do the 1 percent, rather than the 99 percent, seem to critics and moralists to characterize the culture? Most people don't participate in the economy of manipulation and financial gimmickry that seems to have produced our dubious elite. Most people know nothing about it. It is an excrescence of computer-assisted globalization whose existence we learned of when it went into crisis and took us all with it. The 99 percent were swept into the capitalist schema by the phrase "class envy"—these people had what all the rest of us wanted, supposedly. Most of us want a reasonable degree of control over the life of the country—that old democratic expectation that the lives of most of us should not be vulnerable to the whims of a self-interested elite. The ethic, for want of a better word, by which this elite has flourished is ethically repulsive by the lights of the population in general. In the ordinary course of life, there are few occasions when one is simply cheated, and I have never heard anyone praised for being a systematic cheat. The whole notion of class is deeply problematic, but insofar as it has any normative value, I think the consensus among the public would be that cheating shows a lack of class, and that this emphatically is no less true when the cheating is done for money. Of course there are candy bar magnates and party favor magnates, and there are fortunes that come with creating things that are useful or beneficial, fortunes that have themselves been put to good use. This has always been true. But the rather abrupt change in the wealth structure of the United States reflects perverse innovation that has had the effect of making most of us poorer. We know what has happened to the wage.

How is this relevant to my subject, to grace? Grace would give the country back to the people by acknowledging the reality of lives lived patiently and honorably. We insist on the word "capitalist," a word Marx did not apply to us, urging it on ourselves as our defining quality and at the same time deploring it, more on the left, less on the right. It is characteristic of certain terms—capitalist, materialist, consumerist—that their speaker is exempting himself, at least in the sense that any vacancy he feels in his life, any shallowness she feels in her motives, are induced by cultural influences, economic determinism first of all. In this capitalist environment, we can only marvel that we are not quite as grasping as everyone else. Well, not the people we know, really, but those hordes out beyond somewhere who collectively exude this toxic atmosphere. Those nameless wage-fallen others who somehow make Wall Street Wall Street and are overweight besides. Truly, I am sick to death of presumptive contempt of the only human souls most of us will ever have any meaningful relationship with, who offer the only experience of life in the world that most of us will ever have occasion to ponder seriously, that is, respectfully and compassionately, that is, with grace. It is very easy for me to imagine that my life might have gone another way, and that I might be one among those great multitudes about whose inward life nothing is known, upon whom social pathologies can be projected. It really is rather miraculous that someone as ill-suited to the demands of life as I am should have found a niche to flourish in. I have lived long enough to chalk up to age inadequacies that have been with me the whole of my conscious life.

All this is on my mind because we have just come through Christmas. The clichés about Christmas are so utterly weary and worn that it is difficult to mention them even to attempt to be rid of them. Still. The reality of the phenomenon is this—people mob the stores looking for gifts to give to other people. All this is swept into the broad category of consumption so that we can speak of it as if it were greed and self-indulgence in an artificially heightened state. It is really inflamed generosity. All those people are thinking about what someone else might want, need, look good in, be amused by. This by itself must be a valuable discipline. That Martian, and any competent anthropologist, ought to find this great national potlatch extremely interesting. I call it a potlatch because the economics of it are so perverse, from the point of view of the great public on whom it all depends. Every one of them knows that if they chose to celebrate Epiphany, January 6, the day when the Magi actually, traditionally speaking, brought their gifts, or any day after December 25, which most of them know is a date chosen arbitrarily by the early church, they would save a tremendous amount of money. So the investment they are making is only secondarily in stuff, and primarily in a particular evening or morning that is set apart by this singular ritual of giving and receiving. A Martian might conclude that these evenings and mornings focus benevolent feelings that would otherwise be unexpressed, unacknowledged, or merely routine. Families tend to provide, but Christmas reminds everyone that there is joy in it. A small gift to or from an acquaintance is expressive, a kind of courteous language. If we wanted to, we could find a considerable loveliness in all this, but that is prohibited by the conventions of social critique. We would rather think darkly about those materialists who have emptied the shelves of things we had on our lists, who stand with their carts full of loot between ourselves and the cash register.

Since I have mentioned economics—if we abolished December 25 and the de facto sumptuary tax on ritual giving, everything would simply cost more during the rest of the year, since businesses and corporations will have their profits. And the impact on all sorts of countries who manufacture the strange, decorative excesses that are aesthetically comprehensible only at Christmas would be severe. I suspect that in a year or two the phenomenon would simply shift to the Fourth of July. What economic rationalism cannot justify it also cannot destroy—and again, it is the economic perspective of the overwhelming majority that is the issue here.

I began by speaking about grace and alleviation, and now I have suggested that our refusal to interpret graciously a significant aspect of national culture puts a kind of curse on something that is, in itself, far too interesting to fall into the limbo of facile disparagement, though in fact that void yawns for most of what we do. "We" in this context means "you," and "they." It means students who have learned that they are intellectually disabled by the fact of their birth and acculturation and cannot aspire to work of the first order. It means the store clerk who told me in the solemn tone usual when these words are spoken that Americans don't read books—with the implication that we could respect them more if they did. This is a great psychic burden, much in need of alleviation. The Bible pairs the words "grace" and "truth." Truth in this case would be felt as grace—the model of cultural determinism is sloppy Marxism, or worse. Much of the language about society and culture derives from European "thought," so called, in the period leading to Europe's great disasters, from the early nineteenth century to the mid-twentieth and after. This "thought" was taken up with authenticity, rootedness, ethnic purity, all of which made people profound, as they could not be if they were transplanted, ethnically mixed, speakers of an adopted language. These notions spoke ferociously against all Europeans of whom these things were true, and made a nightmare image of dystopia of this country, from Chateaubriand and Baudelaire forward. I will die never understanding why this should be true, but it is true, that Americans enjoy this kind of thing when it is directed against them, or, perhaps, against everybody else on the continent. No, in fact they, we, persist in thinking that profundity only occurs elsewhere.

That they lack authenticity and will never achieve it, that they lack culture and will never be capable of it, that the admixture of foreign influences, actual or perceived, debases culture and language—this is exactly what German nationalists said about Jews. No one should be able to think in such terms without embarrassment. We reject the particulars, relative to ourselves, or try to, but we accept the conclusion. To adopt such thinking as a constraint on one's own hopes, on the hopes of one's society, is a kind of maiming, unforced and inexplicable. We have seen these ideas enact themselves as history, and still they live on in our curricula, notably as botched Marxism—though anyone who has read him knows better than to blame him.

That doubleness again. I have the permission of Emerson and Whitman, both of whom I revere, to contradict myself, though I still can't even seem to do it without discomfort. I have said we have an extraordinary educational culture, which is true, indisputable. Yet I note the oddness of gathering promising youths at great expense into situations where they will learn prejudices against themselves. The culture is itself full of contradictions. Grace is clearly on the side of the impulse to educate, and the burden it must ease is the secondary message that the education is somehow never the real thing, that the students themselves are not potentially creators of civilization, as truly as any thinker or artist they are given to study and admire. Of course there are schools that communicate special entitlement, but this is subject to the same intellectual limits our culture feels generally. My essay collection *Absence of Mind* is listed on Amazon as phenomenology. On a good day it ranks at about 75,000 among books in general, but it is often in the top ten in a category that, in fact, doesn't sell like hotcakes. I'm not sure I'd have thought to call the book phenomenology, but I'm pleased anyway, because I am quite consistently the only woman in the upper reaches of the list and may have made a breakthrough of a kind. More to the point, I'm usually the only American, except for the occasional readers' guide to someone European. Can this be right? Several things may be reflected in it—what is written, what is published, and what goes into the curriculum, which determines sales for books of this kind. Every one of these factors would be sensitive to the assumption that Americans do not write phenomenology. They do, of course, write distinguished philosophy, and Amazon reflects this fact. But Emerson, Whitman, and Dickinson wrote phenomenology before the word, and Melville did, too. Our own tradition, rightly taught, should instruct us. By grace of their example, we might be able to make this beautiful form of thought welcoming to the pensive among us, as all fruitful modes of thinking should be to anyone disposed to them. The gods and heroes of the cities Pindar's athletes come from supply him with analogies for their transcendent achievements in competition. It seems to me that, to the extent that we offer one another models of high achievement, we imply at the same time that we can only admire from a distance, and demonstrate our loyalty to the ideal of excellence by deference rather than by emulation.

This is not to say, is very far from being meant to imply, that excellent things are not done in this population all the time. It is to say that this is true enough to demand, if we are to honor the grace that is in truth, that this fact be acknowledged. I am happy to report that many of my recent students are immigrants or the children of immigrants. Some of them come from backgrounds of severe deprivation. They have new things to say, and the gifts and skills to say them, shaped by public schools in American cities. This is exactly what is to be hoped for, in an immigrant culture with an open and expanding literature, in a democracy. When we say dismissive things about Americans, do we mean the new young citizen from Guatemala, who knows absolutely everything about the Supreme Court? Whom do we mean? The brilliant daughter of the Caribbean domestic worker, who describes characters like her mother with Chekhovian delicacy? Is there any subset of the population we really want to characterize in the terms and the tone we use for the population as a whole? Perhaps the old notion that "Americans" are homogeneously white seems to excuse this—no harm in ridiculing a secure and self-satisfied majority. But this notion of homogeneity corresponds to nothing. The Midwest is a congeries of European minorities, many of them not so far from deprivation and immigration themselves, as well as newer immigrant communities from every part of the world, and African American communities differentiated by their various origins in the South. If you have looked at Sinclair Lewis's *Main Street* lately, part of the literature that has taught us contempt for the vast center of the country, you will know that the recoil is against the ragged and uncouth Europeans flooding into it. These immigrants settled beside communities with whom they had had homicidal histories in the old country, so amicably that it seems pointless to those passing through to look for any differences among them. The stereotype of the population, in any significant part, as homogeneous enough to justify generalization is basically a version of racism and inverted ethnocentricity. If the census reveals patterns that seem to characterize us generally—Americans are more religious than Europeans, for example—this is certainly a consequence of our being populated in large part by minorities who identify with their communities—by our heterogeneity, in other words. Dutch Calvinists and Libyan Muslims check the same box. This may indeed represent a deep consensus, the benign and ironic consequence of the fact that there is no national religion, no Church of America.

That all the numberless affiliations are swept up into one image of ignorance and haplessness is an aspect of the artificiality and insensitivity that saturate the conversation we have among and about ourselves. We are very given to bad-apple sociology—any pathology that flares anywhere within our borders implicates us all and adumbrates deeper and more general pathology. Those who hate Fox News are as persuaded by its representation of the country as are its truest devotees. Yes, the last election was a blow. Things would have been different if there were not so much in the cultural air to imply that cynicism and passivity are a moral stance—the country being so dull-minded, materialist, and so on.

I suppose I might have been expected to speak about grace more theologically, when it is perhaps the major term in my religious tradition. But by my lights I have spoken theologically, since everything depends on reverence for who we are and what we are, on the sacredness implicit in the human circumstance. We know how deeply we can injure one another by denying fairness. We know how profoundly we can impoverish ourselves by failing to find value in one another. We know that respect is a profound alleviation, which we can offer and too often withhold. That doubleness again. A theology of grace is a higher realism, an ethics of truth. Writers know this.

PRESIDENT OBAMA AND MARILYNNE ROBINSON

A Conversation In Iowa

PART I

The following conversation between President Obama and Marilynne Robinson was conducted in Des Moines, Iowa, on September 14, 2015. An audio recording of it can be heard at itunes.com/nybooks.

—The Editors, *The New York Review of Books*

THE PRESIDENT: Marilynne, it's wonderful to see you. And as I said as we were driving over here, this is an experiment, because typically when I come to a place like Des Moines, I immediately am rushed over to some political event and I make a speech, or I have a town hall, or I go see some factory and have wonderful conversations with people. But it's very planned out and scripted. And typically, we're trying to drive a very particular message that day about education or about manufacturing.

But one of the things that I don't get a chance to do as often as I'd like is just to have a conversation with somebody who I enjoy and I'm interested in; to hear from them and have a conversation with them about some of the broader cultural forces that shape our democracy and shape our ideas, and shape how we feel about citizenship and the direction that the country should be going in.

And so we had this idea that why don't I just have a conversation with somebody I really like and see how it turns out. And you were first in the queue, because—

Marilynne Robinson: Thank you very much.

The President: Well, as you know—I've told you this—I love your books. Some listeners may not have read your work before, which is good, because hopefully they'll go out and buy your books after this conversation.

I first picked up *Gilead*, one of your most wonderful books, here in Iowa. Because I was campaigning at the time, and there's a lot of downtime when you're driving between towns and when you get home late from campaigning. And you and I, therefore, have an Iowa connection, because *Gilead* is actually set here in Iowa.

And I've told you this—one of my favorite characters in fiction is a pastor in Gilead, Iowa, named John Ames, who is gracious and courtly and a little bit confused about how to reconcile his faith with all the various travails that his family goes through. And I was just—I just fell in love with the character, fell in love with the book, and then you and I had a chance to meet when you got a fancy award at the White House. And then we had dinner and our conversations continued ever since.

So anyway, that's enough context. You just have completed a series of essays that are not fiction, and I had a chance to read one of them about fear [124–140] and the role that fear may be playing in our politics and our democracy and our culture. And you looked at it through the prism of Christianity and sort of the Protestant traditions that helped shape us, so I thought maybe that would be a good place to start.

Why did you decide to write this book of essays? And why was fear an important topic, and how does it connect to some of the other work that you've been doing?

ROBINSON: Well, the essays are actually lectures. I give lectures at a fair rate, and then when I've given enough of them to make a book, I make a book.

THE PRESIDENT: So you just kind of mash them all together?

ROBINSON: I do. That's what I do. But it rationalizes my lecturing, too. But fear was very much—is on my mind, because I think that the basis of democracy is the willingness to assume well about other people.

You have to assume that basically people want to do the right thing. I think that you can look around society and see that basically people do the right thing. But when people begin to make these conspiracy theories and so on, that make it seem as if what is apparently good is in fact sinister, they never accept the argument that is made for a position that they don't agree with—you know?

THE PRESIDENT: Yes.

ROBINSON: Because [of] the idea of the "sinister other." And I mean, that's bad under all circumstances. But when it's brought home, when it becomes part of our own political conversation about ourselves, I think that that really is about as dangerous a development as there could be in terms of whether we continue to be a democracy.

THE PRESIDENT: Well, now there's been that strain in our democracy and in American politics for a long time. And it pops up every so often. I think the argument right now would be that because people are feeling the stresses of globalization and rapid change, and we went through one of the worst financial crises since the Great Depression, and the political system seems gridlocked, that people may be particularly receptive to that brand of politics.

ROBINSON: But having looked at one another with optimism and tried to facilitate education and all these other things—which we've done more than most countries have done, given all our faults—that's what made it a viable democracy. And I think that we have created this incredibly inappropriate sort of in-group mentality when we really are from every end of the earth, just dealing with each other in good faith. And that's just a terrible darkening of the national outlook, I think.

THE PRESIDENT: We've talked about this, though. I'm always trying to push a little more optimism. Sometimes you get—I think you get discouraged by it, and I tell you, well, we go through these moments.

ROBINSON: But when you say that to me, I say to you, you're a better person than I am.

THE PRESIDENT: Well, but I want to pick up on the point you made about us coming from everywhere. You're a novelist but you're also—can I call you a theologian? Does that sound, like, too stuffy? You care a lot about Christian thought.

ROBINSON: I do, indeed.

THE PRESIDENT: And that's part of the foundation of your writings, fiction and nonfiction. And one of the points that you've made in one of your most recent essays is that there was a time in which at least reformed Christianity in Europe was very much "the other." And part of our system of government was based on us rejecting an exclusive, inclusive—or an exclusive and tightly controlled sense of who is part of the community and who is not—in favor of a more expansive one. Tell me a little bit about how your interest in Christianity converges with your concerns about democracy.

ROBINSON: Well, I believe that people are images of God. There's no alternative that is theologically respectable to treating people in terms of that understanding. What can I say? It seems to me as if democracy is the logical, the inevitable consequence of this kind of religious humanism at its highest level. And it [applies] to everyone. It's the human image. It's not any loyalty or tradition or anything else; it's being human that enlists the respect, the love of God being implied in it.

THE PRESIDENT: But you've struggled with the fact that here in the United States, sometimes Christian interpretation seems to posit an "us versus them," and those are sometimes the loudest voices. But sometimes I think you also get frustrated with kind of the wishy-washy, more liberal versions where anything goes.

ROBINSON: Yes.

THE PRESIDENT: How do you reconcile the idea of faith being really important to you and you caring a lot about taking faith seriously with the fact that, at least in our democracy and our civic discourse, it seems as if folks who take religion the most seriously sometimes are also those who are suspicious of those not like them?

ROBINSON: Well, I don't know how seriously they do take their Christianity, because if you take something seriously, you're ready to encounter difficulty, run the risk, whatever. I mean, when people are turning in on themselves—and God knows, arming themselves and so on—against the imagined other, they're not taking their Christianity seriously. I don't know—I mean, this has happened over and over again in the history of Christianity, there's no question about that, or other religions, as we know.

But Christianity is profoundly counterintuitive—"Love thy neighbor as thyself"—which I think, properly understood, means your neighbor is as worthy of love as you are, not that you're actually going to be capable of this sort of superhuman feat. But you're supposed to run against the grain. It's supposed to be difficult. It's supposed to be a challenge.

THE PRESIDENT: Well, that's one of the things I love about your characters in your novels, it's not as if it's easy for them to be good Christians, right?

ROBINSON: Right.

THE PRESIDENT: It's hard. And it's supposed to be hard. Now, you grew up in Idaho, in a pretty—it wasn't a big, cosmopolitan place.

ROBINSON: The word "cosmopolitan" was never applied.

THE PRESIDENT: Which town in Idaho did you grow up in?

ROBINSON: [Coeur d'Alene] is where I really grew up.

THE PRESIDENT: How big was the town when you were growing up?

ROBINSON: 13,500 people.

THE PRESIDENT: All right. So that's a town.

ROBINSON: Yes, the second-largest city in the state at the time.

THE PRESIDENT: And how do you think you ended up thinking about democracy, writing, faith the way you do? How did that experience of growing up in a pretty small place in Idaho, which might have led you in an entirely different direction—how did you end up here, Marilynne? What happened? Was it libraries?

ROBINSON: It was libraries, it was—people are so complicated. It's like every new person is a completely new roll of the dice, right?

THE PRESIDENT: Right.

ROBINSON: I followed what was for me the path of least resistance, which meant reading a lot of books and writing, because it came naturally to me. My brother is excellent in many of these things, you know? And I think we reinforced each other, he and I, but it was perfectly accidental.

With all respect to that environment, many very smart people do not follow the path in life that people like my brother and I did. You learn from them even if you don't learn from them in a formal sense. But I always knew what I wanted to do in a sense—I mean, not *be*, but *do*. I didn't really have the concept of author until I was in high school. But I was writing.

THE PRESIDENT: But you knew you wanted to read and write.

ROBINSON: Yes, that's what I wanted to do.

The President: Were your parents into books, or did they just kind of encourage you or tolerate your quirkiness?

Robinson: There was great tolerance in the house for quirkiness. No, it's a funny thing because on the one hand, I'm absolutely indebted to my origins, whatever they are, whatever that means. On the other hand, with all love and respect, my parents were not particularly bookish people.

The President: Well, that's why you have good sense along with sort of an overlay of books on top of good sense. What did your mom and dad do?

Robinson: My mother was a stay-at-home mother. My father was a sort of middle-management lumber company guy.

The President: But they encouraged it.

Robinson: You know what, they were the adults and we were the kids, you know what I mean? Sort of like two species. But if they noticed we were doing something—drawing or painting or whatever we were doing—then they would get us what we needed to do that, and silently go on with it. One of the things that I think is very liberating is that if I had lived any honest life, my parents would have been equally happy. I was under no pressure.

The President: Well, you told me about a certain attitude that your parents had that was—there was a certain set of homespun values of hard work and honesty and humility. And that sounded really familiar to me when I think about my grandparents who grew up in Kansas.

And that's part of what I see in your writing. And part of my connection to your books, I think, is an appreciation for—without romanticizing Middle America or small-town America—that sense of homespun virtues. And that comes out in your writing. And it sometimes seems really foreign to popular culture today, which is all about celebrity and being loud and bragging and—

ROBINSON: I mean, I really think that you have to go very far up in American culture to get beyond the point where people have good values. I mean, you really have that feeling sometimes that honesty is more intrinsic in some person that's doing very low-level work than it is in perhaps somebody that's trying to find his way into some sensation—

THE PRESIDENT: These big systems where everything is all about flash. But that's not how your parents saw the world, right? When you said that all they cared about was just you being honest and—

ROBINSON: Yes, exactly.

THE PRESIDENT: —doing your best in some enterprise.

ROBINSON: In whatever. Exactly.

THE PRESIDENT: It's interesting, because we're talking in Iowa; people always, I think, were surprised about me connecting with folks in small-town Iowa. And the reason I did was, first of all, I had the benefit that at the time nobody expected me to win. And so I wasn't viewed through this prism of Fox News and conservative media, and making me scary. At the time, I didn't seem scary, other than just having a funny name. I seemed young. Sometimes I look at my pictures from then and I say, I can't believe anybody voted for me because I look like I'm twenty-five.

But I'd go into these towns and everybody felt really familiar to me, because they reminded me of my grandparents and my mom and that attitude that you talk about. You saw all through the state—and I saw this when I was traveling through southern Illinois when I was first campaigning for the United States Senate—and I actually see it everywhere across the country.

The issue to me, Marilynne, is not so much that those virtues that you prize and that you care about and that are vital to our democracy aren't there. They are there in Little League games, and—

Robinson: Emergency rooms.

The President: —emergency rooms, and in school buildings. And people are treating each other the way you would want our democracy to cultivate. But there's this huge gap between how folks go about their daily lives and how we talk about our common life and our political life. And people describe it as the distance between Washington and Main Street. But it's not just Washington; it's the way we talk about our politics, our foreign policy, our common endeavors. There's this gap.

And the thing I've been struggling with throughout my political career is how do you close the gap. There's all this goodness and decency and common sense on the ground, and somehow it gets translated into rigid, dogmatic, often mean-spirited politics. And some of it has to do with all the filters that stand between ordinary people who are busy and running around trying to look after their kids and do a good job and do all the things that maintain a community, so they don't have the chance to follow the details of complicated policy debates.

They know they want to take care of somebody who's sick, and they have a generous impulse. How that gets translated into the latest Medicare budgets [isn't] always clear. They know they want us to use our power wisely in the world, and that violence often begets violence. But they also know the world is dangerous and it's very hard to sort out, as you talk about in your essay, fear when violence must be met, and when there are other tools at our disposal to try to create a more peaceful world.

So that, I think, is the challenge. I'm very encouraged when I meet people in their environments. Somehow it gets distilled at the national political level in ways that aren't always as encouraging.

ROBINSON: I think one of the things that is true is that many Americans on every side of every issue, they think that the worst thing they can say is the truest thing, you know?

THE PRESIDENT: No. Tell me what you mean.

ROBINSON: Well, for example—I mean, I'm a great admirer of American education. And I've traveled—I mean, a lot of my essays, you know, are lectures given in educational settings—universities everywhere. And they're very impressive. They are very much loved by people who identify with them. You meet faculty and they're very excited about what they're doing; students that are very excited, and so on.

And then you step away and you hear all this stuff about how the system is failing and we have to pull it limb from limb, and the rest of it. And you think, have you walked through the door? Have you listened to what people say? Have you taught in a foreign university?

We have a great educational system that is—it's really a triumph of the civilization. I don't think there's anything comparable in history. And it has no defenders. Most of the things we do have no defenders because people tend to feel the worst thing you can say is the truest thing you can say.

The President: But that's part of what makes America wonderful, is we always had this nagging dissatisfaction that spurs us on. That's how we ended up going west, that's how we—"I'm tired of all these people back east; if I go west, there's going to be my own land and I'm not going to have to put up with this nonsense, and I'm going to start my own thing, and I've got my homestead." . . . It is true, though, that that restlessness and that dissatisfaction which has helped us go to the moon and create the Internet and build the Transcontinental Railroad and build our landgrant colleges, that those things, born of dissatisfaction, we can very rapidly then take for granted and not tend to and not defend, and not understand how precious these things are.

And this is where conceptions of government can get us in trouble. Whenever I hear people saying that our problems would be solved without government, I always want to tell them you need to go to some other countries where there really is no government, where the roads are never repaired, where nobody has facilitated electricity going everywhere even where it's not economical, where—

Robinson: The postal system.

The President: —the postal system doesn't work, or kids don't have access to basic primary education. That's the logical conclusion if, in fact, you think that government is the enemy. And that, too, is a running strain in our democracy. That's sort of in our DNA. We're suspicious of government as a tool of oppression. And that skepticism is healthy, but it can also be paralyzing when we're trying to do big things together.

Robinson: And also, one of the things that doesn't take into account is that local governments can be great systems of oppression. And it's a wonderful thing to have a national government that can intervene in the name of national values.

THE PRESIDENT: Well, that was the lesson of the entire movement to abolish slavery and the civil rights movement. And that's one thing—I mean, I do think that one of the things we haven't talked about that does become the fault line around which the "us" and "them" formula rears its head is the fault line of race. And even on something like schools that you just discussed, part of the challenge is that the school systems we have are wonderful, except for a handful of schools that are predominantly minority that are terrible.

Our systems for maintaining the peace and our criminal justice systems generally work, except for this huge swath of the population that is incarcerated at rates that are unprecedented in world history.

And when you are thinking about American democracy or, for that matter, Christianity in your writings, how much does that issue of "the other" come up and how do you think about that? I know at least in *Gilead* that factors into one major character, trying to figure out how he can love somebody in the Fifties that doesn't look like him.

ROBINSON: Iowa never had laws against interracial marriage. Only Iowa and Maine never had [them]—

THE PRESIDENT: Those were the only two.

ROBINSON: Yes. And [Ulysses S.] Grant really did call [Iowa] the shining star of radicalism, and so on. We never had segregated schools; they were illegal from before, while it was still a territory, and so on. And these laws never changed and they became the basis for the marriage equality ruling that the Supreme Court here [in Iowa] did.

So that whole stream of the culture never changed. And at the same time, the felt experience of the culture was not aligned with the liberal tradition [of the] culture. And so in that book, Jack has every right to think he can come to Iowa, and yet what he finds makes him, rightly, raise the question.

THE PRESIDENT: I'm going to shift gears for a second. You told me that when you started writing, it just kind of showed up in some ways. When you started writing your novels, that it was just forced upon you and that you didn't map it out. Tell me about when you were writing *Gilead* and *Home* and some of my favorite books, how did you decide, I'm going to start writing about some old pastor in the middle of cornfields?

Because by that time you had gone to the East Coast, you had traveled in France.

ROBINSON: The Midwest was still a very new thing for me. I got a voice in my head. It was the funniest thing. I mean, [I'd] been reading history and theology and all these things for a long time. And then I was in Massachusetts, actually, just [waiting to spend] Christmas with my son[s]. They were late coming to wherever we were going to meet, and I was in this hotel with a pen and blank paper, and I started writing from this voice. The first sentence in that book is the first sentence that came to my mind. I have no idea how that happens. I was surprised that I was writing from a male point of view. But there he was.

THE PRESIDENT: He just showed up.

ROBINSON: He just showed up. And the first things that I knew about him—that he was old, that he had a young son, and so on—they create the narrative.

PART II

The President: Are you somebody who worries about people not reading novels anymore? And do you think that has an impact on the culture? When I think about how I understand my role as citizen, setting aside being president, and the most important set of understandings that I bring to that position of citizen, the most important stuff I've learned I think I've learned from novels. It has to do with empathy. It has to do with being comfortable with the notion that the world is complicated and full of grays, but there's still truth there to be found, and that you have to strive for that and work for that. And the notion that it's possible to connect with some[one] else even though they're very different from you.

And so I wonder when you're sitting there writing longhand in some—your messy longhand somewhere—so I wonder whether you feel as if that same shared culture is as prevalent and as important in the lives of people as it was, say, when you were that little girl in Idaho, coming up, or whether you feel as if those voices have been overwhelmed by flashier ways to pass the time.

Marilynne Robinson: I'm not really the person—because I'm almost always talking with people who love books.

The President: Right. You sort of have a self-selecting crew.

Robinson: And also teaching writers—I'm quite aware of the publication of new writers. I think—I mean, the literature at present is full to bursting. No book can sell in that way that *Gone with the Wind* sold, or something like that. But the thing that's wonderful about it is that there's an incredible variety of voices in contemporary writing. You know people say, is there an

American tradition surviving in literature, and yes, our tradition is the incredible variety of voices. . . .

And [now] you don't get the conversation that would support the literary life. I think that's one of the things that has made book clubs so popular.

THE PRESIDENT: That's interesting. Part of the challenge is—and I see this in our politics—is a common conversation. It's not so much, I think, that people don't read at all; it's that everybody is reading [in] their niche, and so often, at least in the media, they're reading stuff that reinforces their existing point of view. And so you don't have that phenomenon of here's a set of great books that everybody is familiar with and everybody is talking about.

Sometimes you get some TV shows that fill that void, but increasingly now, that's splintered, too, so other than the Super Bowl, we don't have a lot of common reference points. And you can argue that that's part of the reason why our politics has gotten so polarized, is that—when I was growing up, if the president spoke to the country, there were three stations and every city had its own newspaper and they were going to cover that story. And that would last for a couple of weeks, people talking about what the president had talked about.

Today, my poor press team, they're tweeting every two minutes because some new thing has happened, which then puts a premium on the sensational and the most outrageous or a conflict as a way of getting attention and breaking through the noise—which then creates, I believe, a pessimism about the country because all those quiet, sturdy voices that we were talking about at the beginning, they're not heard.

It's not interesting to hear a story about some good people in some quiet place that did something sensible and figured out how to get along.

ROBINSON: I think that in our earlier history—the Gettysburg Address or something—there was the conscious sense that democracy was an achievement. It was not simply the most efficient modern system or something. It was something that people collectively made and they understood that they held it together by valuing it. I think that in earlier periods—which is not to say one we will never return to—the president himself was this sort of symbolic achievement of democracy. And there was the human respect that I was talking about before, [that] compounds itself in the respect for the personified achievement of a democratic culture. Which is a hard thing—not many people can pull that together, you know. . . . So I do think that one of the things that we have to realize and talk about is that we cannot take it for granted. It's a made thing that we make continuously.

THE PRESIDENT: A source of optimism—I took my girls to see *Hamilton*, this new musical on Broadway, which you should see. Because this wonderful young Latino playwright produced this play, musical, about Alexander Hamilton and the Founding Fathers. And it's all in rap and hip-hop. And it's all played by young African American and Latino actors.

And it sounds initially like it would not work at all. And it is brilliant, and so much so that I'm pretty sure this is the only thing that Dick Cheney and I have agreed on—during my entire political career—it speaks to this vibrancy of American democracy, but also the fact that it was made by these living, breathing, flawed individuals who were brilliant. We haven't seen a collection of that much smarts and chutzpah and character in any other nation in history, I think.

But what's most important about [*Hamilton*] and why I think it has received so many accolades is it makes it live. It doesn't feel distant. And it doesn't feel set apart from the arguments that we're having today.

And Michelle and I, when we went to see it, the first thing we thought about was what could we do to encourage this kind of creativity in teaching history to our kids. Because, look, America is famously ahistorical. That's one of our strengths—we forget things. You go to other countries, they're still having arguments from four hundred years ago, and with serious consequences, right? They're bloody arguments. In the Middle East right now, you've got arguments dating back to the seventh century that are live today. And we tend to forget that stuff. We don't sometimes even remember what happened two weeks ago.

But this point you made about us caring enough about the blood, sweat, and tears involved in maintaining a democracy is vital and important. But it also is the reason why I think those who have much more of an "us" versus "them," fearful, conspiratorial brand of politics can thrive sometimes is because they can ignore that history.

If, in fact, you don't know much about the evolution of slavery and the civil rights movement and the Civil War and the postwar amendments, then the arguments that are being had now about how our criminal justice system interacts with African Americans seem pretty foreign. It's like, what are the issues here? If you're not paying attention to how Jefferson and Madison and Franklin and others were thinking about the separation of church and state, then you're not that worried about keeping those lines separate.

Robinson: Exactly. I believe very much in teaching history. I spend an enormous amount of time working with primary sources and various sources and so on. And I think that a lot of the history that is taught is a sort of shorthand that's not representative of much of anything. I think that's too bad.

The President: Do you pay a lot of attention to day-to-day politics these days?

Robinson: I do actually. I read the news for a couple of hours every morning.

The President: Right. And how do you think your writer's sensibility changes how you think about it? Or are you just kind of in the mix like everybody else, and just, "ah, that red team drives me nuts, and you're cheering for the blue?"

Robinson: Well, if I'm going to be honest, I think that there are some political candidacies that are much more humane in their implications and consequences than others. I mean, if suddenly poles were to be reversed and what I see as humanistic came up on the other side, there I'd be. I think in my essay on fear [124–140] I was talking about the assumption of generosity in this culture, you know? We have done some very magnanimous things in our history.

The President: Yes.

Robinson: Which seem in many ways unifying, defining. And then you see people running on what seem to be incredibly mean-spirited, tight-fisted assumptions, and you think, *this is not us. This is not our way forward.* Well, I'm getting all too political, but insulting people that you know will become citizens—however that's managed—giving them this bitter memory to carry into their participation in the national life. Why do that?

The President: We're going through a spasm of fear. And you're seeing it elsewhere. This is not unique to the United States. You see the emergence of the far-right parties in Europe. I think that it's a moment of great change, and the change happens fast. And there have been periods in our history where change happened fast like this, and people just are trying to find firm footing.

When you're looking for firm footing, one of the easiest

places to go is, somebody else is to blame. And the market system globally right now does create a situation where workers—ordinary people—have less control.

When you were growing up, when I was growing up, the majority of people had confidence that if they lost their job, it would be temporary, that they often would be with the same company for years, that there would be a pension in place, that they would be able to support a family, and that their kids would probably have a better life than they did. And people feel less confident about that because workers have less leverage, and capital is mobile and labor is not. And we haven't adapted our systems to take into account how fast this is moving.

What's frustrating to me is just that it wouldn't take that much for us to make the system work for ordinary people again.

ROBINSON: If I could strike one word out of the American vocabulary, it would be "competition." I think that that is the most bogus thing that has been entered into our [laughter]—

THE PRESIDENT: Now, you're talking to a guy who likes to play basketball and has been known to be a little competitive. But go ahead. [Laughter.]

ROBINSON: But what we're really telling people is that if they do not acquire nameless skills of a technological character, they will not have employment. It will be shipped out of the country. So basically it's a language of coercion that implies to people that their lives are fragile, that is charged with that kind of unspecific fear that makes people—it's meant to make people feel that they can't get their feet on the ground.

THE PRESIDENT: Right. Now, the argument would be, though, that that's the reality that people are feeling because companies can go anywhere and—

ROBINSON: Exactly, but when I look at these other economies we're supposed to be competing with, they're fragile. They're very fragile. And we're seeing that now. So all the competition has meant, it seems, is that labor is cheap and environmental standards are low. Look at, frankly, China. China has a vile ecology around its industrial centers. It's running out of appropriate cheap labor. And it's going into crisis. And what does that mean? It means that all of that capital will bundle itself up and land in another place that's relatively more advantageous. So what are we competing with? We run China into the ground, is that our great mission?

THE PRESIDENT: Well, in fact, historically, the way we "competed" was we educated our kids better. We put more money into research. We believed in science and facts, as opposed to being driven by superstition. We welcomed talent from all around the world. We put in place a social safety net so people felt that they could take risks without—

ROBINSON: That's crucial.

THE PRESIDENT: —without being utterly destitute.

ROBINSON: And having good bankruptcy laws. We have very liberal bankruptcy laws. But you know, we generate fantastic ideas—ideas move as fast as capital does. We can have the most brilliant population in the world, and if the best ideas that we have are sent offshore, we're still in the same position.

THE PRESIDENT: Right. We made progress on all these fronts. Slowly but surely. Where I completely agree with you, Marilynne, is that we have everything we need to thrive. And it is interesting watching the current political season for me, because I'm not on the ballot. So, although obviously I still have a huge stake in the outcome as a citizen, in addition to soon being an ex-president—and there are times where I'm listening to folks make these wild claims about how terrible America is doing, and I want to just press the pause button here for a second and remind them that by almost every economic criterion, we are hugely better off than we were just seven years ago; that we have done far better than almost every advanced country, and certainly every large advanced country on earth, in terms of growing the economy, driving down unemployment, managing our budgets.

And the only thing that, right now, is holding us back is Washington dysfunction. We could knock off another percentage point on the unemployment rate if we started rebuilding roads and bridges and airports. You travel—it's embarrassing when you go to other airports in other countries. Ours used to be the nicest ones.

Robinson: They were nice first, and then all [laughter]—

The President: Yes. Now they're a little worn down. We got to keep them up. The same is true with our education system. It is outstanding, but we've got—everybody else is caught up.

We got to step it up. So one of the reasons I'm here in Iowa is to talk about two years of college education—or two years of community college education for everybody, as free as high school was before. Research—we have fallen behind in basic research that created all these amazing technological wonders upon which our economic engine ran.

And, finally, making sure that people get paid enough money that they can support a family. Because all the evidence in history shows that when workers get paid a reasonable salary, then they spend it, businesses do better, the economy does better, and our political system does better. I mean, what is true is that when people feel pinched, then the generosity that you describe narrows to my immediate family, my immediate community, my immediate group.

ROBINSON: It's amazing. You know, when I go to Europe or—England is usually where I go—they say, "what are you complaining about? Everything is great." [Laughter.] I mean, really. Comparisons that they make are never at our disadvantage.

THE PRESIDENT: No—but, as I said, we have a dissatisfaction gene that can be healthy if harnessed. If it tips into rage and paranoia, then it can be debilitating and just be a self-fulfilling prophecy, because we end up blocking progress in serious ways.

ROBINSON: Restlessness of, like, "why don't we do something about this yellow fever?" There's generous restlessness.

THE PRESIDENT: That's a good restlessness.

ROBINSON: Yes, absolutely. And then there is a kind of acidic restlessness that—

THE PRESIDENT: "I want more stuff."

ROBINSON: "I want more stuff," or "other people are doing things that I'm justified in resenting." That sort of thing.

THE PRESIDENT: Right.

ROBINSON: I was not competing with anyone else. Nobody knew what my project was. I didn't know what it was. But what does freedom mean? I mean, really, the ideal of freedom if it doesn't mean that we can find out what is in this completely unique being that each one of us is? And competition narrows that. It's sort of like, you should not be studying this; you should be studying *that*, pouring your life down the siphon of economic utility.

THE PRESIDENT: But doesn't part of that depend on people having different definitions of success, and that we've narrowed what it means to be successful in a way that makes people very anxious? They don't feel affirmed if they're good at something that the society says isn't that important or doesn't reward.

Probably the best example for me is the teaching profession, where I can't tell you how many kids I meet—and I used to meet them in law school when I was teaching there—who had taught for two, three, four years, they loved teaching, and they thought it was just the most important thing. And you could tell that this was their calling, and at a certain point they couldn't afford to raise a family on it and they got discouraged, and—

ROBINSON: Somebody was looking over their shoulder.

THE PRESIDENT: Somebody was looking—or they'd get some comment from a classmate who had gone on to become an investment banker, they just eventually got discouraged and you didn't have a society that supported what they were doing, despite the fact that—talk about a complicated, magnificent art. Teaching. Being able to transmit ideas to young minds.

And so I like your definition of what America and freedom should be. But it does require all of us to have different definitions. And you have systems—or it requires a broader set of definitions than we have right now. And that's true for businesspeople, as well. I can't tell you how many businesspeople I meet [for whom] their joy is in organizing things to create products and services, and to help people be useful in various ways. And because they've got quarterly reports to shareholders and if they've made a long-term investment that may pay off way down the line, or if they're paying their employees more now because they think it's going to help them retain high-quality employees, a lot of times they feel like they're going to get punished in the stock market. And so they don't do it, because the definition of being a successful business is narrowed to what your quarterly earnings reports are. . . .

So my last question to Marilynne is, when you think about your books and you think about your faith and you think about your citizenship as an American, when do you feel most optimistic? What makes you think, *you know what, this experiment is going to keep going, I feel encouraged*?

ROBINSON: Well, you know, I mean, when I do book signings, for example, and people come up one by one and talk to me about their lives, if there's time [to] do that, how earnest they are, how deeply committed they are to sustaining people they feel close to or responsible for and so on—there they are, the people that you think of as the sustainers of a good society.

And it's only—really, if we could all just turn off media for a week, I think we would come out the other side of it with a different anthropology in effect. I wish we could have a normal politics where I disagree with people, they present their case, we take a vote, and if I lose I say, "yes, that's democracy," I'm on the losing side of a meaningful vote.

THE PRESIDENT: And "I'll try to make a better argument the next time."

ROBINSON: Exactly.

THE PRESIDENT: "I'll try to persuade more people the next time."

ROBINSON: And I think in little groups, like my department at the university or something—people get together, talk something over, take a vote, and that's it. And it's a little microcosm of democracy. That's what it's supposed to be.

THE PRESIDENT: Yes, but that does require a presumption of goodness in other people.

ROBINSON: Absolutely.

THE PRESIDENT: And that's not just what our democracy depends on, but I think that's what a good life depends on. Occasionally, you'll be disappointed, but more often than not, your faith will be confirmed.

ROBINSON: I believe that.

NOTES

All Bible passages are from *The New Oxford Annotated Bible: New Revised Standard Version with the Apocrypha*, ed. Michael D. Coogan, 3rd ed. (Oxford: Oxford University Press, 2001).

REFORMATION

21 "their wicked preachings and doctrines": *De Haeretico Comburendo*: 2 Henry IV, Cap. 15, in Henry Gee and William John Hardy, *Documents Illustrative of English Church History* (London: Macmillan, 1914), 134, 137.

21 "that such punishment may": *Documents of the Christian Church*, ed. Henry Bettenson (New York: Oxford University Press, 1947), 248–54.

21 "Meanwhile some poor wretch may cry at their gate": William Langland, *Piers the Ploughman*, trans. J. F. Goodridge (London: Penguin, 1966), 114.

22 "If God spare my life": John Foxe, *Foxe's Book of Martyrs: Select Narratives*, ed. John N. King (New York: Oxford University Press, 2009), 15.

22 "being born in a stable": John Calvin, *Sermons on Isaiah's Prophecy of the Death and Passion of Christ*, trans. and ed. T.H.L. Parker (Cambridge, U.K.: James Clarke & Co., 1956), 51.

22 "was nourished in such poverty as to hardly appear human": Ibid., 54.

23 "In disquisitions concerning the motions of the stars": John Calvin, *Institutes of the Christian Religion*, trans. John Allen (Philadelphia, 1813), book 1, chap. 5, paragraph 2, 64.

23 "Fetch down some knowledge from the clouds": Isaac Watts, *The Improvement of the Mind: A Supplement to the Art of Logic* (London, 1833; Morgan, PA: Soli Deo Gloria, 1998), 32–33.

26 "the manifold agility of the soul": Calvin, *Institutes*, book 1, chap. 5, paragraph 10, 67.

28 "he should have so much of a natural candour and sweetness": Watts, *Improvement*, 64.

28 "learn to know, and taste, and feel a fine stanza, as well as to hear it": Watts, *Improvement*, 294.

GRACE

34 "My ending is despair": William Shakespeare, *The Tempest*, ed. Northrop Frye (Baltimore: Penguin, 1959), epilogue, lines 15–18, 90.

SERVANTHOOD

53 "Great slaughter and burning": Anne Askew and John Bale, *The Examinations of Anne Askew*, ed. Elaine V. Beilin (New York: Oxford University Press, 1996), 8.

56 "But all the clergy of the church": Langland, *Piers the Ploughman*, 149–50.

57 "Faith alone is sufficient": Ibid., 190.

58 "being Written in times of Freedom": Roger L'Estrange, *Considerations and Proposals in Order to the Regulation of the Press* (London, 1663), 10. quod.lib.umich.edu/cgi/t/text/text-idx?c=eebo;idno=A47832.

58 "Death, Mutilation, Imprisonment, Banishment": Ibid., 31.

59 "For the Authors, nothing": Ibid., 30–32.

60 "We must listen": Karl Barth, *The Theology of John Calvin*, trans. Geoffrey W. Bromiley (Grand Rapids, MI: Eerdmans, 1995), 177.

60 *"Hoc est corpus meum"*: *Elizabeth I: Collected Works*, eds. Leah S. Marcus, Janel Mueller, and Mary Beth Rose (Chicago: University of Chicago Press, 2000), 47.

63 "I know the inconstancy": Ibid., 66.

64 "Earthly princes deprive themselves": Christopher Hill, *The English Bible and the Seventeenth-Century Revolution* (London: Penguin Books, 1993), 59.

64 "In the palaces of kings": John Calvin, *Commentaries on the Book of the Prophet Daniel*, trans. Thomas Myers (Grand Rapids, MI: Baker Book House, 1996), 350–51.

64 "Whence, then, does it happen": Ibid., 166.

67 "If the poor man": Langland, *Piers the Ploughman*, 174.

68 "Manslaughter is committed not": *Wycliffite Spirituality*, eds. and trans. J. Patrick Hornbeck, Stephen E. Lahey, and Fiona Somerset, The Classics of Western Spirituality (New York: Paulist Press, 2013), 189.

69 "Among all the sins": *Wycliffite Spirituality*, 17.

69 "the simple response is": Ibid., 70.

69 "Thou shalt not take": Ibid., 224.

70 "One can be saved": Ibid., 74.

72 "Our joy and our healing": Langland, *Piers the Ploughman*, 132.

GIVENNESS

75 "men who, in the name": Alexis de Tocqueville, *Democracy in America*, trans. Arthur Goldhammer (New York: Literary Classics of the United States, 2004), 13.

77 "The motion of the blood and animal spirits": Jonathan Edwards, *A Treatise Concerning Religious Affections*, ed. Edward Hickman (Edinburgh: Banner of Truth Trust, 1834, 1974), 1: 242.

89 "We have got so far": Ibid., 1: ccxxi.

AWAKENING

93 "My general remark is": Owen Lovejoy, "Sermon on Religion and Politics, July 21, 1842," in *Lovejoy, His Brother's Blood: Speeches and Writings, 1838–64*, eds. William F. Moore and Jane Ann Moore (Champaign: University of Illinois Press, 2004), 36.

98 "The crack in the teacup": W. H. Auden, "As I Walked Out One Evening," in *The Norton Anthology of Poetry*, 3rd ed. (New York: Norton, 1970), 1099–100.

105 "many will say to me": Matthew 7:22–23.

105 "the sword of the Spirit": Ephesians 6:17.

DECLINE

121 "Braver men never lived": Thomas Wentworth Higginson, *Army Life in a Black Regiment and Other Writings* (London: Penguin Classics, 1997), Kindle edition.

122 "the fortunes of a race": Ibid.

FEAR

125 "in the beginning with God": John 1:2–5.

125 "the eternal life": 1 John 1:2.

126 "The sound of a driven leaf": Leviticus 26:36–37.

PROOFS

142 "When the Scripture speaks": Calvin, *Institutes*, book 1, chap. 13, paragraph 7, 145.

142 "upholds all things": Hebrews 1:3.

144 "Of [God's] wonderful wisdom": Calvin, *Institutes*, book 1, chap. 5, paragraph 2, 64.

145 "Were it not that": John Calvin, *Commentary on the Gospel According to John 1–10*, trans. William Pringle (Edinburgh, 1847; Grand Rapids, MI: Baker Book House, 1999), 1:4, 11.

145 "All circumstances are the frame": *The Complete Poems of Emily Dickinson*, ed. Thomas H. Johnson (New York: Little, Brown, 1960), 398.
146 "All who are *not*": Calvin, *Commentary on John*, 1:5, 33.
147 "Let not thy heart": James B. Pritchard, ed., *Ancient Near Eastern Texts Relating to the Old Testament*, 2nd ed. (Princeton: Princeton University Press, 1955), 412, 423.
147 "You go and take": Ibid., 425, 426, 429.
147 "[The Evangelist] speaks here": Calvin, *Commentary on John*, 1:4, 32.
151 "The most beautiful thing": Albert Einstein, in *Living Philosophies: A Series of Intimate Credos* (New York: Simon & Schuster, 1931), 6.
151 "Scientific views end in": Richard Feynman, *The Meaning of It All: Thoughts of a Citizen Scientist* (Reading, MA: Perseus Books, 1998), 39.
152 "God was always invented": Richard Feynman, *Superstrings: A Theory of Everything*, eds. P.C.W. Davies and J. Brown (Cambridge, U.K.: Cambridge University Press, 1998), 208–209.
155 "For from the fact": René Descartes, *Meditations on First Philosophy with Selections from the Objections and Replies*, ed. John Cottingham (New York: Cambridge University Press, 1996), Sixth Meditation, 62.
156 "arbitrary constitution of the Creator": Jonathan Edwards, "The Great Christian Doctrine of Original Sin Defended" in *The Works of Jonathan Edwards*, ed. Edward Hickman (London, 1834; Edinburgh: Banner of Truth Trust, 1974), 1:223.

MEMORY

169 "this species of property": Jefferson Davis, speech in the U.S. Senate, February 8, 1858, in *Jefferson Davis: The Essential Writings*, ed. William J. Cooper, Jr. (Modern Library, 2004), 141.
169 "This relationship [that subsists]": Henry Ward Beecher, "The Conflict of Northern and Southern Theories of Man and Society" (speech, New York, January 14, 1855). http://www.gutenberg.org/files/25653/25653-h/25653-h.htm.
171 "in the image of God": Genesis 1:27.

METAPHYSICS

189 "what a darkness we are involved in": John Locke, *An Essay Concerning Human Understanding*, ed. Alexander Campbell Fraser (New York: Dover Publications, 1959), vol. 2, book 4, chap. 3, 222.
189 "is the image of": Colossians 1:15 ff.
192 "the knowledge of God's": Colossians 2:2–3.
192 "let loose our thoughts": Locke, *An Essay Concerning Human Understanding*, vol. 1, Introduction, 31.

197 "to be fixed on Christ": Calvin, *Commentary on John*, 3:16, 124.
198 "I, I am He": Isaiah 43:25.
199 "vital force": H. S. Chamberlain, *Recherches sur la sève ascendante* [Studies on rising sap], (Neuchâtel, 1897).
200 "Those who were full": 1 Samuel 2:5.
200 "He has put down": Luke 1:52–53.
200 "Whoever exalts himself": Matthew 23:12.
202 "in a golden gown": Pico della Mirandola, *On the Dignity of Man*, trans. Charles Glenn Wallis (Indianapolis: Bobbs-Merrill, 1965; Indianapolis, Hackett Publishing, 1998), 12.
203 "I understood why man": Ibid., 3–4.
203 "I have placed thee": Ibid., 5.
204 "Human nature it is": De Docta Ignorantia, in *Unity and Reform: Selected Writings of Nicholas de Cusa*, ed. John Patrick Dolan (Notre Dame, IN: University of Notre Dame Press, 1962), 65.
204 "an order that by nature": Ibid., 67.
205 "the highest nature that comprises": Ibid., 64.
205 "Since this light, of which the Speech was the source": Calvin, *Commentary on John*, 1:4, 32.

THEOLOGY

210 "Physicists have discovered": Natalie Wolchover, "A Jewel at the Heart of Quantum Physics," *Quanta*, September 17, 2013. http://www.simonsfoundation.org/quanta/20130917-a-jewel-at-the-heart-of-quantum-physics/.

SON OF ADAM, SON OF MAN

243 "equality with God": Philippians 2:6–7.
245 "the Son of Man came not": Matthew 20:28; Mark 10:45.
245 "were everywhere in abundance": John Chrysostom, Homily 32, section 11, in *Saint Chrysostom: Homilies on the Epistles of Paul to the Corinthians*, ed. Philip Schaff, vol. 12, *A Select Library of the Nicene and Post-Nicene Fathers of the Christian Church* (Edinburgh: T & T Clark, n.d.; reprint, Eerdmans, n.d.), 191.
247 "Do not presume to say to yourselves": Matthew 3:9.
247 "Do not begin to say to yourselves": Luke 3:8.
248 "The Lord says to my lord": Psalm 110:1.
248 "If David thus": Matthew 22:45.
248 "What do you think of the Christ?": Matthew 22:42–45.
251 "He took to himself": Chrysostom, Homily 24, section 8, in *Saint Chrysostom*, 143.

254 "Doubtless he says *one*": Calvin on Hebrews 3:5 and 3:7, in *Calvin's Commentaries*, trans. John Owen, vol. 44, *Hebrews* (Edinburgh, 1847–1850), 56, 59.
255 "He who sanctifies": Hebrews 2:11.
255 "through whom also he": Hebrews 1:2–3.

LIMITATION

258 "Nor let anyone think": John Locke, *Human Understanding*, vol. 1, book 2, chap. 7, 164–65.
262 "I suppose nobody will": Ibid., chap. 1, 132.
262 "[Atoms in the brain] can remember": Richard Feynman, "The Value of Science," in his *"What Do You Care What Other People Think?": Adventures of a Curious Character*, ed. Ralph Leighton (New York: Norton, 2001), 244.
263 "The whole world is preserved": John Calvin, *Commentary on a Harmony of the Evangelists: Matthew, Mark, and Luke*, trans. William Pringle (Edinburgh, 1845; Grand Rapids, MI: Baker Book House, 1996), Matthew 4:4, 24.
264 "occupy themselves with myths": 1 Timothy 1:4–5.
268 "And being found in human form": Philippians 2:8.
268 "Though he was in the form": Philippians 2:6–7.
269 "For it has been delivered": Luke 4:6.
271 "Foxes have holes": Calvin, *Harmony*, Matthew 8:20, at http://www.ccel.org/ccel/calvin/comment3/comm_vol31/htm/ix.lxxiii.htm.
272 "It is strange": Calvin, *Harmony*, 1:388.

REALISM

274 "One born to prowess": Pindar, *The Odes*, trans. Cecil Maurice Bowra (New York: Penguin, 1969), 107.
274 "lit / By the lovely light": Ibid., 109.

ACKNOWLEDGMENTS

I would like to thank the following institutions where these essays, sometimes in different form, were originally delivered as lectures: the Nexus Institute; the First Presbyterian Church of New York City; Santa Clara University; University of California, Berkeley; Yale University; Theos Think Tank; University of Notre Dame; Western Theological Seminary; the International Society, Wittenberg, Germany; Union Theological Seminary; Regent College, Vancouver; the Divinity School, Oxford University; the Soul Conference at Oxford University in conjunction with the University of Nottingham; the School of Divinity at the University of Edinburgh; and Key West Literary Seminar.

365
45
1825
1460
16,425